WAYNE GRETZKY'S GHOST

ROY MacGREGOR

WAYNE GRETZKY'S GHOST

AND OTHER TALES

FROM A LIFETIME IN HOCKEY

RANDOM HOUSE CANADA

PUBLISHED BY RANDOM HOUSE CANADA

COPYRIGHT © 2011 ROY MACGREGOR

All rights reserved under International and Pan-American Copyright Conventions. No part of this book may be reproduced in any form or by any electronic or mechanical means, including information storage and retrieval systems, without permission in writing from the publisher, except by a reviewer, who may quote brief passages in a review. Published in 2011 by Random House Canada, a division of Random House of Canada Limited, Toronto. Distributed in Canada by Random House of Canada Limited.

www.randomhouse.ca

Random House Canada and colophon are registered trademarks.

Page 373 is a continuation of this copyright page.

LIBRARY AND ARCHIVES CANADA CATALOGUING IN PUBLICATION

MacGregor, Roy, 1948–

Wayne Gretzky's ghost : and other tales from a lifetime in hockey /
Roy MacGregor.

Issued also in electronic format.

ISBN 978-0-307-35741-0

1. Hockey players—Canada—Biography. 2. Hockey—Canada.
3. Sportswriters—Canada—Biography. 4. MacGregor, Roy, 1948– . I. Title.

GV848.5.A1M297 2011   796.962'092271   C2011-901975-2

Cover image: © ANDY CLARK/Reuters/Corbis
Printed and bound in the United States of America

2 4 6 8 9 7 5 3

For my older brother Jim, in appreciation of his
hand-me-down skates, his table-top game,
a million first-one-to-ten shinny matches and
his own great passion for the national game.

CONTENTS

11. THE WORLD'S GAME

WAYNE GRETZKY'S GHOST

PREFACE: A GAME FOR LIFE

My mother, bless her heart, kept things that otherwise would have been tossed years ago. My grade twelve report card, for example — where the principal has written, in red pen, "Going! Going! _____!!" along the bottom of a long list of marks in the thirties and forties, leaving me to fill in the blank he thoughtfully provided — "gone!!" — the following term when I flunked every subject but English and phys-ed. I keep that report as a lesson that comebacks are possible in life, as well as in hockey.

She also kept a red Empire scrapbook. It is little more than a cheap manila folder with the price — fifteen cents — still pencilled on the cover. The first page opens on me, eight years old, smiling out from a newspaper photograph that was taken on a day when our little northern town put on a special display for one of the Toronto dailies to show that life goes on in summer cottage country in the winter as well. Below that picture is a clipping from the weekly *Huntsville Forester*: "Goals by MacGregor Gives Auxiliary Tie With Hay & Co. 2–2." The story begins:

The Legion Auxiliary's Roy MacGregor turned two spectacular solo rushes into a 2–2 tie with Hay & Co. Saturday morning.

A highlight of a Huntsville Hockey League Squirt playoff
game, MacGregor's goals marked the second time Auxiliary
had battled from behind a one-goal deficit.

Young defenseman Michael Allemano was especially
good for the Hookmen, breaking up many Auxiliary rushes.
Both of the Hay & Company goals by Brent Munroe and
John Newell, were scored on power plays.

It is important to know here that this is squirt hockey, age seven
and eight, that the full name of the team is the Legion *Ladies'*
Auxiliary, and that the game was played on only one-half of the ice,
a line of boards being temporarily erected so two games could go on
at once. But no matter. This is what small-town hockey was all
about in Canada in the 1950s and 1960s. So what if there were no
"spectacular solo rushes." I remember both goals vividly, one on a
scramble, one on a slow shot the length of the ice that the goaltender
fanned on. But the local paper knew what it was doing. Creating
local heroes. And the day the paper came out there were grown-ups
on Main Street who had noticed. An old relative even stopped me
and said I'd soon be in the NHL. Damn right I would.

Today the glue has dried and some of the clippings fall out
when the fifty-five-year-old scrapbook is opened. "Pee Wee's Cut
Down Orillia," "Pee Wee's Batter Burks Falls." The day we won
the prestigious Wardell & Company trophy, the story began:
"Anglo Canadian's one-two punch of Harry Snowden and Roy
MacGregor continued to spark the Hidemen at the Arena on
Tuesday night . . ."

This was pure glory. The teams had nicknames — the Hidemen
meant you were sponsored by the local tannery, the Hookmen
meant the local lumberyard — and the tiny goal scorers were
transformed magically in the local paper into *somebodies*.

I see on one page of the scrapbook where I have practised writing my autograph. I see with the grace of time how totally absurd the notion was that I would one day be signing programs and team jerseys thrust at me by adoring fans. But I smile at the small-town myth for the harmless, happy days it gave me and God knows how many thousands of others. Hockey, for many of us, was the first time—and often the only time—we felt we truly mattered.

Dreams fade, but there is no reason for fun to follow. I may have peaked at age twelve or so, but so be it. I kept playing long after it was obvious there would be no BeeHive Corn Syrup picture of me in a Chicago Blackhawks uniform. I played house league every year, on Huntsville all-star teams several seasons and one winter played juvenile hockey for another town, which involved driving yourself to and from games around the District of Muskoka. Not much of a "career" in competitive hockey, but enough to instill in me a love of this game that is as strong today as it was the first time I looped a ridiculously vain "R" in that red scrapbook.

I do, however, have one great regret in hockey, and that is that, like so many other average players, I stopped playing once there was no more competitive hockey available. For almost a dozen years I never played, only to be drawn back to the game in the late 1970s by the rise of recreational hockey. And once back, I returned with a vengeance, playing several times a week, coaching minor hockey for a dozen years in three different centres and even coaching one of our daughters, Christine, and our son, Gordon. My greatest achievement in the game today is to be on the same ice as Gord and his pals each Monday evening for an hour, where for a brief fantasy hour no one points out the obvious thirty-five-year-gap between the players still sticking fast to wooden sticks and the players with the two-hundred-dollar composite sticks. In part, that is because there is no one there to point out anything— no fan ever showing up to watch a game far better seen from the bench than from the stands.

My father played hockey. There is a picture on the wall of him—dark hair parted like a centre line—posing with the 1927–28

Eganville Senior Hockey Team. He "retired" at twenty-two when he headed into the Algonquin Park bush, where he would stay for the rest of his working life. In his eighties, retired, he came a couple of times to old-timer tournaments I played in with the Rusty Blades of Ottawa. "You have no idea how lucky you are," he once said. "We had no opportunity to keep playing."

I do know. And I plan to keep on playing for as long as it makes sense. Or doesn't—who really cares?

It is somewhat ironic that I would dream as a child of a life in hockey and end up with a life in hockey far removed from that original dream. At age eight, I could never have imagined how this would happen. But long after the NHL career dream broke, I chased another in journalism and eventually found my way back to hockey.

Even that was not planned. Though I often wrote profiles of NHL players while working in magazines during the mid- and late '70s, my journalism ambition was to write about politics. For more than a dozen years I covered Parliament Hill, beginning with *Today* magazine and gradually working through the *Toronto Star*, *Maclean's* magazine and the *Ottawa Citizen*. Though I handled sports for *Maclean's* and, while with the newspapers, periodically would be assigned to hockey stories—world championships and Canada Cups—I never figured to work full-time in hockey.

All that changed in 1992. The *Citizen* was going through a policy change, wanting Hill reporters to pay for their own parking rather than accept the free parking made available to all Hill workers. There was some thought, however silly, that by accepting the parking spot—a heavy hike down a steep hill to the side of the river—we were somehow compromised. Fine, I said in a memo to the editor, Jim Travers, but the paper will have to pay for at least a good portion of a downtown parking spot. One summer day, I got a call from Travers, who sadly would pass away in 2011, asking me to join him for lunch.

"I have a solution for your parking concerns," he said.

"Excellent," I gloated.

"You're covering the Ottawa Senators from now on."

I was stunned. I thought I was a political columnist. I thought I had the pulse of the nation, as we like to say, but I didn't even have a finger on my own pulse, it seemed. I never saw this coming, though perhaps if I had thought about it I might have. A couple of years earlier Ken Dryden and I had written *Home Game: Hockey and Life in Canada*, and the book had been a huge success.

The Ottawa Senators were just starting up and Travers wanted to reorganize the sports department, installing me as the hockey columnist and the national editor, Graham Parley, as sports editor. Both of us were given a day to think about it. Neither of us required a day: we jumped at the opportunity.

And so began my return to the life that had first been imagined in that old frayed scrapbook. I wrote a book, *Road Games*, about that first year covering the Senators—easily the funniest and most enjoyable assignment I ever had—and then *The Home Team: Fathers, Sons & Hockey*. In 1995, publisher Douglas Gibson of McClelland & Stewart approached me with an idea: to produce a series of hockey books aimed at the young "reluctant reader," a.k.a. *boys*. I had never written a children's book but agreed to try one, thinking that would be it. Soon there would be twenty-four books in the series, now also published in Sweden, Finland, the Czech Republic and China.

Once the *National Post* started up in 1998, the chain took me from the *Citizen* and gave me a general column, though each spring I would move into sports to join fellow columnist Cam Cole on the hockey beat. In 2002 I left for the *Globe and Mail* and a general five-days-a-week column that touched so regularly on the national game that in 2010 they asked me to turn full-time again to hockey.

The NHL—with all its growth, excitement and undeniable flaws—had obviously changed since my great heroes were Gordie Howe and Bobby Hull, wingers stayed to their sides and games were broadcast once a week, usually beginning in the second period; but so too had I.

The one important thing that had never changed since that red Empire scrapbook first opened was a complete love of this magical sport that has, somewhat to my own great surprise, and totally to my great delight, become a game for life.

Kanata, March 2011

★

ONE

WAYNE GRETZKY'S GHOST

"*One more year!*" the 18,500 gathered at Ottawa's Corel Centre began to chant with 4:43 left in regulation time. "*One more year! One more year! One more year!*"

He heard them—he even raised his stick in salute—but he wasn't listening. Wayne Gretzky was finished. This would be his final National Hockey League game ever played in Canada, his home country, a 2–2 tie on April 15, 1999, back when the NHL still had ties, between the Ottawa Senators and his New York Rangers. It seems a silly thing to say so many years on—"his New York Rangers"—as in Canadian eyes and hearts, and even imaginations, he is an Edmonton Oiler forever.

Wayne Gretzky was thirty-eight years old that early spring day in Ottawa. He was, by his own measure, merely a shadow of what he had once been as a player. He had 61 points for his final season—"99" retiring in 1999—whereas he had once scored 215. He was, however, still the Rangers' leading scorer, and had several of his lesser teammates only been able to finish on the perfect tape-to-tape passes from the corners, from the back of the net, that he had delivered all this game, not only would the Rangers have easily won but his point total would have been in familiar Gretzky territory.

Still, he had missed a dozen games due to a sore disc in his back. He knew it was time. He had once said he would be gone by thirty, but his great hero, Gordie Howe, who had retired early and then returned to play till age fifty-two, had warned him to "be careful not to leave the thing you love too soon." He had continued on past thirty but would not, he swore, be hanging on at forty.

It had been a magnificent lifetime of hockey. Six teams—Indianapolis Racers and Edmonton Oilers of the World Hockey Association, the Oilers, Los Angeles Kings, St. Louis Blues and Rangers of the NHL—and he had won four Stanley Cups, all with the Oilers, while establishing a stunning sixty-one scoring records, many of which will never be broken. He had scored more goals than anyone who had ever played the game, and just to put that into context, he was never even really considered a goal scorer but a playmaker.

He had been hearing the accolades since he was ten years of age and scored 378 goals for the Nadrofsky Steelers in his hometown of Brantford. "You are a very special person," his father, Walter, had told him around that time. "Wherever you go, probably all your life, people are going to make a fuss over you. You've got to remember that, and you've got to behave right. They're going to be watching for every mistake. Remember that. You're very special and you're on display."

On display constantly—whether scoring 92 goals one season for Edmonton, getting married to Janet Jones in Canada's "Wedding of the Century," getting traded to the Kings in a deal that will be debated as long as Confederation, becoming the country's most recognizable pitchman for corporate sponsors—and measured endlessly. They called him "Whiner" Gretzky for a while. They once said he skated like a man carrying a piano on his back when he went through his first back troubles. They blamed his wife for the trade to Hollywood, where she was an actress. Yet if there were minor stumbles there was never a fall, almost impossible to imagine in this era of over-the-top sports celebrity, temptation and gotcha journalism. He never forgot Walter Gretzky's good advice.

They tried, but could never quite describe the magic he brought to the ice. Gordie Howe jokingly suggested that if they parted the hair at the back of his head, they would find another eye. Broadcaster Peter Gzowski said he had the ability to move about the ice like a whisper. It was said he could pass through opponents like an X-ray. He himself liked to say he didn't skate to where the puck was, but to where it was going to be. During the 1987 Canada Cup—when he so brilliantly set up the Mario Lemieux goal that won the tournament—Igor Dmitriev, a coach with the Soviet team, said: "Gretzky is like an invisible man. He appears out of nowhere, passes to nowhere, and a goal is scored." No one has ever said it better.

But here in Ottawa on April 15, 1999, the invisible man seemed like the only man on the ice by the end. Walter Gretzky and his buddies from Brantford were on their feet, Janet and their three children, Paulina, Trevor and Ty, were on their feet. The NHL commissioner was on his feet. There is no possible count of the millions watching on television who were on their feet, but it is a fair bet that a great many were.

"*Gret-zky!*" the crowd chanted as the final minute came around.

"*Gret-zky!*"

"*Gret-zky!*"

"*Gret-zky! Gret-zky! Gret-zky!*"

The horn blew to signal the end of overtime, still a tie, and both teams remained on the ice while the cheers poured down. Then, with a gentle shrug of his shoulders, Ottawa defenceman Igor Kravchuk broke with the usual protocol and led his teammates over to shake Gretzky's hand and thank him.

It was over.

Months passed between Wayne Gretzky's retirement from hockey and a meeting that took place later that summer at the *National Post*'s main offices on Don Mills Road in Toronto. The newspaper's publisher, Gordon Fisher, said he had something important to discuss with me. I was invited to a meeting with him, editor Ken Whyte and sports editor Graham Parley. It was all to be kept top secret. I had no idea when I entered the room what was up.

"We're bringing on a new sports columnist," Ken said with his enigmatic smile. A *new* sports columnist? I wondered. They already had Cam Cole, the best in the business—snatched from the *Edmonton Journal*—and I was pitching in regularly as well as doing some political work. What did we need with another sports columnist?

"He'll be writing hockey," Ken said. I blanched. But . . . but . . . but *I* write hockey. And Cam writes hockey.

"It's Wayne Gretzky," Gordon finally said.

I remember giving my head a shake. *Wayne Gretzky? As a hockey columnist? How did they even know he could type, let alone write?*

"It's a huge coup for us," said Gordon. "This will get us a lot of publicity and bring in a lot of readers. He has one condition, though."

"What's that?" I asked, half expecting to be told to back off and stay out of the rinks.

Gordon smiled. "He wants to work with you."

"We want you to be his ghostwriter," added Ken.

Gretzky's agent, Mike Barnett, had done the negotiations for the column and this request had been part of the deal. No one but the senior executives knew what the financial part of the deal was to be—rumours went as high as $200,000, as low as for free in order to keep the recently retired player in the public eye—but soon everyone at the paper, and many beyond, would know that I was also part of the agreement.

This quite surprised me. We hardly knew each other. Unlike Cam, I had never covered the Oilers in their glory years. I had even, long, long ago, written one column, tongue rather in check, suggesting Wayne Gretzky was the worst thing that ever happened to hockey— his brilliance and popularity causing NHL expansion to places that made no sense, his high ability raising fans' expectations for skill level that would sag once he retired—and I had even gone on the CBC's *As It Happens* back in the summer of 1988 to predict, with uncanny foresight, that Gretzky would be swallowed up in Hollywood and never heard of again. Instead, of course, he became even more famous in the years that followed.

In the late fall of 1994, however, I joined a handful of other journalists to accompany the "99 All-Stars" on a barnstorming trip to Europe during the NHL's first owners' lockout. It was mostly a lark: Gretzky and pals like Brett Hull, Paul Coffey, Marty McSorley and Mark Messier heading off on a tour of Europe with their hockey bags, wives and girlfriends and even, in the case of Gretzky, McSorley, Messier and Coffey, their dads. They played in Finland, including one game in Helsinki where Jari Kurri joined the fun, Sweden, including matches against teams featuring the likes of Kent (Magic) Nilsson and Mats Naslund, Norway and Germany. It was a wonderful experience, the stories filed back to Canada given wonderful play by newspapers starving for hockey and the stories, many untold, of the trip itself something to be treasured forever.

In the intervening years, we'd become casually friendly as Gretzky moved to St. Louis and then on to New York to round out his career. His kids, along with the children of Mike Barnett, were even reading the Screech Owls hockey mystery series. Gordon Fisher asked if I would agree to help out the paper by dropping one of my four weekly columns and using that time to help out. Of course, I agreed. He was, after all, the publisher.

And besides, it sounded like fun.

His first column appeared on September 18, 1999. "No regrets," it began. "I still feel good about my decision."

It was a long first column, sixteen hundred words, and it covered everything from his feelings about retirement to his plans to keep busy to his thoughts on Alexei Yashin's contract holdout with the Ottawa Senators. "There's a lot of talk now about players refusing to play out their contracts," he wrote. "I never refused to honour mine."

He said he had no "pangs of regret" when training camps started up and he wasn't going anywhere. His Los Angeles neighbour and friend Claude Lemieux, then with the Colorado Avalanche, had pestered him all summer about getting fit and ready but he had held to his promise to call an end to it after twenty-one seasons. He had visited with the New York Rangers and coach John Muckler had tried to talk him into coming back, saying he needed someone who could get the puck to newly signed Theoren Fleury, but he had not been tempted. "Somebody asked me the other day if I'm going to be involved in hockey," he wrote. "I don't have any time. I really don't."

It seemed like a casual chat from one of the few players in the game identifiable solely by his number, 99, but the work that went into it far, far surpassed what would have gone into the one column a week I had given up in order to help out. First I had interviewed him at length over the telephone, then I had written a draft and faxed it to Mike Barnett, his agent. (This was in the early days of e-mail, and fax machines still dominated.) Mike had faxed back suggestions and changes, and then he had run it all past his main client and Wayne had suggestions and changes. I changed and rewrote and recast and refaxed, and finally they faxed back a version that they were okay with.

The first column had gone to print.

I was beginning to think I had made a horrible mistake, that a single column looked as if it might take up a full week's work—and the column wouldn't even be appearing under my byline. I would *disappear* from the paper.

But gradually we worked it all out. From initially dealing with one telephone number, Mike Barnett's, I soon had a half-dozen numbers including his and Janet's cell phones. I even struck up a relationship with the housekeeper to let me know where he was and how he could be reached. Calls took place on the road, on golf courses (I could hear the click of ball on metal in the background), by the pool, in his office and, increasingly, on the run. As he became more familiar with my style and I became more familiar with his thoughts, the columns became easier and easier.

He wrote columns about overtime, shootouts, playoff heroes, various teams, individual players from Mark Messier to Jaromir Jagr, about junior hockey, minor hockey pressure and the value of playing sports other than hockey in the summer. He wrote about how he came to wear No. 99—not his idea but that of his junior coach in Sault Ste. Marie, as an older player already had 9—and how at first people laughed at the number that is today retired throughout the NHL. He left hockey from time to time to talk about the Grey Cup, the Super Bowl, Tiger Woods' domination in golf, his grandmother and her rocking chair.

Here are some of the highlights from that year of weekly columns:

★ He said if he were starting his career again, he would wear a visor to protect his eyes. That week, during a match between the Ottawa Senators and Toronto Maple Leafs, an accidental high stick had struck the eye of young Toronto defenceman Bryan Berard, threatening to destroy a promising career. If he had grown up playing with one, Gretzky said, he would have continued to wear it, not thrown it away as so many juniors were doing when they reached the NHL, where such protection was not obligatory. "Without question," he wrote, "in my opinion, the National Hockey League now needs to grandfather a rule that would require all players who have come up through the system wearing a visor to continue to do so in the NHL." In what now seems an eerie exchange, he talked about how the year before, when he was still playing in New York, he had talked to young Manny Malhotra about keeping the visor on. "He was just a rookie and he wanted to keep it off. 'You're crazy,' I'd tell him. 'Keep it on.'" A dozen years later, while playing for the Vancouver Canucks, a visorless Malhotra would be hit in the eye by a deflected puck and require extensive surgery to save his vision.

★ Following a devastating hit on Dallas Stars forward Mike Modano by Anaheim Mighty Duck Ruslan Salei, he called for the league to take a strong stand on hits from behind. He also suggested that something be done about modern equipment, though he was fully aware that "I'm in no position to preach." But he said that today's game was so fast and the players so big and strong that "I would never let anyone get on the ice with the helmet I wore."

★ With Canadian teams struggling to survive in a time of escalating salaries and a low Canadian dollar, and with the Calgary Flames rumoured to be on the brink of failure, he said it would be a "tragedy" if hockey failed to support "small-market" franchises. Calgary, he said, had won a Stanley Cup and had been "a hockey hotbed" throughout its history. "Sometimes it makes you wonder. If hockey can't make a go of it in places like this, there must be something wrong."

★ He wrote about Dominik Hasek, then starring for the Buffalo Sabres, and he argued that in the 1998 Nagano Olympics "Canada played as well as—and I'd say better than—any team in the tournament, but we couldn't score against him. It took a lucky deflection to put our game against the Czech Republic into overtime, and we knew they were just going to play for the tie. We spent the entire overtime in their end, but we still couldn't score. We knew it wouldn't be on a two-on-one and we knew it would never be on a shot from the blueline. It would have to be on a scramble. We'd have to crash the net and we'd have to distract him somehow. When we couldn't do that, that was it. I always say we didn't lose in the Olympics, we lost in a skills competition. But that doesn't mean Dominik Hasek wasn't brilliant. He was."

★ He was forced to comment, no matter how uncomfortable it was, on another incident that caused national outrage in Canada: Marty McSorley's stick attack on Donald Brashear that led to

McSorley being charged with assault with a weapon and subsequently found guilty. McSorley, a former teammate of Gretzky's and long one of his closest friends, was suspended for the remainder of the season. "It's no secret that Marty's one of my best friends," Gretzky began, detailing their years together in Edmonton and in Los Angeles. But, he added, "nobody, absolutely nobody, is going to stand up and say it was right to do or that it wasn't Marty's fault. He's a grown man. And he'd be the first to agree that he has to take full responsibility for what happened. I deplore what happened, but I can still admire the fact that Marty didn't take the easy way out. He didn't slip out the back door. He stood up front and centre and immediately apologized to Donald Brashear, to both teams and all hockey fans. No excuses. Full responsibility." He hoped both players would eventually return to play in the NHL. Brashear did; McSorley never played another game.

★ He talked about his minor hockey days and tournaments, remembering how his Brantford team insisted on billeting the players in order to save the parents money. He talked about fundraising through draws and candy sales. He spoke fondly of the famous Quebec International Pee-Wee Hockey Tournament, where more than ten thousand people packed the Colisée to see them beat a team from Dallas 25–0. Best of all, though, was when a knock came at the dressing room door and in walked Jean Béliveau, who shook every child's hand as if he were already in the NHL.

★ He wrote about the death of golfer Payne Stewart, killed in a plane crash. He admitted to his own legendary fear of flying and how he had once been afraid even to board airplanes, how he had tried hypnotherapy to cure him and how he only grew more comfortable after Air Canada pilots let him sit in the cockpit to watch the takeoffs and landings and he saw how confident and sure they were even under tough weather conditions. In speaking of Stewart, whom he knew, he confessed to his own deeply religious side. "I believe—I'm not at all ashamed to say so—and I also believe in life after death."

★ He allowed himself, at one point, to gaze into hockey's future, and saw expansion into Europe, the levelling off of salaries (though not for the top players), the survival of the then-struggling Canadian teams and improved equipment to cut down on collision injuries. He predicted three rule changes—dropping the red line and "touch-up" offsides that would allow the defence to fire the puck back into the offensive zone without waiting, and opening up the game by having officials call obstruction penalties—all of which eventually came to pass.

★ He addressed the rumours of his own return to hockey as a potential investor in Steve Ellman's purchase of the Phoenix Coyotes. "I never made any bones about my intent of one day returning to what is, essentially, the only thing I've ever known. Hockey has been a large part of my life, it's given me and my family a great deal, and I still love the game and all the crazy, wonderful people involved in it. There were a few chances early on, but I knew immediately that the timing wasn't right. Nor, for that matter, was the location." Location, it turned out, was of extreme import, as he then said what had long been believed. "What living here most gives us," he said about the family's home in California, "is the opportunity to live a fairly normal family life." Phoenix, he said, would also give the family that chance. Phoenix, he said, was "a natural fit. Tougher to ignore. It was made clear right from the start of discussions that I wouldn't be expected to move. I wouldn't be the coach. I wouldn't be the general manager. I wouldn't be the team president. . . . One thing I am certain on is it couldn't possibly be coaching . . ."

Naturally, there was criticism over his column. Those who wanted him to slam the league over whatever was the issue du jour were disappointed, but slamming had never been his personality. He has always been a team player when it came to the overall league, as well as when it came to whatever team he was on, and while he might prod and suggest, he was loath to condemn.

The criticism came my way, too, one journalist charging I was somehow in a conflict of interest in doing the column. It seemed a strange charge, given that virtually all newspapers have from time to time featured columns written by staff members that appear under the byline of a well-known athlete. Even the paper that threw up this charge had been doing it with a well-known Canadian golfer, the column ghostwritten by staff. I was a staff writer assigned by my editor and publisher to help out on the column. And not only did I not receive a single extra penny for doing so, I actually *lost* on the deal, given that for a year I had to give up a column of my own each week in order to produce Gretzky's.

It was, in fact, my second experience at ghostwriting, the first coming way back in 1973 when I was just beginning my journalism career at *Maclean's* magazine. In the months following the 1972 Summit Series, the young goaltender in that epic battle, Ken Dryden of the Montreal Canadiens, was approached to put his name to an article on his experiences, and as I was the only staffer with a keen interest in the game, I was assigned to be Ken's "ghost." The Cornell graduate and law student had kept copious notes, some dictated, some scribbled, and his thoughts filled a couple of red binders that he passed on to me to see what might be made of the musings. I was impressed. I took the notes, wrote one version of an article, and he took my version and returned it to me, rewritten. I went to the editor, Peter C. Newman, and suggested that Ken was a strong enough writer that he didn't really need a ghost, but rather an editor who might guide him. Newman agreed, and Ken and I set to work on what would become his first-ever published work.

We became great friends during the experience and, once it was done with, I talked to Ken about one day turning his attention to a book on hockey. We spoke on and off about the idea for years, and Ken kept up his note taking as he and his Montreal team seemed to win Stanley Cup after Stanley Cup. I was eventually able to connect him and Douglas Gibson, the young publisher of Macmillan, with whom I was discussing a work of fiction. More years and many more discussions passed until 1983, when Doug simultaneously published my work of hockey fiction, *The Last Season*, and Ken's non-fiction epic, *The Game*, possibly the best book on sport ever written by an athlete. Ken's book absolutely swamped mine in sales and attention, but I was proud then, and remain so, to have been a small contributor to what stands as a major work in sports literature. The ghost who wasn't required.

Halfway through my year of working with Wayne Gretzky, the *American Journalism Review* even took notice and published a short piece entitled "Ghostwriting for The Great One." The *National Post* column had been picked up by United Feature Syndicate and was appearing increasingly around the United States. When I first heard about the piece, I figured it would be another attack. But it was nothing.

Writer Sean Mussenden fingered the ghostwriter by name but rather surprisingly added that *The Washington Post* had also tagged me "the closest thing there is to a poet laureate of Canadian hockey." The article quoted one journalism professor saying he believed any ghostwritten article should "disclose" the ghost-writer with a credit at the end, but *National Post* sports editor Graham Parley said this was hardly necessary, as it was quite well known that I was the ghost. In fact, Gretzky himself often joked about it and would call me his "ghost" on the few occasions we bumped into each other that 1999–2000 season in which the column ran. "The Great One," Mussenden concluded in his very mild piece, "whom *National Post* columnist Cam Cole recently described as being harder 'to get an audience with [than] the Dalai Lama,' could not be reached for comment."

—

At the end of the 2000 Stanley Cup finals—New Jersey Devils defeating the Dallas Stars in six games—the Wayne Gretzky column "retired" for the summer, never to appear again.

He was getting increasingly involved in the game again—first as executive director of Team Canada heading into the 2002 Salt Lake City Winter Games, where Canada won its first gold medal in men's hockey in half a century, then as coach of the Phoenix Coyotes.

I still have that last column. He was talking about the devastating check laid on Eric Lindros by Scott Stevens during an earlier playoff round between Stevens' Devils and Lindros's Philadelphia Flyers. Lindros was left with a concussion that, ultimately, would play a role in his early retirement from the game he had, for a very short while, dominated.

He argued that "clean" hits or "dirty" hits were not the issue here, that all that matters is the health of the players. He advised changes in equipment and called for better testing and evaluation to understand just how severe the concussion threat is to the game. "My fear, my real concern," Gretzky wrote, "is that we are just scratching the surface. We're still a long way from getting a good handle on what concussion is and how it can be prevented, and yet we also have to be moving as quickly as possible to find a remedy for this very real threat to the game."

Sounds like a strong stance to me.

Just think, if the NHL and NHL Players' Association had only moved on this issue "as quickly as possible to find a remedy," perhaps today's concerns over headhunting and the threat to the careers of the likes of Sidney Crosby would not be an issue.

Rather prescient and powerful, Columnist Gretzky, if I do say so myself.

TWO

THE NATIONAL GAME

"THE DANCE OF LIFE"—
THE OPENING OF A NEW SEASON
(*The Globe and Mail*, October 7, 2010)

Hockey has no founding father or mother or identifiable moment of birth. It was invented in the imagination and is reinvented every day from early fall on in the backyards and—where still permitted—side streets of this hockey-mad country.

As the National Hockey League returns to the ice on Thursday, this much is undeniable: Hockey is Canada's game. There is nothing to be gained by pointing out that a Mesopotamian tablet dating from the third millennium BC makes reference to men using wickedly curved sticks—apparently not illegal in those days—to propel a wooden ring over the dirt. There is no ear here for the argument that Pieter Bruegel's *Hunters in the Snow*, painted in 1565, appears to contain a game of shinny in the background. Nor do we really much care about the more localized claims that the game was first played in the Far North by the men on the Franklin expedition, and if not there then on a pond near Windsor, Nova Scotia, or if not there then at Kingston, Ontario, or even that there are newspaper clips to prove that the first organized game took place in Montreal.

Soccer might claim more numbers, but hockey leads, as it always has, in nightly dreams and daily conversation. The grip this "national drama"—Morley Callaghan's phrase—has on people is difficult to explain to those who did not grow up in its grasp or, as happens increasingly these days, came to embrace the game as they and, in particular, their children came to terms with a new climate.

Lester Pearson tried to convey this sense in 1939 when the future prime minister of Canada told an audience in London, England: "It is perhaps fitting that this fastest of all games has become almost as much of a national symbol as the maple leaf or the beaver. Most young Canadians, in fact, are born with skates on their feet rather than with silver spoons in their mouths."

Hockey had to be Canada's game. Had Canada invented baseball instead, players would have frozen to death between pitches. "In a land so inescapably and inhospitably cold," Bruce Kidd and John Macfarlane wrote many years ago, "hockey is the dance of life, an affirmation that despite the deathly chill of winter we are alive."

Very soon after Kidd and Macfarlane published their book on hockey, however, something happened to the national game. It was called the 1972 Summit Series.

The famous series is generally hailed as Canada's greatest victory on ice—Paul Henderson's dramatic goal surely the "singular moment in time" for generations of Canadians who can recall not only where they were but what they were wearing. The remarkable comeback in Moscow by the spunky Canadians launched a celebration that had as much, if not more, to do with relief as it did with triumph. Heading into the eight-game series—supposedly a friendly exhibition—the Soviets had not been given a chance. They had no goaltending. They had no shots. They had no coaching. Canada would probably sweep the series because hockey is Canada's game. When Henderson scored that final goal, it meant that Canada had won by the narrowest of margins imaginable—a single goal scored with only thirty-four seconds left in the final game.

"When the country's celebration ended," Ken Dryden and I wrote in *Home Game: Hockey and Life in Canada* back in 1989, "the new day looked different. A lot had happened in the twenty-seven days since the first game in Montreal. A symbol, something about us, that we had always taken as self-evident, had been rocked. Our innocence, our confidence and enthusiasm, our urge to jump into the world's deep water—we had changed."

This lack of confidence, so often buried under bravado, would rise and fall for decades following the 1972 series. The 3–3 tie between the Soviet Red Army and the Montreal Canadiens on New Year's Eve, 1975, would be spoken of as "the greatest game ever played," yet if that were true—and many still believe it was—then it meant that the Russian robots had risen to a level equal with the very best of Canadian hockey. And if the Russians were coming, how soon the Americans?

Outsiders could still be beaten by Canadian players in Canada Cups or in NHL exhibitions, but too often the difference maker would be brawn (as when the Philadelphia Flyers pummelled the Red Army back into the dressing room in early 1976) or, as it was so often said, heart—despite medical proof that Russians, Swedes, Finns and Czechs all got their blood from a similar pump.

Canada had entered an uneasy time with its own game. Every loss, no matter how close it might be—the 1981 Canada Cup, Rendez-Vous '87, various world championships and junior championships—seemed to cause another jolt of identity angst. Having wished for a century or more that the world would appreciate the game that Canada had given it, many Canadians seemed unable to accept that the game had indeed been taken up by others and that others could play it.

This anxiety came to a crisis point as the game entered its second century. Canadians had always believed that if only NHLers were allowed to participate in the Olympics, world dominance would be automatic. When it happened in 1998, and the Canadian men's team failed even to win a medal, the blow to national pride was devastating. That year also saw the beginning of seven consecutive world junior championships in which the best hockey country in the world could not prove itself best.

By 2002, in Salt Lake City, this growing national anguish was expressed perfectly by the country's greatest player, Wayne Gretzky, when he told a startled media gathering that "the whole world wants us to lose."

A few days later, however, the whole world (at least the small world that gives a damn about hockey) saw Canada win, and not only the men's gold medal but the women's as well.

In retrospect, the self-doubt and anxiety played an important role. Canada began questioning its own sense of superiority in the 1990s—never so much as at the 1999 Open Ice Summit, which could basically be summed up in three words: What went wrong?

To the great credit of those who have a say in shaping the way the game is played as well as those who play the game—from Hockey Canada down to the smallest local minor hockey organization—everything from coaching to skill level was re-examined and, often, reconsidered. You would have to be naive and foolish to call it perfect, but there can be no doubt that the game is in better shape in Canada today than it has been for decades. The 2010 hockey summit held in Toronto this last summer seemed oddly unpressing, almost unnecessary.

Canada is once again comfortable in its hockey skin.

The men and women won gold in Vancouver. If the juniors don't win gold, they at least play for it. Young Canadians such as Sidney Crosby (captain of the 2009 Stanley Cup champion Pittsburgh Penguins), Jonathan Toews (captain of the 2010 Stanley Cup–winning Chicago Blackhawks) and the two top draft picks of the 2010 draft, Taylor Hall of the Edmonton Oilers and Tyler Seguin of the Boston Bruins, are all . . . Canadian.

There remains, however, one itch still to be scratched. One

that has grown increasingly irritating since 1993, when the Montreal Canadiens last accomplished the feat.

And that is to bring the Stanley Cup home. Where it began— and where a great many Canadians believe it belongs.

THE HEART OF HOCKEY

(*Legion* Magazine, January/February 1999)

Long after I had stopped asking about Santa Claus, I still believed that hockey in this country was a creation of The Royal Canadian Legion.

In the fall of 1956, the year I turned eight, my mother gave me the two dollars necessary to sign up for town league hockey. With the two-dollar bill and my birth certificate in pocket, I walked with Brent and Eric, then and still the very best friends in the world, down the hill and along the leaf-splattered Muskoka River to the Memorial Arena in Huntsville, a small town on the edge of Ontario's famous Algonquin Park. It was a typical rink of its day, large and bulky, erected in honour of those who had fought for their country, and the women of Branch 232 ran the snack bar. I was placed on the Legion Auxiliary team, which naturally meant we would be called the "Legion Ladies." We were, as I recall, proud to be called this, for the simple sweater—blue, with a white maple leaf—not only made us feel like miniatures of the real Leafs, but it guaranteed quick service at the hot chocolate counter.

The Legion itself, further up the hill from the river, was also where the minor hockey organization held the year-end banquet and would one day, a few years later, be the site of the one moment for which Brent and Eric and I are forever remembered in Huntsville minor hockey lore. Unfortunately, it had nothing to do with what we could do on the ice. One of us—history has conveniently forgotten which—passed wind so loudly during Mayor Frank

Hubbell's opening remarks that it brought the awards ceremony to a dead halt. The three of us, giggling and red-faced, crawled and crouched beneath the drooping white cloths of the long table assigned to the bantams—and we stayed there, the room silent, the mayor clearing his throat, until Mrs. Kelly, resplendent in Legion uniform, stuck her stately head under the cloth and informed us, in no uncertain terms, that we would all be given one chance to smarten up or else. It was, and remains, the best piece of advice the three of us ever received.

Forty-three years after I laid down that first two-dollar bill, I am still a hockey player. There have been small glories and large disappointments. I have made teams and been cut from teams, played in front of crowds and, today, play in front of no one. As an old-timer, I have passed recently from teams that worried about the goaltender showing up to a team that worries whether or not the doctor on left wing will be out tonight, and yet the love of the game remains as intense, if not as simple, as it was that very first season of 1956–57, when I was fortunate enough to wear the blue and white colours of the Legion Auxiliary.

The "highlight" of that season was the day the *Toronto Daily Star* and *Toronto Telegram* and the *Globe & Mail* all came to town to see the wonders that had been created by a few townsfolk who had cared enough to build a rink and organize the kids. The following Wednesday the local *Forester* ran a photograph that shows me with two teammates and the coach of the town's all-star teams, the cutline reading:

> Last minute adjustments to the goalkeeper's pads are made by Huntsville's top notch hockey coach Mye Sedore before Roy MacGregor, Terry Stinson and Donny Strano of the Legion Ladies' Auxiliary team took the ice to perform before Maple Leaf scouts Bob Davidson and Pep Kelly and Toronto newspapermen at the Arena last Saturday morning when 270 Huntsville kids showed the visitors how the Town

Hockey League functions. They put on a grand show and the three Toronto daily newspapers told the story in big pictures and lots of type in their Monday and Tuesday editions, attracting countrywide attention to this Muskoka town and its surrounding district.

Perhaps the cutline ran on a bit, but so too did our imaginations back then. Having been scouted, at age eight, by the Leafs' very own Bob Davidson, who had even come into our dressing room, it would only be a matter of time, surely, before I was in the National Hockey League.

Time, however, doesn't always co-operate. It is now 1999, racing toward 2000. No one pays two dollars to play the game anymore. It costs me about $500 a year just for ice time, to say nothing of the sticks and tape and the endless sharpening that never seems to have me skating as I stubbornly believe I once could. Hockey, I must now concede, has played as much a part of my life as family, school and work. In fact, it has at times been both family and work, for I treasure the years when I coached first Christine and then Gordon, two of our four children who also played the game, and for the past six years my full-time job has been to cover the Ottawa Senators and the National Hockey League as a sports columnist. There have also, along the way, been four books on the game and a sprawling, now up to ten, series of hockey-based children's mysteries.

This is not to suggest there is no ambivalence in such a confession. Like everyone else in this country who has become caught up with the national game, I have my moments when I shudder over what it has become. I cannot abide the corporate suites and multi-million-dollar salaries of today's NHL. I grow easily bored at the style of the game at the professional level. I find the violence unnecessary, the clutching and grabbing unnatural. I consider Don Cherry's commentaries as destructive to today's game as Howie Meeker's once were instructive.

As coach and hockey writer, I have seen more than my fair share of boorish parents, men who bait referees not much older than their own children, women who sit in stands with stopwatches, insecure men and women so determined that they are able to say their child plays "competitive" that they have allowed house leagues to be ransacked in order to create levels of inter-community play where the youngsters can barely skate. As a coach, I have fielded the incessant calls from fathers who want practice hours turned into exhibition games so that the parents have something to watch, and measure, even if it means our children now practise so little that it is no wonder we are losing out to those who believe there is a magic to hockey that cannot be learned in game conditions where every experiment earns a reprimand.

There are times when I sit in cold Canadian rinks, shivering lips blowing over a cup of coffee that tastes like boiled pucks, and agree with the long-time official of the Canadian Amateur Hockey Association who admitted to me one day that the one great regret in his career was that 1960s campaign to get parents to "take, don't send" their children to the local rink. Once some of those parents began to see their involvement in minor hockey as an investment, both in time and in money, they began to look for a return on that investment. And that is when hockey in Canada became more career than recreation.

Rising above all these unfortunate points, however, is the game itself, and the happy majority of parents and coaches who remain, today, not all that much different from Mrs. Kelly and Mye Sedore of so many years ago. For every hideous story of minor league politics that is passed on to me, I come across two or three incidents that give hope. The kids up the street playing road hockey in the dead end. The teacher who turns an hour of gym class over to an old-fashioned game of shinny. The coach who takes his team out on an open-air rink so that they will know what it is to play, and feel, this extraordinary game when sweat rolls down your spine and a January wind finds its way through your collar. When people talk to me of Triple-A hockey and summer hockey schools and power-skating clinics, I am reminded of a quiet conversation I had with Wayne Gretzky one slow afternoon during the 1996 World Cup. In the words of the greatest player the game has ever seen, he didn't get that way through fifty-minute ice slots, but "in my back-yard and basement." Where he could try things and, when they didn't work out, try them again and again and again until they did. Where he could experiment without being criticized.

Where he could play.

That, of course, is what should give us all hope for this game that is, at the moment, going through some rough times in this country. Gather sportswriters anywhere and they will always mention two things about the game of hockey. The first, and the one Canada should be most proud of, is how remarkably "decent" the vast majority of hockey players have remained at a time when boorish behaviour among professional athletes is far more the norm than the exception. Ken Rappoport, who has covered sports out of New York City for the Associated Press for decades, once told me he thought there must be a connection to all those early practices hockey players head out for with their mother or father. "Someone's got to make those drives," he said. "If there's no family support they won't have the right equipment and they won't be able to afford to play the game. There has to be that family environment or they don't become hockey players."

The other thing they invariably mention is the sheer pleasure that this game seems to bring all those who play it, from the smallest children to the most jaded professional to the overweight old-timers Thursday nights at midnight. Sportswriters rarely see baseball, football or basketball players still playing their games, but it is not at all unusual to come across a group of NHL multi-millionaires playing with a roll of tape in the rink corridors, or finding a group of players—Russians, Swedes, Finns, Czechs, Canadians—staying out on the ice at the end of a practice to see who can put the most point shots off the crossbar.

It is the sheer joy of hockey that will save it from money and television ratings and obsession with size and poor officiating and so much expansion that soon clutching and grabbing will become part of the "skills competition" at the annual All-Star Game.

For even if every NHL team in Canada left this country for New Mexico, there would still be someone willing to go out with a wide shovel and the firehoses and flood the school rink for nothing but the pleasure of knowing that a child might put on his or her skates and pick up a stick and chase a puck and feel, if even for the briefest moment, what it is to play the sweetest game of all.

I worry about the game, but do not despair. Each mail delivery brings another pencil-printed letter from a Screech Owls reader who wants me to know that he—and ever more often she—loves this game as no other play they have found. Nor will I ever forget that eighteen months when I covered, full-time, the Citizens' Forum on Canada's Future, the Spicer Commission, and how every session in all those church basements and community halls and large-enough living rooms began with the same question, a commissioner asking the people gathered that evening—usually older, always concerned—what it was they loved about this great big country. Medicare, they answered. And hockey. Always the first two mentioned.

The reason is simple: Hockey means more to Canadians than mere sport. "Hockey is Canada's game," Ken Dryden and I wrote in the book *Home Game.* "It may also be Canada's national theatre . . . it is a place where the monumental themes of Canadian life are played out—English and French, East and West, Canada and the U.S., Canada and the world, the timeless tensions of commerce and culture, our struggle to survive and civilize winter."

It is also fun. Fun tomorrow in that little Prairie rink when no one else in their right mind would be up. Fun this weekend when the child, or grandchild, is standing at the end of the bed pulling on your blankets to get you going. Fun tonight, when no matter how much your bones and muscles say no, there is something in your imagination that will send you down to the basement where that heavy bag of disgusting equipment lies—and where there is always at least one more pretty goal in the stick that looks good for one more game.

In 2011 I turned sixty-three and still play, now "cutting back" to three hours a week. The greatest delight is playing with son Gordon and several of his friends, those of us old enough to be their fathers grateful for passes and accepting of the ridicule that is reality in a hockey dressing room. I now use an expensive composite stick that has done nothing, absolutely nothing, for my game.

★ ★ ★

THREE

LEGENDS OF THE GAME

MARIO LEMIEUX'S LONG JOURNEY

(The Globe and Mail, January 1, 2011)

He hasn't lost a step.

There are not many players you can say that about at age forty-five and five years removed from his skates, but the truth is Mario Lemieux never had much of a step to begin with. Never needed it—not when you could fire the puck over the net from centre ice at age eight, not when peewee goaltenders used to weep at the mere prospect of facing you, not when you score on your very first shift in the National Hockey League.

There was not much to cheer about at the Winter Classic Alumni Game. Once the introductions are done with, interest in old-timers playing shinny drops as quickly as the puck at the opening faceoff.

In Pittsburgh, however, they came out ten thousand strong in the early morning to cheer the player who saved the franchise so many times he now owns it. They cheered as, toque replacing helmet, Lemieux made his way out from the football stadium locker room to the outdoor rink where Saturday's much-hyped "Classic" game will be played between his Pittsburgh Penguins, featuring Sidney Crosby, and the Washington Capitals, with Alexander Ovechkin.

They cheered when hockey's former superstar won the opening faceoff and cheered again when, predictably, he floated into the opponents' end, sailing more than skating, and promptly set up the first goal of the game.

"Some things never change," chuckled his long-time friend and one-time teammate Paul Coffey.

They would have cheered even louder had the NHL shown the common sense to send the dreary alumni game to a shootout when it ended 5–5—a move that would have allowed Lemieux the chance at one more hockey heroic, even if rather meaningless compared to all the others.

It has been a long journey for the one they called The Magnificent One. I met him first in 1985 at the world championships in Prague, where his play as a teenager was the talk of the tournament. He was shy, reluctant, and spoke little English. His personality transformation over the years has been almost as remarkable as his on-ice accomplishments. He once refused to play for the Canadian juniors because he did not like the coach. He refused to shake the hand or don the jersey of the NHL team, the Penguins, that drafted him. He learned English, but rarely bothered talking, preferring to duck out the dressing room's back doors than to face the press.

His on-ice brilliance was undeniable. From that goal on the first shift—stealing the puck from the great Ray Bourque, no less—he chased Wayne Gretzky through a decade of NHL records that still stand. He won every trophy available. He scored that most brilliant goal during the 1987 Canada Cup. He purposely let that puck slip through his legs to Paul Kariya during the 2002 Winter Games as he captained Canada to Olympic gold. He battled remarkable health issues—back operations, cancer—retired from the game, was chosen for the Hall of Fame, and came back not only to play again but to star.

However, he changed his personality when he had to sell the

game, not merely play it. When bankruptcy threatened to destroy this franchise and take the millions of deferred salary he was owed with it, he somewhat reluctantly became an owner and today, with a brand-new rink for his team, seems at ease in his new life.

Lemieux sat on a stool after the shinny match, microphone in hand, and talked about whatever subject was raised. He was asked about Crosby, the youngster Lemieux took into his own home and who is now on his own, captain of the 2009 Stanley Cup champion Penguins and leading scorer in the NHL this season.

"Incredible," Lemieux said. As for the twenty-five-game scoring streak Crosby recently put up, incredible doesn't even begin to measure it. "It's not the same as it was twenty years ago," Lemieux said in considering his own remarkable forty-six-game streak of 1989–90. "What he's doing now is much more impressive than anything I did. It's tougher to dominate the way the league is today."

He then talked about how the rivalry he had with Gretzky might compare to all the current talk concerning Crosby and Ovechkin. Hard to say for sure, he mused, as the game has changed so dramatically, particularly in terms of overall speed and in the skating ability of today's defence. Gretzky, he said, liked to hold the puck and had a signature play of curling back with it to buy a little extra time. "You can't do that anymore," he said.

He said nothing of his own style. He didn't need to. As former teammate Luc Robitaille once put it, "A fire hydrant could score forty goals with him."

Ovechkin, Lemieux said, has an extraordinary physical presence and, of course, that "shot." Crosby, on the other hand, is "more controlling" out there, seeking out pucks and using incredible speed and strength to create opportunities in a game that, today, seems all about speed.

"Two different styles," he said, "two different eras."

But still the same game—and always better for a top-notch rivalry. Gretzky and Lemieux. Crosby and Ovechkin. Someone else tomorrow . . .

In the real game that followed, Crosby was hit by Washington's David Steckel—perhaps by accident, as Steckel maintained—and likely suffered the concussion that was exacerbated a few days later when hit by Tampa Bay Lightning defenceman Victor Hedman. The absence of Crosby from the game begat a debate over head-shots that would come to dominate the NHL's 2010–11 season. When a brawl broke out between the Penguins and the New York Islanders in February, Lemieux spoke out, calling the game "a travesty" and saying if such action reflected the state of the NHL, he needed "to rethink whether I want to be a part of it." Pittsburgh general manager Ray Shero became one of the strongest advocates for cleaning up headshots and, later in the year, when the NHL suspended Penguins forward Matt Cooke for the remainder of the season and the first round of the playoffs for just such a hit, the Penguins not only accepted the suspension but applauded it.

GOING IT ALONE: MATS SUNDIN

(*The Globe and Mail*, February 5, 2007)

He may be the loneliest star the game has known.

His name links with no other player, not even with any very special team. Lemieux and Jagr. Hull and Mikita. Lindsay and Howe. Sittler and McDonald. But unlike them, his name automatically rings no other bell.

Esposito had Orr back on the blueline. Gretzky found himself maturing with Messier, Coffey, Kurri, Fuhr. Lafleur had Lemaire and Shutt and the best defence in all of hockey to feed up the puck. Henri Richard was so lucky that, when he retired, he found he had more Stanley Cup rings than fingers.

Even today there are combinations people speak of in some awe: Lecavalier and St. Louis, Spezza and Heatley, Crosby when he is on the power play with Malkin.

But no name has ever connected for long with that of Mats Sundin. And it begs the question: How good was—and, to a degree, still is—the captain of the Toronto Maple Leafs?

Sundin is now thirty-five years old. He has lost every golden hair that shone that day in 1989 when he became, at eighteen, the first European hockey player ever to go No. 1 in the entry draft. He has played for only two teams: the Quebec Nordiques, who traded him before they headed off to Denver and the Stanley Cup, and the Leafs, who have been poor to middling to not-quite-good-enough in the dozen years that he has been, by far, the team's most consistent player. He has never won a Stanley Cup, never played in a Stanley Cup final.

He scored twenty-three goals as a solid six-foot-five rookie and has scored twenty goals or more every single season since, a remarkable record given the teams he has suffered and the certainty of injury in today's NHL. When he scored his twentieth last week—the game winner against the New York Rangers—he set a new Leafs record for consecutive twenty-goal seasons, surpassing the likes of Darryl Sittler and Dave Keon. He played his twelve hundredth game that week and, a month earlier, had recorded his twelve-hundredth point—again, the picture of consistency.

Saturday night in Ottawa, he scored the second Toronto goal on a calm and deliberate pause move that had Ottawa goaltender Ray Emery helplessly sliding out of the net and out of the way. And then, when overtime still ended in a tie, he scored on a magnificent backhand in the shootout to give Toronto the chance to win, which they eventually did. All in a night's work, with no one in particular to play with. This night it was Alexei Ponikarovsky and Nik Antropov, two forwards who benefit hugely from playing with him but are otherwise unremarkable. When they were injured earlier, it was at times Alex Steen and Jeff O'Neill, both of whom saw their games pick up thanks to Sundin.

It is a curious story of bad luck. The best winger Sundin ever had with the Leafs was Alexander Mogilny, then near the end of his glory days. When Sundin was with the young and rising Nordiques, the team decided to trust in centres Joe Sakic and newcomer Peter Forsberg, trading Sundin off to the Leafs for former Leafs captain Wendel Clark, two others and a draft pick.

The Nordiques became the Avalanche and, for a while, such an elite team that it seemed every star had a star to play with, while Sundin headed off to Toronto and a seemingly endless string of wingers simply not up to his level. Because he was replacing Clark, one of Toronto's all-time most popular players, Leafs fans warmed slowly to the big Swede and never have warmed as much as they would if he brought them a Stanley Cup. But, of course, they have yet to make the finals with him and, again this year, are middle of the pack.

Every few years, however, Sundin shows the hockey world that he stands among the best who have ever played. In World Cup play, he has been the best player in the tournament, though Sweden has come up short. In Olympics play, the same. In Salt Lake City in 2002, the Swedes were by far the best team, only to implode mysteriously against Belarus. In 2006, he finally led his country to the gold medal in Turin.

"With the national team, he's tremendous," says Ottawa captain Daniel Alfredsson, who has been Sundin's linemate over several of those tournaments. "He just dominates out there."

At thirty-five and after sixteen seasons, it is likely that the best of Mats Sundin has been seen in the NHL—but also likely that the best was never allowed to be seen. Simply because of chance. Simply because, in careers as well as in games, the bounces sometimes go different ways.

"Sports is hard to explain," Sundin said Saturday night in regard to another question. But it was also a good enough answer for a remarkable career that has been, pretty much, one man alone in a team game.

*In the summer of 2008, unrestricted free agent Sundin was ponder-
ing retirement and turned down a two-year, $20-million offer*
from the Vancouver Canucks. He later reconsidered, however, and
signed a one-year deal in December. It was not a good decision, as
he managed only 9 goals and 19 assists in 41 games, though he rose
to a point a game in the playoffs. Sundin did retire this time,
leaving with 1,349 points in 1,346 games, Hall of Fame numbers
by any measure.*

NO "ORDINARY JOE"

(*National Post*, May 28, 2001)

The star thing just isn't me. — Joe Sakic, 1996

It still isn't. It is now five years since Joe Sakic, hockey's "Ordinary
Joe," won the Conn Smythe Trophy as he led his Colorado
Avalanche to its first Stanley Cup.

A second is suddenly looming, thanks to Sakic's extraordinary
play in Game 1 of this final series, in which he scored the winning
goal, added a spectacular insurance goal and set up another in the
Avalanche's 5–0 romp over the New Jersey Devils—a game also
notable in that Sakic, the team captain, turned New Jersey captain
Scott Stevens, last year's Conn Smythe Trophy winner, inside out and
upside down and outside in as he quietly went about his business.

They are talking today about a second Smythe for the player
with the early lead on playoff MVP honours. He is already nominated for the Hart Trophy as the league's most valuable player
during the regular season, the Selke Trophy as the league's best
defensive forward and the Lady Byng as the NHL's most gentlemanly player.

---

* Player salaries and franchise values in U.S. dollars

Not since 1991 has any player been nominated for three regular-season awards (goaltender Ed Belfour for the Hart, the Vezina as the top goaltender and the Calder as top rookie), and if Sakic were somehow to pull off a Tiger Woods–like sweep of four major awards—plus the Stanley Cup—it would stand as one of the best individual seasons the game has ever witnessed. Only Boston's Bobby Orr, in 1969–70, pulled off a similar feat (winning the Hart Trophy, Conn Smythe Trophy, Art Ross Trophy as the NHL's top scorer and Norris Trophy as top defenceman to go with the Bruins' Stanley Cup title).

Perhaps then they would spell his name right, as one paper here failed to do back in 1996 when he brought the Avalanche a championship in the franchise's very first season. Perhaps a few people might even start pronouncing his name correctly— "Sack-ich," his parents claim, not "Sak-ic," as it has become—and, who knows, he might one day even escape the only nickname he has in hockey, which also happens to be incorrect information.

"Burnaby Joe," they call him in Canada. It should be "Vancouver Joe," if anything. Born there, raised there—and only off to Burnaby to play his minor hockey and pick up the moniker that still somewhat irritates his parents, Marijan and Slavica Sakic.

Joe Sakic himself is unlikely to set the record straight. What he learned from his father, Marijan—a Croatian stonemason who ended up working in construction on the West Coast—is that "talking meant nothing," and there is certainly ample evidence of this to be found in the thirteen years of reporters' notebooks that track his career. He does, actually, have one more nickname among the NHL press: "Quoteless Joe."

Even in the heady minutes following Saturday night's impressive win over the Devils, Sakic was his usual librarian self. The Devils—frozen to the ice in the eyes of everyone else—were "a great hockey team" in the eyes of Joe Sakic. His lovely first goal, a quick snap shot between the legs of New Jersey goaltender

Martin Brodeur as Sakic flew down the right side, was the result, he claimed, of "a great pass" from Rob Blake to Milan Hejduk who then "just got it over to me."

As for Sakic's second goal—in which he flew down the same side, curled, set Stevens in place as if he were more ice auger than defenceman, stepped into the clearing and blasted a quick shot to Brodeur's stick side, well . . .

"I really don't know what happened."

Perhaps it is better, then, that we do the talking for him. Sakic, an amazed New Jersey coach Larry Robinson said when it was over, could have played the game carrying "eggs in his pants" for all his Devils were able to do to catch him. And Ray Bourque, Sakic's relatively new teammate who played so many years for Boston, suggested that once Sakic gets his full speed up with the puck, even a defenceman of Scott Stevens's stature is helpless.

"If you miss," said Bourque, "forget it."

But there is so much more to Joe Sakic's season than this one night. He might win all four trophies. He will almost certainly win the Hart as the clear MVP of the entire league. He already came second in both the race for that Art Ross Trophy that went to the top point getter (Pittsburgh's Jaromir Jagr) and the Rocket Richard Trophy that went to the top goal scorer (Florida's Pavel Bure).

Joe Sakic is thirty-one years old. He has spent his entire career with this organization, dating back to when the Avalanche were the Quebec Nordiques. He had been a junior sensation with the Swift Current Broncos but, likely because of his slight size, was not even the Nordiques' first choice in 1987, his draft year. They took Bryan Fogarty, who never worked out, first (ninth overall), and on their next choice—after such names as Wayne McBean, Jayson Moore, Yves Racine, Keith Osborne and Dean Chynoweth had been called out by other teams—they went for the quick little centre from Western Canada with the fifteenth overall pick.

Thirteen NHL seasons later and Sakic is numbered among the very best players in the league, with an impressive 1,178 points (including 457 goals) in his 934 regular season games played. His playoff performance is equally impressive, his 53 goals (and counting) the most any NHLer has scored over the past decade.

Yet if he fails to get the public and media attention that such numbers demand, it cannot be said that he has passed unnoticed in hockey. He was, with Mario Lemieux, the most obvious among the first eight chosen to represent Canada at the 2002 Winter Olympics. It has not been forgotten that, had Sakic not been injured in Nagano in 1998, there might have been no need of a shootout.

The New York Rangers certainly noticed his worth a few years back when they tried to lure the then-restricted free agent away from Colorado with an offer sheet that forced the Avalanche to match and, for one season, made Joe Sakic hockey's only $17-million-a-year man. Sakic's financial value is of increasing interest in hockey circles, for on July 1 he will become an unrestricted free agent, able to choose wherever he wishes to play. He missed full agency by a mere six days last year and elected to sign a one-year deal for $7.9 million in order to be entirely free this summer.

The Avalanche, however, will do what they can to keep their captain. The franchise is extremely rich and already pays teammate—and fellow former Quebec Nordique—Peter Forsberg $10 million a year. The gathered media wanted to talk about that yesterday afternoon. About that contract and free agency and what he would make and where he would want to play and . . .

"I haven't thought too much about it," he said.

It sounded much the same as the Joe Sakic of 1996, who was asked how he thought hockey fans regarded him. "I . . . don't know," he stammered. "I guess they can see for themselves on the ice—just a guy who works hard out there."

And gets the job done.

The next year, Sakic was a pivotal player in Team Canada's Olympic gold medal victory at the Salt Lake City Winter Games, where he was named tournament MVP. He played several more years but back issues finally forced retirement in 2009. He played 1,378 games, scoring 625 goals and 1,016 assists. He won the Stanley Cup twice, the Conn Smythe, the Hart as the league's most valuable player and the Lady Byng as the league's most gentlemanly. Today, Sakic works for the Avalanche in an executive capacity.

THE LONG JOURNEY FROM DOUBT TO BELIEF: STEVE YZERMAN

(*National Post*, June 14, 2002)

DETROIT, MICHIGAN

They are known, as well, by the way they come and go. At the rear entrance to the Joe Louis Arena, the diehard fans with their disposable cameras and autograph binders wait in a small red-and-white cluster at the point where the Red Wings players leave following the final practice before what these fans, and the players, trust will be the final game of the 2002 Stanley Cup playoffs.

Chris Chelios and Brett Hull travel together in a thirty-year-old black Cadillac convertible, roof down, enjoying the spotlight and the cheers even if refusing to acknowledge their adoring fans. Young Russian Pavel Datsyuk stops his dark Mercedes and happily signs a few caps and jersey backs. Popular forward Darren McCarty stops his big SUV and signs his name and poses for photographs for as long as it takes, the lineup to get out of the players' parking lot growing ever longer and ever more impatient.

One of those stuck in the lineup is team captain Steve Yzerman. He sits, in a black Yukon behind darkly tinted glass, with his back oddly turned to the window and his stare self-consciously averted. He looks much more like a waiting getaway driver in a bank holdup than the sentimental favourite to win his second

Conn Smythe Trophy as the MVP of the playoffs. If the Wings were to have defeated the Carolina Hurricanes in Game 5 last night, the Smythe was expected to go him or to defenceman Nicklas Lidstrom, who has also performed brilliantly this spring for Detroit.

Some of the players who blow by the diehards are lightly booed if they fail to slow or even acknowledge the fans' presence. But not Yzerman. He sees his opening, stares straight down at the road ahead, turns even more away from them and guns his vehicle out onto the main road—and still they cheer and shout his name.

To them, that's just the way Steve Yzerman is.

There was a time, only a few years ago, when he would disguise himself as he moved about the city. Dark glasses, hat pulled down. At one point, in late 1997, he even admitted that "the last five years I didn't want to be recognized." But that was before the one they call "Stevie Y" finally came true. Before the Stanley Cup victories in 1997 and 1998, before he won his first Conn Smythe in 1998 and later added such honours as the 2000 Selke Trophy as the league's best defensive forward, and before Salt Lake City, where he may well have been the best player on the ice this spring when Canada won the Olympic gold medal.

After nineteen years in the same Red Wings uniform, no one doubts Yzerman anymore. He has his Stanley Cup rings, the Olympic gold medal, the Hall of Fame is a lock—and yet he is still essentially the same shy, unfailingly polite, introspective young man who came out of Nepean, Ontario, two decades ago and discovered there was precious little recognition to go around in hockey after Wayne Gretzky and Mario Lemieux had taken their fair share.

It has been a long journey. His has gone from the twenty-one-year-old captain who seemed and acted too young to hold authority to one whose leadership today is lauded. He has gone from sixty-five-goal seasons and incredible scoring feats—"They were so long ago now I don't even remember them"—to being known as much for his checking as for his scoring. "It just never got noticed until I stopped scoring," he once said rather ruefully.

He has gone from the fresh-faced eighteen-year-old who broke in in '83 to a veteran who hobbles between games on a right knee so damaged it very nearly kept him out of the Olympics and will almost certainly require surgery in the off-season. It is, today, hard to believe that for years after Scotty Bowman came here in 1993, the Detroit coach was not a great believer in Yzerman, whom he regarded as somewhat one-dimensional. He fell out of favour. He was, at one time, on the verge of being shipped off to the Ottawa Senators, where it was presumed he would quickly live out his career and soon be gone. He was seen, then, as a brilliant player who could not quite deliver, the Stanley Cup just slightly beyond his grasp.

"A guy like Yzerman," former Montreal Canadiens general manager Serge Savard once said, "he's never won anything."

Always there were doubts. He was twice cut from Canada Cup lineups and had even reached a point where he wondered himself if he was a winner. After that first Stanley Cup win five years ago he admitted, "I don't have to battle other people's doubts, or even my doubts, for that matter." The new confidence changed him. He ceased having problems with Bowman as if, at last, each understood the other—though there may, in fact, be no understanding to be had for Bowman's coaching genius.

"How to get along with him," Yzerman said earlier this week, "is to show up, work hard, and keep your mouth shut." And then he paused, thinking to add one more critical point: "And play well defensively."

He is thirty-seven now, and while some have suggested the wonky knee may mean the Hall of Fame will come earlier than expected, others are convinced he has found new life with this late arrival of such success. Three Stanley Cups, after all, are one more than Lemieux, one short of Gretzky—the two figures in whose shadows he has skated all these years.

"Age," he now says, "has really become irrelevant in the league. It doesn't necessarily mean we're going to be the same team five years from now, but age right now means nothing."

In fact, it does mean something significant: experience.

Injuries began to take a terrible toll on Yzerman. He played but sixteen games in 2002–03, scoring twice. The next year he recovered to 51 points but the following year was lost to the owners' lockout. He scored 14 goals and 20 assists in 2005–06 and then chose retirement. His 1,755 points left him sixth in all-time scoring and he was the longest-serving captain in NHL history. In 2009, he entered the Hall of Fame and in 2010 was named general manager of the Tampa Bay Lightning.

SAINT PATRICK OF THE NETS
(*National Post*, May 29, 2001)

Tucked into a corner of Patrick Roy's locker in the Colorado Avalanche's suburban practice facility is a small photograph of Bobby Orr in a Chicago Blackhawks uniform. The two Hockey Hall-of-Famers—one ensconced, one on his way—have much in common despite their different eras and different positions, for just as Bobby Orr revolutionized the way defence is played in the modern game, Patrick Roy has done the same for goaltending.

Where they may part company is in the second uniform. Bobby Orr looks out of sorts out of a Boston Bruins sweater. Patrick Roy—twice a Stanley Cup champion with the Montreal Canadiens, twice winner of the Conn Smythe Trophy as the Habs' most valuable player in the playoffs—is today almost as familiar in the maroon, blue, grey and white of the Avalanche as he once was in the red, white and blue of *Les Glorieux.*

It is now nearly six years since that fall evening in 1995 when the Detroit Red Wings trounced the Canadiens 11–1 and a furious Roy announced that "I've played my last game in Montreal" when coach Mario Tremblay finally relented and pulled him off the ice. But time is only part of the story. In the years since, Patrick Roy has delivered one Stanley Cup almost immediately to the Avalanche, and is three victories away from a second. He is, once again, counted among the early favourites for the Conn Smythe. But that too is only part of it.

At thirty-five, Roy has reached that time of his life when the legacy is cemented. This was the season when, in an Avalanche uniform, he surpassed Terry Sawchuk to become the winningest goaltender in NHL history. He was already the winningest goalie in playoff history, but this spring added most playoff shutouts (eighteen and, perhaps, counting) to that record and, heading into tonight's Game 2 against the New Jersey Devils, stands within reach of a few others:

★ A victory tonight and Roy would tie another Hall-of-Famer, Montreal's Ken Dryden, for the most consecutive wins in final playoff series: eleven.

★ Sixteen minutes and eleven seconds without a goal being scored by New Jersey and Roy would slip past Clint Benedict for the longest shutout streak in finals play. Benedict did it with the 1923 Ottawa Senators and extended it with the 1926 Montreal Maroons. Roy hasn't been scored on in finals play since the first period of Game 3 against the Florida Panthers, way back on June 8, 1996.

He cannot even remember who it was that beat him (it was Rob Niedermayer). He will not predict when it will happen next. "There's no rush," he says.

It has already been a fascinating spring for Roy. He was, early on, thought to be a problem for the Avalanche, an aging goaltender who had lost his edge, particularly after an opening game loss to the Los Angeles Kings in Round 2. The early criticism was, at times, as strong as the recent praise. "You're not amused by that," he says, "but you have no control over that, so you just try to remain focused. I always believed things would turn around."

In a way, the entire season has been like this for Roy. In the fall, he was embroiled in a domestic dispute in which charges were eventually dropped. Today, what debate there is around Roy has died down to speculation as to where he would be playing next year and whether or not he would be considered for the Canadian Olympic Team headed for Salt Lake City in early 2002.

Roy is in the final year of a contract that pays him $7.5 million a year and will become a free agent this summer. Had his inconsistencies not improved, he might have been headed for his third NHL team. Should Colorado win another, the pressure will be on to keep him. Pressure is also suddenly building to include him on the Olympic squad, though it was Roy who allowed the critical goal in the 1998 shootout against the Czech Republic and Roy again who played somewhat listlessly as Canada came up short against Finland in the bronze medal game.

But the good sense in waiting until the final moment to name the Canadian goaltenders is somewhat apparent this week as New Jersey's Martin Brodeur looked rather ordinary in Game 1, while Roy sparkled when necessary. It may be that the same three goaltenders from Nagano will be headed for Salt Lake—Roy, Brodeur and Toronto's Curtis Joseph—with the current "money goalie" the choice to start. And so far, neither of the others have proved to be the money goaltender that Roy so undeniably can be.

"It's something that I haven't thought about, to be honest with you," he says of the Olympic possibility. "It's something that I don't want to think about. I have no control over their selection. The only thing I can control is what's going on right now."

And that, for the moment, is the Devils' attack, which surely will not be as unimpressive from here on out as it was in Game 1.

One NHL coach says that the Devils need to rattle Roy more by making him play the puck behind his net as much as possible. Roy is, by nature, so obsessively competitive, says the coach, that he will not be able to resist going one-on-one against Brodeur, who Roy concedes is the best puck-handling goaltender in the game. "Patrick," says the coach, "can get out of control."

Certainly Roy's reputation is of a fiery, at times unpredictable, competitor. His mannerisms—the once-novel butterfly style, talking to the goalposts, refusing to skate over the bluelines—made him both noticeable and often controversial right from his very first season in Montreal, and there remains a bit of an edge to him.

He does not care to be reminded of his inevitable retirement. He says, somewhat curtly, that he has never considered the fact that he could be on the verge of becoming the first goaltender to win Stanley Cups in three different decades. He bristles when someone suggests that he and New Jersey coach Larry Robinson were once teammates in Montreal a long time ago. "Maybe for you," he says, "but not for me."

He does concede, however, that experience, not time, has had its effect on him as a goaltender. "There are things that are different," he says. "I don't think I'm as quick as I was then, but experience sometimes will make up for that. I'm still moving pretty good side to side, but I know there are things that I was doing better then than I do now, and there are things that I do now that are better than I was doing then."

No matter how it's done, however, the results seem to remain exactly the same: Patrick Roy finds a way to win final series. No wonder Colorado coach Bob Hartley calls him "the spine" of the hockey club.

"Patrick has given us a chance to win every game," says Hartley. "He's given us the belief that if we give him the necessary offensive support, he's going to take care of the rest."

Patrick Roy retired in 2003 after a still-remarkable season in which he went 35–15–13 and posted an impressive .920 save percentage. He won four Stanley Cups, three Conn Smythe trophies as the top player of the playoffs and three Vezinas as the NHL's top goaltender. In 2006 he was elected to the Hockey Hall of Fame. In retirement he became owner and general manager of the Quebec Remparts junior club, taking over the coaching duties and winning yet another championship: the Memorial Cup.

WITHIN ARM'S REACH: RAY BOURQUE

(*National Post*, May 26, 2001)

DENVER, COLORADO

Perhaps there should be a statute of limitations on playoff beards.

Ray Bourque should be excused, for there is something about his snow-dappled chin stubble that makes him look more like a middle-aged executive at the end of a two-week canoe trip than an elite NHL defenceman at the beginning of what he hopes will be the best two weeks of his career.

Without the stubble Bourque could pass for thirty, a superbly conditioned athlete without an ounce of fat and with a head of hair so thick and water resistant it has been compared to an otter's pelt. With the stubble he looks more than what he is, forty, and it serves as a prickly underline to the daily sidebar attached to this year's Stanley Cup final: "Win One for Ray."

Raymond Bourque is forty going on forty-one. He is in his twenty-second NHL season. He won the Calder Trophy as the league's top rookie in his first season and five Norris trophies as the league's top defenceman in the seasons that followed. He has scored, in that time, a remarkable 410 goals and 1,169 assists for

1,579 regular season points and added another 178 points, and counting, in post-season play. He has played 1,612 regular season games and, this evening against the New Jersey Devils, will dress for his 208th playoff game. He has, however, one small shortcoming in that remarkable record: "I've never won my last game."

This will only be Bourque's third final in those twenty-two springs. In 1988 and 1990 he led the Boston Bruins, the team he played almost twenty-one seasons for, to the final against the Edmonton Oilers, but both times the Bruins were easily defeated. This, he feels, is his best chance—and likely his last—to accomplish the one great dream of his life.

All hockey players, of course, have that same dream. None, however, may dream it as intensely as Bourque, the shy, reserved young kid who grew up in Montreal during the Canadiens' last great dynasty, and who used to skip school to watch what seemed to him the annual Stanley Cup parade. He has been to the Hockey Hall of Fame to stare at the trophy. He has, on several occasions, drawn close enough to read the names on it.

He has never, however, touched the Stanley Cup. He has had chances but never reached for it, never believed he had the right to hold something he had not earned. Bourque—who once said he would both retire and die a Bruin—came to Colorado for one reason only, to have that final chance to win his final game of a long hockey season. It was supposed to be last year, but the Avalanche fell unexpectedly to the Dallas Stars in the Western final. This year, the "Win One for Ray" theme has only been heightened by the fact that he is one year older and the Avalanche, this time, made it to what Colorado goaltender Patrick Roy likes to call "The Big Dance."

"It would be nice," Roy said earlier this week, "for him to touch the steel."

It is a feel-good story that, it must be said, not everyone feels equally good about. The swaggering, rich Avalanche sometimes feel like hockey's version of the New York Yankees, and some find it difficult to cheer for Bourque if it also suggests that Stanley

Cups can be bought by bringing in late-season, very expensive additions like Bourque a year ago and defenceman Rob Blake at this year's trading deadline.

Bourque himself has always been dutiful in his dealings with the public and the press, but his reserved personality has also meant not everyone warms to him. There is, as well, some lingering resentment among older players toward Bourque's perceived "softness" in dealing with the Bruins on contracts, a matter some agents will argue cost all elite players in that hockey bargaining is done through comparison shopping. Bourque, however, is hardly suffering. He made, and saved, tens of millions with the Bruins and is currently on a one-year, $5.5-million deal with the Avalanche.

Most fans would applaud a Stanley Cup to cap off one of the game's greatest careers. Great athletes who never win the championship—baseball's Ernie Banks, hockey's Marcel Dionne— seem to carry an asterisk about with them, and Bourque would prefer not to enter the Hall of Fame with anyone whispering, "He was great, but . . ."

Each day when Bourque drives down Peoria toward the Avalanche's suburban practice facility, he passes by a long line of such reminders. John Elway, the great Denver Broncos quarterback, was destined to go down in sports history as the superstar who could never win the big one until, at the end of his long career, he suddenly won back-to-back Super Bowls. Today, Elway's name graces a long string of affluent automobile dealerships along Peoria, proof that a name without a "but . . ." has extra currency long past retirement. Bourque admits no one cheered more than he did when Elway finally won the championship that seemed destined to elude him.

He calls his own championship chase "Mission: 16W." Sixteen wins, four rounds of successful best-of-seven series, and the Cup would be his to raise. He even had baseball caps made up to hand around the dressing room and the notion has caught on to the point where they are beginning to sell the caps to the public. It has even been noted that "16W" also stands for the exit off the New Jersey Turnpike that will take Bourque and his teammates to the Continental Airlines Arena for Games 3 and 4 and, if necessary, Game 6.

"A good omen," says Bourque, " . . . I hope."

He finds the story quieter this year than it was last, when he became the surprise trading-deadline deal that so many presumed meant a second Cup for the powerful Avalanche and a first one for Bourque. It was a trade he had requested from Boston toward the end of what had become one more frustrating season of coming up short.

"There came a time in that season where I knew it wasn't going to happen," says Bourque. "And if I hadn't made the move, I really don't know if I would still be playing. I might have just packed it in and retired."

The idea of not retiring came to him from an unlikely source, Chris Chelios, another aging defenceman, who had left the Chicago Blackhawks for the Detroit Red Wings and seemed, to Bourque, to be thriving.

"We had a nice little chat," Bourque remembers. "It looked like he was really enjoying himself. He was in a situation that was similar to mine in terms of being in a place where they weren't being very successful. You're playing a lot of minutes, tough minutes, and really not playing up to the level that you're used to. When I saw him move and then the way he was playing in Detroit, I talked to him about it. And I certainly thought about what it would mean to me to move somewhere else and what kind of effect it would have to have me playing my game again."

He talked it over with his wife, Christiane, and their three children, Melissa, Christopher and Ryan, and when he had their approval he decided to "go for it." The effect turned out to be astounding, considering his years. Bourque was an instant success in Colorado last season and one of their best playoff performers in what ultimately turned into another disappointment. This year he began slowly, but soon was playing his regular thirty minutes of hockey a night and impressively enough to be named a finalist, once again, for the Norris.

He slipped again early on in these playoffs, but is again healthy and playing like he once did when his playoff beard was red to the roots. "It's been a great move for me," he says. "Last year, we made it to the semis and this year to the finals. That's what it's all about. You forget that feeling and how good it feels, and it's good to feel it again."

Other players on the team say it is an "inspiration" to see Bourque working so hard to win the Cup they all want. "You hear about guys in this game who have passion," says Blake, who is often paired with Bourque on defence, "but to give so much to one team and one organization for so long and then to make a change late in your career and to have that same outlook, that's a passion for the game not many guys have."

Blake, who came to Colorado from Los Angeles in February, says his game has picked up since he's been playing with Bourque. "I don't think you ever stop learning during your years in the NHL," Blake says. "I still have a few years left in my career, but I can learn so much from Ray. He's going to help me from now until I retire."

Bourque's own retirement is a subject that comes up as often as the missing Cup. He candidly admits to being "in denial" about his age — "You don't want to think about that" — and believes he is in good enough shape to play several more seasons if he really wants to. But that decision he will put off until this coming summer. "I'm going to wait," he says. "I really don't know when, or how I'm going to go about it."

Summer, however, is still a few weeks off, weeks in which it will be decided whether or not a man with a grizzled beard will actually get to raise the Cup of his dreams or one more time be left staring at the one prize neither he, nor fate, has ever allowed him to touch.

At the moment, there is only one thing he knows for certain: "I'm running out of time."

Ray Bourque finally got to raise the Stanley Cup that spring. He was the first player captain Joe Sakic handed the prize off to. He then retired, having played 1,612 games and recorded 1,579 points—and another 180 in 214 playoff games. The Hall-of-Famer's two sons, Christopher and Ryan, have both been drafted by NHL teams. He returned to Boston to live and work for the Bruins.

THE QUIET PERFECTION OF PAUL KARIYA
(*Ottawa Citizen*, April 30, 1996)

There is a curious off-ice game being played here at the world championships between Canadian goaltender Curtis Joseph and Canadian sharpshooter Paul Kariya. They take the overnight summaries from the NHL playoff games—who scored, when they scored, and how they scored—and the one holding the summary will ask the other to describe, without knowing, exactly how the goal was scored. The only information the other is given is who shot and who was in the net. Nothing else.

"Joe Sakic."

"Low to the stick side."

"Right!"

It is not unusual for a goaltender to know so much of players' habits and styles, but most unusual for a player—especially a twenty-one-year-old in only his second NHL season. Most unusual. But then, Paul Kariya is a most unusual young man. To improve his eye-hand co-ordination, he taught himself to juggle. He used to spend so much time sitting quietly before a game "envisioning" exactly what would happen this night that he would actually "get all screwed up" when games did not go precisely as imagined. He has read every word that has to do with Wayne Gretzky, and the way a player should prepare and behave. He has studied the films of Bobby Orr, who retired when Paul Kariya was two years old, to understand better the values of surprise acceleration. He will spend his summer sitting alone, quietly thinking about others playing their game—Joe Sakic, low to the stick side—and how he might take from them and give more to himself.

"I've never seen a player so focused," says Team Canada general manager Pierre Gauthier, who three years ago drafted the Vancouver youngster when Gauthier was still with the Mighty Ducks of Anaheim. Gauthier, like everyone else, respected Kariya's fanatical devotion to bettering himself. Unlike many others—several of them NHL general managers—Gauthier did not think Kariya lacked the size or the strength to play in the NHL. Three general managers went before Anaheim and took, in order, Alexandre Daigle (Ottawa), Chris Pronger (Hartford, now with St. Louis) and Chris Gratton (Tampa Bay).

Kariya has quickly emerged as the crown jewel in what was supposed to be the richest draft in years. In only his second year, he scored fifty goals for the Mighty Ducks. He has already scored four times for Canada at the world championships and is, head and shoulders, the best Canadian on the ice—even if he only comes up to some of the other players' shoulders.

He never played junior. He went from British Columbia to the University of Maine on a scholarship and, in his freshman year, was given the Hobey Baker Award as the best player in college hockey—but still he never imagined he would one day be an NHL star. "I never thought about the NHL," he says. "I was perfectly prepared to be a businessman or a teacher."

He stayed away from the NHL for a year and played, brilliantly, for the Canadian national team—he missed the shot in 1994 that gave Olympic gold to the Swedes; he won a world championship two months later—and then signed a huge contract with the Ducks that pays him $3 million a year. Disney, obviously, saw a future star in the making.

On the ice, it has worked out beyond even Disney's dreams. Paired with Finnish forward Teemu Selanne, Kariya is now half of the most exciting pair of wingers in the game. With Wayne Gretzky thirty-five and fading, the spotlight is shifting, and Paul Kariya can feel it coming. Off the ice, it has not been such a simple matter. He is only twenty-one, and they say he is cool. Aloof. In a recent Southam poll of Canadian hockey writers, his name surprisingly was on a list of those few players in the game who are generally considered "jerks."

This early and unexpected image problem has perplexed and, in some cases, angered those who know him best, the officials who have worked with him and the players who have played with him. Gauthier considers him "one of the nicest kids I have ever met." Canadian Hockey Association people find him dedicated, loyal and selfless. While several Canadian stars bailed out on the world championships, claiming everything from tiredness to lack of contract, Kariya immediately said yes, despite the fact that he had just spent ten hours in a dentist's chair getting repairs to four broken teeth.

The focus is hockey, and it leaves very little room for anything else. He doesn't read the papers or listen to the radio, and one suspects it is because he has not trusted what can be said about celebrity in a world that both craves and criticizes it. "I don't go out and try and create an image," he says. "I'm a pretty quiet person. You're not going to get an outrageous quote from me."

But what you will get is an insight into the game that only Gretzky before him has been able to offer. Gretzky once said he didn't go to where the puck was, but to where the puck will be. Kariya says: "Hockey is a lot like chess. You have certain moves that are always repeated and, knowing that, you can plan your next move."

He is convinced that hockey prowess is a learned, rather than an inherited, ability. "My father never played the game," he says, "so you can't say it's natural. It's all learned." He studies hockey as a scientist might study cultures. He talks to players and builds mental scouting cards on what everyone might do in a certain situation, just like baseball managers will study the opposition. He studies film to see how Gretzky would attack, how Lemieux will pass. When he discovered Bobby Orr on film, he found the secrets of acceleration.

"You're going to be a lot more effective," he says, "if the defence has your speed pegged at seventy–eighty and then you can suddenly jack it up to a hundred. Bobby Orr had four to five speeds. I've only got two."

So far. But he is also twenty-one, and on the verge of hockey superstardom. He will need to acquire more tricks of the trade, both in Bobby Orr acceleration and in Wayne Gretzky's renowned ability to pull out of something that seems to be spinning out of control.

Gretzky in fact met with Kariya, by arrangement, at the NHL All-Star Game in Boston, and they talked about image and responsibility and being ready for the spotlight when it finds you. Teemu Selanne, perhaps hockey's friendliest star, has been brought to Anaheim both to help Kariya score points and to help him adjust to being in the limelight.

There is no doubt in anyone's mind that this slight twenty-one-year-old who never imagined he would even be here is being groomed to become the game's next big star. Paul Kariya did not have a Walter Gretzky to warn him that he'd be on display all his life, with people watching for every mistake. He didn't have that because he was never a ten-year-old phenomenon, and his father did not understand that world of hockey. He did, however, understand responsibility.

"What my parents taught me," he says, "is that it doesn't matter what you do in life. Whether you're a businessman or a garbage man, you've got to be a good person."

And that, he believes, will have to be enough.

Any assessment of Paul Kariya's career would have to take bad luck into consideration. He left the Ducks before they won the Stanley Cup in 2007, playing for the Colorado Avalanche, Nashville Predators and St. Louis Blues. Kariya was supposed to be the key to Canada's 1998 entry in the Nagano Olympics but had his hopes crushed by a vicious cross-check to the head when Chicago's Gary Suter reacted to a Kariya goal. Kariya missed the Olympics and the rest of the season with post-concussion syndrome. He was concussed again when hit by New Jersey Devils defenceman Scott Stevens during the 2003 Stanley Cup finals, which the Devils won. He sat out the entire 2010–11 season with post-concussion syndrome. With 989 points in 989 games, his record remains remarkable, despite the harsh realities of head injuries.

A FLOWER FOR ALL SEASONS: GUY LAFLEUR
(*Maclean's*, October 16, 1978)

I retired in 1971, the same year Guy arrived, and he came to me and asked me what I thought about him taking my sweater number. "If you want it, take it," I told him. "But don't you think you already have enough on you? Why don't you pick another number and make it famous yourself?" —Jean Béliveau

The new smell of Quebec is known by its trademark: No. 10. The odour may be appropriately described as *flowery* as it rises this fall out of pre-shave, after-shave, cologne, deodorant and the true saviour of Christmas, soap-on-a-rope. The same number can be found pushing automobiles, skates, sticks and yogourt. No. 10 surfaces on the binders, pencil cases and exercise books the children carry to school. Even the company is called Number 10 Promotions Inc., and the president—for those without programs—is Guy Lafleur.

The company Guy Lafleur keeps as a hockey player, however, has narrowed down year by year until today there is only himself. While the National Hockey League launches its sixty-second season this week, there are only the long-shot mutterings of the insane left. Will Lafleur's team, the Montreal Canadiens, which has already won more than one-third of all NHL championships, somehow fail to win yet another? Will Lafleur himself—most valuable player over the past two seasons, scoring champion over the past three—outdo even his last year's feat of sixty goals? The answer is already with us, lying in a sealed envelope in a suburban office outside Montreal. Inside is written Guy Lafleur's annual prediction for his coming season, and the hint is that—despite a broken nose suffered at the end of the exhibition schedule—he will indeed do better.

It is Lafleur's enormous gift that makes him special, certainly not his walk—the steps too long—nor his face: greaser soft, it is more the look of someone who should be topping up your battery. The eyes, however, brown and shimmering, seem to ransack the immediate area about him. Not in fear—though that was once the case when undercover detectives took every step he took—but in simple anticipation. Everywhere, even in the USSR, where customs agents asked for his autograph, they know the man who, like Bambi's skunk, is proud to be called "Flower." Crossing Maisonneuve Boulevard, the eyes intercept a sultry woman who steps sideways just long enough to kiss Lafleur on the lips. Out of a hydro manhole two workers rise and call his name. A woman brings her son forward for a laying on of his hands. Those who don't want just to touch would like to give. A man promises a new suit, a girl a present. An unnamed European country this summer offered a butler, a housekeeper, a villa on the water, a new luxury car and a hockey lord's ransom, all tax-free. To collect it, he only had to change his sweater.

The man an entire province prayed for when Jean Béliveau moved on has arrived at his full bloom. It is hardly possible to believe today that those same hands that ruffle children as if their imaginations were crops he himself had planted once struggled to put down his desperate feelings in poetry. It is harder still to realize these same friendly eyes could have spilled tears over the red, white and blue Canadiens-coloured chesterfield in Jean Béliveau's office as Lafleur sat crying over whatever it was that had gone so wrong with his promised life.

But eyes can also weep for joy. And Antoine Viau, who has waited much of his life for this moment, is dampening slightly as he stands watching his beloved Canadiens skate and shoot and actually breathe. The Montreal Forum is empty of fans, but Guy Lafleur—who an hour earlier has said "What good is money when you play and lose?"—is skating with Stanley Cup intentions during a $25-per-player pre-season scrimmage. His wispy hair matted with the cream cake his teammates have used to celebrate his twenty-seventh birthday, Lafleur commands his magic to turn a 4–2 deficit into victory. In the dying minutes he scores, sets up the tying goal, then single-handedly wins the game in overtime with a phantom shot from the point. He has served notice against the best hockey team in the world, his own, that Lafleur is ready for the new season. For Antoine Viau, who sweeps floors nights at the American-owned IBM plant, the state of *les Canadiens* is, in many ways, the state of his own well-being. The team and Lafleur are an unspoken vindication.

"Ah, Lafleur," Viau says, courteously speaking English to the reporter who helped him sneak in. "Lafleur ... Lafleur ... I love it!"

Guy Lafleur is more symbol than human to a great many Québécois. "There is," says Jerry Petrie, Lafleur's agent, "probably more pressure on him to perform from the people in this province than there is on René Lévesque."

We may be, as Irving Layton has said, "a dull people enamoured of childish games," but Layton is certainly not speaking for those to whom hockey is a far more mature passion than politics. For them, Lafleur occupies the highest office in the land.

"Guy is the true throwback," says Ken Dryden, the Canadiens' goaltender. "I look out sometimes and see the St. Lawrence skater, not the player, and it is a beautiful thing to behold."

Pierre Larouche, who came to Montreal from Pittsburgh last year, says he actually used to cheer for Lafleur when their teams played: "They'd be ahead 6–1 and I'd be on the bench wishing he'd score more, just so I could watch and see how it is done."

The last to recognize this special status has probably been Lafleur himself. In Moscow this summer he was asked by the head of hockey and the director of all Soviet sports to pick his own world all-star team and when he came to right wing he blushed deeply and said "Me!"—quickly covering his embarrassment with a laugh that implied it was merely his own little joke, but the Soviet officials gravely nodded in total agreement.

"The Flower is a very strange person," says Lafleur's linemate and good friend Steve Shutt. It is not for any obvious idiosyncrasy such as his superstitious tap of the goal netting to start each game and period; what is truly odd, in Shutt's evaluation, is that Lafleur is "the furthest thing from an athlete you'd ever want to see off the ice." A loyal consumer of Molson's ale (the brewery owns his team) and a chain-smoker who two weeks ago switched to a pipe, Lafleur does little more than work out with suntan oil in the off-season.

"He shows up at camp, puts on his skates and it's the first time he's been on them since the playoff," says Larry Robinson of the Canadiens. "And the frightening thing is he just flies by everybody immediately."

For people like Jean Béliveau, who even in retirement runs two to three miles a day, it is a continuing mystery how Lafleur—who hasn't attended an optional practice in years—remains so fit. "The most amazing thing about him is his physical resistance," says Béliveau. "It's because he's so hyper," says Shutt. "He winds himself up like a coil."

The bad nerves are a mixed blessing: what Lafleur gains in

reflex and metabolism he gives up in what it does to his mental fitness. Before particularly important games he has been discovered in the dressing room at three o'clock in the afternoon—his equipment on, his skates tightened—fully five hours before game time. By the time the puck drops he is drained, which partially explains his periodic slumps in critical games. Before the pipe came along he tried to smoke out the devils inside, and there have been games, one teammate says, when he would begin chain-smoking hours before a game and continue through the intermissions.

The best solution, he has discovered, is to rinse the mind completely of all hockey thought. He spends the jittery pre-game hours reading car magazines, clipping from architectural books for the dream-home file he keeps or taking bubble baths. On the road he and his roommate, Shutt, fight over the television, Shutt constantly looking for sports events and Lafleur's bad nerves making any contest, even tennis, an unbearable agony. He is at his happiest watching reruns of *The Three Stooges*.

It can be argued that the premium theorizing on most sports has fallen to the journeymen players—the Sheros and Nesterenkos of hockey, baseball's Jim Bouton—and that the magnificently gifted—Rocket Richard in hockey, Pete Rose and Mickey Mantle in baseball—often appear to be in lifelong thinking slumps. Lafleur would rather keep things simple. His priorities always place the team and the game first, and either his fans or family second. Only once, when the team was in a rare slump, has Lafleur deliberately tried to inspire by anything but his own standard of play. He moved from his locker to the play blackboard near the showers, picked up the chalk, thought a moment, and then scribbled, "A winner never quits and a quitter never wins." He then moved back to his locker where he sat staring up at the approving, legendary faces of *les Canadiens* of past years, and he read again the lines of poet John McRae that are stencilled just below the ceiling: "To you from failing hands we throw the torch; be yours to hold it high."

—

I've always been there when he needed somebody.
He knows I'll always be there. —Jean Béliveau

"I may never be able to play like him," Lafleur once said of Béliveau. "But I'd like to be the man he is." It is a hero worship that has been both inspiration and salvation to Guy Lafleur. Twenty years ago in the Ottawa River town of Thurso, Quebec, Lafleur's parents found him sleeping in his new hockey equipment, and though the dream of that night has long since faded, it is not unlikely that Jean Béliveau threaded a breakaway pass to his new young winger and that the roar of the Forum crowd for Lafleur's goal sounds yet in whatever dimension dreams retire to.

As Béliveau had before him, Lafleur left the small town for Quebec City, and their resulting glory was comparable. As an "amateur" junior, Lafleur made close to $20,000 a year, drove a free Buick and dressed in the finest "gift" clothes. He wore No. 4, Béliveau's signature in Montreal, and Lafleur made sure he kept a poster of his idol taped to the wall beside his locker.

In Lafleur's final year—when he scored an astonishing 130 goals—it was arranged that the sensation would come to Montreal. By rights, as the best amateur in the country, he should have gone to the last-place California Golden Seals, but a celebrated sleight of hand involving trades and draft picks engineered by Montreal's general manager Sam Pollock saw the Canadiens come up with Lafleur.

It was accepted that Lafleur was carrying Béliveau's torch even before the 1971–72 season began. Ken Dryden remembers an exhibition game against the Boston Bruins when he overheard Phil Esposito growl to his linemates, "Which one is Lafleur?" The season before, Esposito had scored a record seventy-six goals, but there was obvious concern in his voice. So much was Guy Lafleur on people's minds—despite never having played a

single professional game—that a manufacturer was rushing production to get a Lafleur-endorsed table-hockey game out in time
for Christmas. Its main competition, naturally, would be the Phil
Esposito game.

By the third winter, however, the Lafleur game was off the
market. Not only had the rookie award gone to his teammate Ken
Dryden, but the word around the league was that Lafleur was
"yellow." The junior promise had become a professional deceit.
"He'd been somewhat of a bust, you might say," says Steve Shutt.

"My legs were in Montreal," Lafleur says, "but my heart was
in Quebec City. My mind wasn't on hockey." With the press constantly demanding what was wrong, Lafleur took to hiding in his
Montreal apartment and writing depressing poetry about the
meaninglessness of life and unfairness of death—a melancholia
that still surfaces from time to time—and his game deteriorated
even further. To give him confidence the Canadiens countered a
$465,000 (over three years) lure from the Quebec Nordiques of
the WHA with a new contract for Lafleur—$1 million over ten
years, fully guaranteed. He responded with his worst season of
all: twenty-one goals.

The unhappy sessions in Jean Béliveau's office weren't providing a solution either. It took a gamble by Béliveau in the spring of
1974 to provide the remedy. Béliveau let it be known that he was
less than pleased with the performance of his heir, and he casti-
gated Lafleur for not working hard enough. The effect, at first
devastating, became "a wake-up" for Lafleur, and he emerged
from his sulk by announcing, "I'll show the bastards."

When training camp opened, he discarded his "yellow" stigma
with his helmet and the new Guy Lafleur suddenly and aggres-
sively emerged as Béliveau reincarnate. A broken finger probably
cost him the scoring championship that year, but he has held the
title for the three years since.

The legendary team that in the past revered such names as
"Battleship," "Boom Boom" and "Rocket" found itself following

the "Flower," but as Pierre Larouche says, "He's as gentle as a flower, but plays like Superman. In Quebec, hockey is a religion, and Lafleur is the new god."

In the four years since the rebirth, there have been times when Lafleur has found himself in his office in Pointe-Claire looking at the tiny skates with the red laces that now keep the door open, the same skates he began on, and poring over the two massive albums, one a foot thick, that are offered to his glory. "It is like a dream to me," he says at these times. "Even now it is like a dream."

There have, however, been darker sides that are not pasted in any album but linger anyway. And this has led him to wonder rather than gloat. In April of 1976, the Montreal police were investigating the holdup of a Brinks truck when they stumbled on a plot to kidnap Lafleur before the playoffs began and hold him for a rumored $250,000 ransom. He will never forget what it was like when Jean Béliveau told him.

"I was at home and the phone rang," Lafleur recalls, the memory sending his fingers searching for cigarettes. "It was Jean and he said he wanted to see me. I said okay, tomorrow. He said no, right now, and he'd come over because we couldn't talk about it over the phone. I hung up and my wife said 'What was that?' I didn't know what to say—I thought I'd been traded. Then Jean arrived with two big guys and they're cops and they tell me I have two choices. I can go to Miami and the club would pay for it and make excuses for me, or I can stay. I said I just wanted to play hockey."

For a full month Lafleur lived in sight of two detectives. His wife, Lise, and eight-month-old son, Martin, stayed for a while in a hotel and then with her parents in Quebec City. The Lafleurs had a home in the country at that time—a renovated two-hundred-year-old farmhouse at the end of a long, dark drive, and his nerves, never reliable, erupted. A squirrel would drum-roll across the roof and Lafleur would scramble for cover. Night after night he couldn't sleep, and once he knelt shaking by the windowsill as a large, black car pulled partway up the drive and sat idling. All he could make out was the glow of four cigarettes, rising, burning brightly, then falling. After a torturous hour the car left, but the reality of the threat stayed. Lafleur's play disintegrated and when the fans and press squeezed him for answers he had to fight to keep it from pouring out.

The very next year he made up for that small lapse by winning the Conn Smythe Trophy as the most valuable player during the playoffs. But there was a new threat to deal with. One of the Boston Bruin players, John Wensink, whose hockey talent is to Lafleur's what punk rock is to Beethoven, proudly announced: "If I get on the ice, Lafleur will not come out alive."

Lafleur survived, of course. Wensink, who has trouble catching his own wind, had to make do with Lafleur's as the Canadiens star flew by and led his team to its record twentieth Stanley Cup. Still, the incident had its effect on Lafleur. "It's supposed to be a sport," he says of his beloved game, "not butchery."

It is such things as this that cause Lafleur to measure just what it is all worth. Even a simple vacation with his family must now be spent in the south of France, so badly have the adoring fans crippled his freedom in Canada. He turned up at a charity baseball game this summer but was forced to give up in the third inning when the worshippers insisted on running out and playing the field with him. He is now paid—thanks to the team renegotiating his ten-year contract—approximately $200,000 a year, a sum that is vast only until it is recognized that Lafleur's salary would not place him in the top twenty of professional hockey. His present contract depresses him to the point where he refers to it as an "iron collar" and is currently pressing the Canadiens for yet another renegotiation.

There are times when he rises in the dead of night and goes into his son Martin's room and crawls in beside the boy. Martin is only three and though he has seen first-hand what it means to be Guy Lafleur—the fawning attacks at shopping malls, the crowds that wait in the streets—he has already announced to his father that he too will be a great hockey player one day. Lafleur, who saw his own youth pummelled by fame, is concerned. "I tell him to sit down and relax," he says. "I know he'd have even more pressure on him than I had. And that? . . . Well." He shrugs and can say no more.

Little wonder, then, that the heir to Jean Béliveau has thought of abdicating one day. The mysterious European offer of this past summer has more attractions than its tax-free value (possibly $400,000 a year). The freewheeling style of international hockey is where Lafleur's immense grace on skates would be best served, and playing a short thirty-five-game schedule for one of those countries—Shutt says West Germany, logic says Finland and Lafleur isn't saying—would leave him both time and places for escape.

"I still haven't said no," he says, the chipped tooth adding mischief to the statement (undoubtedly to throw a scare into his present employers). "The offer came too late for this year, but maybe next year." Lafleur looks out from the comforting shadows of the restaurant and sees those who shortly will be stalking him as he works his way back to the Forum.

"The other thing is," he says as he pushes back his chair, "you have to live sometime."

Lafleur played for another seven years with the Canadiens and retired in 1985. He entered the Hall of Fame but was unhappy away from the game and "unretired" in 1988, spending one season with the New York Rangers and returning to the site of his original fame, Quebec City, for two years with the Nordiques. He had gone from a dominant player to a modest threat, scoring only a dozen goals in each of his seasons in Quebec. In 1991 he retired for good, having scored 560 goals and 793 assists in only 1,127 games—numbers that would have been even more impressive had he not lost three years to "retirement." Five Stanley Cups, three Art Ross trophies as the league's leading scorer, two Hart

trophies as the league's most valuable player and one Conn
Smythe Trophy as the MVP of the playoffs. Today, Lafleur is a
restaurateur in the Montreal area.

KING OF THE KINGS: MARCEL DIONNE

(*Maclean's*, March 24, 1980)

Before it is over the death toll will reach twenty-seven. But on this, the first of ten days of California downpour, the rain is but a small annoyance, lightly chording on the clover-shaped pool. A dark, stubby man with the build of a Chubb vault stands beneath the eaves of his $400,000 home and scowls toward the mist lingering over his neighbour's corral. He stops talking, grabs his head and bends over double, the strain turning the eighteen-stitch cut over his left eye into a black caterpillar. Yet it is neither injury nor weather that bothers Marcel Dionne; it is the future. "I have got to think positive," he says in a rising voice. "Pos-i-*tive!*"

For four hours he has sat working over a few cans of Coors beer and the past. He has touched on the sacrifice—the marriage breakup his parents once faked, the baby his Aunt Denise lost— all tied to the young Marcel's hockey. He has traced himself from Quebec's Drummondville through Ontario's St. Catharines, from Detroit to Los Angeles, once running from his own demanding family, once from his own damning mouth. In awe, he has spoken of Guy Lafleur, first the boy and now the man, and whom, boy and man, Dionne has "been chasing since he was ten years old," in the words of his own best friend, Mickey Redmond.

Only this past weekend, with Dionne a distant sixteen points ahead of Montreal's Lafleur in the National Hockey League scoring race, has that eighteen-year chase seemed won. And with that accomplishment may come another: with agent Alan Eagleson demanding a $500,000-per-year plus contract from the Los Angeles

Kings, Marcel Dionne is about to become the best-paid performer in the sport's history. Either that or Marcel Dionne, ever caught on the far edge of his promise, will move on yet again. Perhaps to Switzerland, where the offers are already being made. It is all too much to consider at once. Dionne changes the subject by pointing across the private road toward a neighbour's yard where another expatriate, an Australian eucalyptus, leans wearily over the drive lane. "I hate those trees, you know," he says. "They've got no roots, nothing to hold them up."

North on Crenshaw Boulevard, up and just off the San Diego Freeway, Jerry Buss walks his fingers around the rim of a second rum and Coke. Buss's jeans, Texas boots and open-necked cranberry shirt say nothing of the more than $500 million that has grown from the $83.33 a month he and a friend each began setting aside in the summer of 1958. A year ago, perhaps sensing the sexiest thing about real estate was his rising profit curve, Buss masterminded a $67.5-million deal to buy the Los Angeles Kings hockey team, the Lakers basketball team, the Los Angeles Forum and a thirteen-thousand-acre ranch from Californian-Canadian Jack Kent Cooke. And so, on May 29, 1979, at the age of forty-six, Buss capped an American dream, which began in Wyoming as the son of a divorced waitress, by driving to pick up the keys to the Forum in a Rolls-Royce Camargue.

This particular Jerry Buss night, like most others, has its visible assurances—new friend Gordon Lightfoot in to share a drink, a satin-eyed, raven-haired comfort waiting to go home with him—yet Buss is a man whose confidence needs few external trappings. "If you can learn medicine in four years," he says in a soft, sure voice, "you should be able to learn hockey in four years."

Having known the joys of indulgence, Jerry Buss does not believe in denial. For his sweet tooth he has stocked his office with jelly beans and lollipops. For his ego he has filled a large, black picture album with scores of the women he has known. For his ambition, he has locked into a vision of the Stanley Cup. And though he may tower over his star by six inches, he has come to recognize that this particular dream lies more within the reach of Marcel Dionne than himself.

"Look," Buss says, tapping a cigarette tight, "you either subscribe to the crazy world we live in or you don't. I do. I have seen people get up on a stage, shuffle their feet, and get $100,000 a week. If you can get people to pay to see you, then I don't think we should interfere with that process . . . So Marcel Dionne is worth whatever he can get from me."

"In what sport," the KLAC Los Angeles sportscaster asks as a leadoff to his noon report, "is the Stanley Cup symbolic of overall supremacy?" Cut to commercial while laid-back listeners throughout the state mull over the possibilities: African exploration? . . . tool manufacturing? . . . making love to Mrs. Roper? "The answer," the sportscaster shouts incredulously on return, "is *hockey!*"

In this city ice comes crushed for margaritas. It is a sports city that nail-bites over the Rams and Dodgers and Lakers coming second, not the Kings standing eleventh, a city where a Marcel Dionne—who came for money and escape more than hockey potential—is lost among the Garveys and Jabbars, who in turn lose out to Paul Newman's cars and Johnny Carson's tennis.

"You couldn't get recognized here if you were Bobby Orr," says actor Larry D. Mann, a Canadian who attends all the Kings' home games.

"Have *something* good tonight," the Forum's All-American Salted Peanut–seller shouts as he mounts the stairs during a listless Kings game against the Washington Capitals. "At least nuts ain't so hard to swallow as *this!*"

Down on the ice Marcel Dionne is doing what comes naturally— "dancing with the puck," his linemate Charlie Simmer calls it—but to no avail. His delicate, perfect set-up is to a defenceman who simply cannot complete the obvious. A Trudeau shrug and Dionne skates off the ice, thinking to himself what he later puts into words. "What do we have?" he asks in his living room. "You see what we have. It's *terrible!*"

But that is the team, not Marcel Dionne. His is a career poorly served by mere statistics. When he was awarded the Lester B. Pearson trophy last year as hockey's most valuable player, the significance was that this award is voted on by peers, not sportswriters. And it may reflect his outspokenness and daring as much as his ability. Still, for most of this season the talk has been about Los Angeles' Triple Crown Line of Dionne, Simmer and Dave Taylor. But for mid-season knee injuries to Simmer and Taylor, the Dionne-led line probably would have become the highest-scoring line in hockey's history. Even so, Dionne's 126 points with nine games remaining may have established him as the premier player of the game.

Dionne even brags he could score two hundred points if only he played for a decent team, but he also claims, unconvincingly, that this is not what matters most to him. "He's always saying how phony those awards are, the trophies, the all-star teams," says Dave Taylor. "But I'd bet on him wanting to win it badly."

Victory, should it come, would finally stop its nearly two decades of teasing. In 1971, their first year as professionals, Lafleur was drafted first, Dionne second; and Dionne's phenomenal first year (a record 77 points compared to Lafleur's 64) was soured when Montreal goaltender Ken Dryden won rookie of the year honours. Until this year, Marcel Dionne was known for but a single first—the five-year, $1.5-million contract he signed with Los Angeles in June of 1975.

"Marcel Dionne can be our Moses," Jack Kent Cooke announced on that occasion. "Marcel Dionne is no Moses," retorted Ned Harkness, the Detroit Red Wings manager who had just lost Dionne. "The only tablets he should bring down are Aspirin tablets because with him around Cooke and the Kings are going to need plenty of them."

But now it is 1980 and the game of hockey is beginning to emerge from a prolonged mid-life crisis. In the year since the North American game discovered it could no longer get it up for the Soviets, merger between the NHL and the World Hockey Association has come about and the gutted house is showing signs of falling back in order. Though ten of the new league's twenty-one teams are projected to lose money this year, attendance is up 5 percent thanks to sellout crowds in such new NHL cities as Edmonton. Because of the Soviet example, the guerrilla hockey of the 1970s may be forced to switch to a creative hockey for the '80s. And as for the sport's main bugaboo, violence, an outcry against it is just now beginning to come from a few of the truly talented players, led by Marcel Dionne and echoed by the likes of Guy Lafleur, Phil Esposito and Mike Bossy.

"If I had my way," says Dionne, who now serves as vice-president of the NHL Players' Association, "we would have a full debate of violence."

But Jerry Buss is naturally less concerned with the violence than he is with financial loss. "Other people think in words," he likes to say. "I think in numbers." That being so, he might well consider the following points: his Kings will lose him $900,000 this year, attendance at Forum hockey games has declined steadily since Dionne's arrival five years ago, and Dionne is currently looking for a new five-year contract in the area of $3 million.

But J.B., as he likes to be called, is hardly a fool. He does, after all, have a PhD in physical chemistry and his idea of fun is to play Monopoly from memory. If he heard Team Canada's Dr. Derek Mackesey say that, over the past few years, "Marcel Dionne has been the heart and soul of the teams we have sent to Europe," Buss would acknowledge that this is also true of Dionne in Los Angeles, where his popularity and respect have finally risen to match his ability. The headaches have not come from Dionne, as Harkness predicted, but from those who are supposed to help him. Buss would also acknowledge the truth of what Marcel

Dionne has to say about his own team, though he would be well advised to grit his teeth while listening.

"I can't do everything," Dionne said one afternoon. "My hockey's suffering. When you have a lot of people who are inferior and they don't think like you do, then a lot of people suffer. They look for leadership but it isn't going to come, because there's not enough people to back it up."

Buss believes he can remedy that in a mere four years. "I'm a quick study," he says. His remarkable real estate success was not by accident, but the result of careful computer programming applied to property and land. Having at one time mathematically determined how many footsteps would wear out a carpet, he may be on the verge of discovering how many head fakes will bring him the Stanley Cup.

Should Buss have any thoughts about reducing Marcel Dionne to an equation, however, he may as well forget them. Marcel Dionne is not merely a hockey player, but also an idea, one that was originally created by a huge family back in Drummondville, Quebec, and is protected and prodded by that family even today.

What computer could measure the grey stucco, seventeen-room house at 89 13th Avenue, l'Épicerie Dionne in the front, the large kitchen behind packed with many of his thirteen uncles, each with a personal touch of advice for *Le P'tit Marcel*? And what of those late Saturday evenings, the big men sitting seriously, their territories traced in empty "quart" Molson's bottles, the sound of sliding coins rising up toward the boy's bedroom where he lay awake knowing that in the morning he would have the price of a new hockey stick? How could a computer be fed the letter from *les Canadiens* that arrived there when Marcel was barely in peewee hockey, telling his parents to take special care of him because Senator Molson and the organization were watching? Or how Marcel would skate about the rink after a victory, the fans reaching down to touch him, and how, when he undressed, he would find dollar bills stuffed in his gloves?

And who but Marcel Dionne himself will ever understand why he dared not once to dream of playing in the NHL, knowing that dream would be ridiculed each time he had trouble reaching over the boards to sign autographs, or when his uncles whispered in the kitchen, thinking him asleep? He was *too small*. It made the pressure even worse. "Hockey . . . hockey . . . hockey . . . hockey," he says, his voice dropping to a tense whisper. "I was going nuts."

When faraway St. Catharines' Black Hawks wooed him at seventeen, he jumped from the Quebec to the Ontario junior league. And when outraged hometown fans threatened court action—to keep him where he belongs—his parents, on a lawyer's advice, fabricated a ploy to make it seem as if they were separating. His mother, Laurette, brother and three sisters ended up in totally foreign St. Catharines, expenses to be met by the delighted new team.

He calls that his moment of truth. He began putting on weight, his playing blossomed and after four months his family returned to the icy stares of Drummondville. The darling of Drummondville became the darling of St. Catharines, spoiled and worshipped. Two successive junior scoring titles followed, climaxing in 1971 when St. Catharines met the Quebec Remparts to decide the best junior team in Canada. More accurately, to decide the best junior player in Canada, for Quebec's star was none other than his old nemesis, Guy Lafleur. Sadly, the series turned to such violence— Dionne was savaged as a "traitor" in the Quebec press, his family had garbage thrown at them and his Aunt Denise miscarried shortly after a near riot in Quebec—that St. Catharines refused to complete the series and Quebec won by default.

Incredibly, this was not to be Marcel Dionne's low point. He was billed as "the next Gordie Howe" from the moment he arrived in Detroit, but his four years there are remembered more for the tears and anger and open fights with management than they are for his hockey. Small talk to a *Detroit Free Press* reporter about his two Dobermans and the baseball bat he carried in his car ended up as the next day's headlines: DIONNE CAN'T WAIT TO QUIT. With his dislike of the city and the team in print, Dionne was advised not to dress that night for a game against Minnesota, but he refused, sitting sobbing as he dressed and then finally standing up and, in a cracking voice, telling his teammates: "I'm sorry. I get confused. I make mistakes." Then he went out and scored two goals, leading the team to victory.

Leaving Detroit was less a problem than where to go. Montreal wanted him. And Toronto. "You bring that young man out here," Edmonton's Wild Bill Hunter told Eagleson associate Bill Watters, "and we'll put his name on the licence plates: Alberta—Home of Marcel Dionne." Los Angeles, however, offered both the best money and the farthest escape. "It was the easiest way to go," Dionne says. With the accusations trailing him—"He can rip a team apart," Johnny Wilson, one former coach offered—he came to a team that had just had its best season, standing fourth overall, and was offering defensive, disciplined hockey under coach Bobby Pulford.

He was suspect from the beginning. Pulford hadn't even been told about Cooke's deal and was so distraught at first sight of his stocky little star that he assigned him immediately to the team's "Fat Squad," forcing him to skate extra laps at practice with plastic sheets wrapped around his swollen stomach. But this time Dionne did not walk out on practice, as he had done in Detroit. And instead of sulking, as he might once have done, he worked and listened.

"Pully thought I was a zipper-head," Dionne now says. "If he could've made me crawl, he would have. I wouldn't crawl. I respect him for what he did because after a while he knew I was not what he had heard."

Pulford discovered, as so many others have, that the tallest part of Dionne is his pride. "I don't want to kiss anyone's ass," he had decided just before turning professional and, though he has certainly suffered for his refreshing frankness, hockey's own belated maturing over recent years has meant that Detroit's "big baby" is now seen as Los Angeles's leader and highly articulate spokesman—without Dionne himself having changed much. He once said, "There seems to be a tiny part of me I can't control." But his railing against archaic management and gang-warfare hockey has in truth been extremely calculated. "If I had to do it again," he says, "I'd do it. And I'll tell you why—because I know I can play for any team in this league."

Before Dionne, the outspoken hockey player was a rarity—Ted Lindsay in the '50s, Bobby Hull to a lesser extent later—but today, with Darryl Sittler fighting management in Toronto and Guy Lafleur attacking lazy, wealthy hockey players in Montreal, the cures for the ill health of hockey are coming, as they should, from the game's healthier cells.

"I had to say to hell with it," says Dionne. "If that's what hockey's all about, I'll say it depends on how much guts you have and how much you believe in yourself."

This game is over, thankfully. Washington has come from behind to win 4–2, the contest as interesting as seeing which brand of paper towel will give away first under the faucet. Dionne, the singular example of grace and caring among so many of those he contemptuously refers to as "slackers," dresses quickly and alone in a far corner of the dressing room. His teammates know better than to speak to him following a loss, as do the local reporters. Hair still dripping from the shower, he buttons up his jacket and walks away from the disgrace, momentarily pausing in the clutch of Jerry Buss and Gordon Lightfoot. A quick handshake and Dionne leaves, silently.

Outside, in the accelerating rain, he climbs into his Mercedes and pulls away, the weight of his anger falling on the gas pedal. It is a time for avoiding thought. There is little concern for making more than $500,000 a year or even for one day being as well known in Los Angeles as Lightfoot, as Buss has promised he one day will be. Playing for the Kings, there is little to be gained by contemplating the game of hockey, where failure is beyond a single man's prevention. Better instead to think of baseball, a sport he loves better, and how he treasures those suspended moments in the batter's box because "when you're up there you're only one man, alone—nobody can help you."

He knows that it is nearing midnight. With the time difference it will shortly be morning in Drummondville, and the radio in the big house on 13th Avenue will report that the hometown wonder managed but a single assist in the loss, and he knows that it will not be enough. "They want me to win the scoring title so badly," he will say next afternoon. "More than I want it."

But he will also know that words are not necessarily truth. "If I was not Marcel Dionne and he was not Guy Lafleur," he will say slowly, "maybe then it wouldn't matter so much."

Then he will say, "But . . ." And after that nothing.

Dionne did win the scoring championship in 1980, but only because he had scored more goals than a youngster in Edmonton called Wayne Gretzky, who surged at season's end to tie Dionne in overall points. In 1987, Dionne joined the New York Rangers in a late-season trade. He played another full season for New York and part of another before ending his career in the International Hockey League in 1989. His regular season totals were most impressive—1,771 points in 1,348 games—but he scored only 21 times in a mere 49 playoff matches. He never won the Stanley Cup. In 1992 he was admitted to the Hockey Hall of Fame. He is today a businessman living in Niagara Falls.

CAPTAIN MARVEL: BOBBY CLARKE

(The Canadian, spring 1976)

As it turned out, the "cradle of liberty" is also an uncomfortable bed of paranoia. The good citizens had determined that since political freedom (as they saw it) was created in their city, then it was only fair that it be defended there as well; so by the time the "Thrilla in Philadelphia" actually got under way on January 11, the marvellous American mind had devised a workable domino theory of international hockey: the Soviets had fought seven times and New York had fallen twice, Chicago, Boston and Pittsburgh once each, Montreal had drawn even and only Buffalo had managed to turn back the red tide.

In the eighth and final match of Russian hockey vs. NHL hockey, the citizens of Philadelphia conveniently forgot the Soviets had already taken the series with five wins; for them, it had come down to their best against our best, and the blessed Flyers, led by their captain Bobby Clarke (who had himself set the mood by announcing "I don't like the sons of bitches anyway"), were assigned to strike the fatal blow for American liberty.

"They're playing this for God, motherhood and NATO," local clothing salesman Mel Pastiloff said as he arrived at the arena, and elsewhere, at least two of the Flyers claimed they'd be representing "the free world" when they skated out. It was only a hockey game, but sitting in the press box that afternoon was not far removed from being an extra in a John Wayne war movie.

Philadelphia had been surly to the Central Red Army team since it had arrived. At practice the morning before, the Soviets had complained they were being held up by a late ice flood, and a fat man with a cigar had offered only his sympathetic "Tough shitsky." It had become quickly obvious that this was to be no mere game, that—to the Americans, anyway—hockey is hell, too.

As expected, it was Clarke who set the standard in the match, attacking from the moment he lost the opening faceoff, and his actions were backed by a continuous barrage of various salvos named Moose Dupont, Mad Dog Kelly, Bird Saleski, Hammer Schultz and Ed Van Impe. The team had obviously taken to heart the typed message coach Fred Shero had tacked to the dressing room bulletin board, a quote from Theodore Roosevelt: "The unforgivable crime is soft hitting. Do not hit at all if it can be avoided, but never hit softly."

Comparing the Flyers' 4–1 victory of January 11 to the Montreal contest on New Year's Eve (a 3–3 tie) is like comparing a skin flick to a Bergman film, but Philadelphia still managed to demonstrate some skills other than merely mugging, and that Fred Shero may well be the greatest strategist the game has seen. After the depressing first period, the Flyers won by hockey skills alone, but it was still not what local TV announcer Gene Hart told his Philadelphia audience: "This has been an artistic success. This has not been the Broad Street Bullies."

And long after it was all over, the man who had worked hardest for the victory still stood, naked and trembling, pinned to his dressing cubbyhole by a swarm of glad-handers, journalists and photographers. Most of the other Flyers had showered, dressed and were either drinking beer or gone, but Bobby Clarke had not showered, nor even put his front teeth back in. Someone had given him a towel and he had hitched it around his waist, though it might better have been used to soak up the blood that oozed from an accidental ten-stitch cut above the hairline and down over starchy skin that looked sick, if not actually dead, when compared with the robust colour of Clarke's friend Reg Leach, whom the photographers had pushed forward a few minutes earlier with their communal yell, "Kiss him, Bobby! Kiss Reggie on the cheek! C'mon boys, we need a shot!" Leach had laughed, but Clarke kept looking down, as he had all through the interviews, peeking up only when a photographer shouted. He was, as he always is in the dressing room, courteous and charmingly shy, which is why the media love him. He will always talk, and seldom gets impatient, while he's in the dressing room.

Getting words out of Bobby Clarke is not difficult—providing the words have a proper distance to them, meaning they relate to the game finished or the game coming, or to a teammate, an opponent, a coach. Words that hit at home do not sit as well.

In any manner possible, Clarke will avoid letting people into his personal world, as this magazine has twice discovered. The first time we pursued him, about three years ago, a magazine writer flew down to Philadelphia only to have Clarke refuse to grant an interview, though a Flyers public relations man had promised one. So this time we checked first with Clarke personally, and he approved, but three days after the reporter's arrival Clarke was still reneging on his promise, arguing that no one had told him about it—though he himself had approved it just the week before. "*You're not being fair!*" he virtually screamed when asked if it was possible to talk before the departure of my already booked flight back to Canada. Finally, on the fourth day of the pursuit, he did agree, but only after much coaxing—and also after the flight had left.

The Bobby Clarke who answers questions so readily about his games and the Bobby Clarke who reluctantly discusses himself are actually one and the same: the Jekyll and Hyde of pro hockey. He is a study in contrasts—a choirboy in white cassock who sneaks nips from the sacramental wine. He exudes innocence with boyish, Donny Osmond charm, but beneath the angel hair and baby fat coils one of the chippiest, dirtiest hockey players in the history of the game—a brat who is very possibly the best.

Clarke is a rarity in the self-centred world of professional hockey: someone who will not talk about himself or his accomplishments, a star who never brags. It is a charming mannerism, one usually taken as his humility, and he is revered as a modest player in an era when modesty often seems as popular as brushcuts. However, modesty may not be a fair interpretation of Clarke's reluctance to talk about himself. Could it not also be a fear of opening up, a dread of coming to terms publicly with what a teenage crisis drove Bobby Clarke to do?

When the magazine set out to learn more about Clarke, it was to profile him as hockey's most valuable player (now that Bobby Orr is hobbled and Phil Esposito is fading) and not as hockey's well-known diabetic who made good. But the more we got to know about him—and to *not* know about him—the clearer it became that everything he is today is rooted in an incident that took place on May 24, 1965, when he was sitting in the family living room in Flin Flon, Manitoba, and realized that his mother's image kept going blurry. They rushed him to the hospital and he stayed a month and a half, completely missing his grade nine exams. (The school put him ahead anyway, but he left for good the next year.) His problem was diabetes, severe enough that even today a special diet is not enough, and he must give himself an insulin injection every morning.

The year they discovered the diabetes, the doctors advised him that if he intended to stick with hockey he should switch to goal, but he wouldn't listen, and that's where who he is today began. Instead, he charged into junior hockey as if he were driven by another force, and soon passed other local players who were far more gifted but much less dedicated. He took his average talents and stretched them until he was judged one of the finest players in the entire Western Canada junior league, and though he had proved there was no need for him to become a goaltender, he was not yet satisfied. His family would sometimes hold meetings with him and tell him things might be fine now, but what about later—but he wasn't listening then, either. He had changed into what he is today.

"He just shut up about it when he was about sixteen," his mother says. "I don't think he ever blamed us, but he must have wondered 'Why me? Why am I going to be different?' We'd go and get him from the hospital and he'd want to walk back alone, and think. He never said a word about it, just left things like diet and medicine up to us. We don't talk much about it even now."

"I've had it for ten or eleven years, so it's a part of life," says Clarke, now twenty-six. "But when I first came up, all anybody wanted to talk about was the diabetes, so I just stopped giving interviews about it. When I first got it, it made me feel different from the other kids, and there was a lot of insecurity that went with it."

The insecurity wasn't helped much when Clarke became the seventeenth choice in the 1969 amateur draft. He'd already proved himself a more capable player than a dozen or more of those selected before him—the Flyers' first pick, Bob Currier, never made it to the NHL—but the teams were shying away from him because of the diabetes.

"What really bothered me was that hockey scouts were making themselves medical experts by saying I couldn't last," Clarke says. "But the Flyers at least invested in a phone call to their doctor who said sure, I'd be able to play."

It gave him another point to prove, and he set about it with such intensity that within a few years he was indisputably acclaimed the best defensive player in hockey. (Somewhat ironically, at mid-season this year the defensive master was leading the league in offence as well.) He is, as the clichés about him go, one who never quits trying, a player so determined to win that he will do absolutely anything to accomplish it—and often with disturbing results. ("Professionals are paid to win, not play" is the way he words it.)

In 1972, he was first given national attention as a surprise addition to Team Canada. Coach Harry Sinden had selected all the best centres in hockey—the Espositos and Mikitas—and had wanted to add Walt Tkaczuk of the New York Rangers, as a possible insurance centre. Tkaczuk, however, had prior commitments to his hockey school, and Sinden's choice came down to either Clarke or Dave Keon of the Toronto Maple Leafs, and he selected Clarke. Playing far above what was expected of him, Clarke contributed greatly to the Team Canada victory by eliminating the top Soviet threat, Valeri Kharlamov, when he disabled Kharlamov with a well-aimed chop to the ankles. Clarke was accused of, and did not deny, hurting the Soviet star deliberately, and quickly became the ultimate anti-hero in the USSR. "He jabbed me and I chased him," says Clarke of the incident, "but I wasn't swinging to break his leg. If I was swinging to hurt him, I'd have swung at his head."

Last year, Clarke swung again to deliberately hurt someone, and, ironically, it was at an old friend, Rod Seiling of the Toronto Maple Leafs, who had been Clarke's roommate with Team Canada. During a game in Toronto, Clarke speared Seiling—considered to be the cruellest of all hockey tactics, as it involves the chance of puncturing a spleen or kidney with the blade of the hockey stick— and when Seiling went down, Clarke jumped on him and pounded Seiling's face bloody.

"That's probably the worst thing I've ever done in my career," he says now. "I was just fired up and I was frustrated. I said the first guy that comes around I'm going to get, and it happened to be him. That was definitely my low point."

And often, it is not his stick but his mouth that brings on the trouble. A year ago he called publicly for NHL president Clarence Campbell to step down, claiming he was too old to handle the job. Clarke was furious about Campbell's suspension of two of his teammates for an incident during a game; he claims now he spoke without thinking, and wrote to Campbell later to apologize. He also apologized to Rod Seiling by phone the day after the spearing episode, and in Philadelphia after the game he was again apologizing, this time for referring to the Soviets as "sons of bitches."

"I didn't mean I hate them as individual players. I just hate all the junk that goes with it. On Friday they showed up a half-hour late for lunch. They also said our presents weren't good enough. Why should we give everything to them when they don't appreciate it anyway? They smile and they're friendly but really they're crapping all over us. It seems like we've got to always kiss the Russians' asses, but I don't believe in all that. They should show us a little respect when they're here. When we were there, we did as they said."

All this nastiness, of course, is in direct contrast to the image the Philadelphia Flyers would like you to believe in, as they so religiously do. During his seven seasons in the NHL, Clarke has become something of a travelling media event, one who comes wrapped in his own mythology. There were early stories that he suffered diabetes so badly he had to inject himself with insulin between periods. There was a story told of how, during a team meeting before the playoffs, a veteran Flyer had raised the question of fees being paid for work done around the city for various groups. Clarke had reportedly risen, thrown a $100 bill at the man and then asked those present if they could now get on with the serious business. And there are the many stories of how he is so often available for banquets and such, free of charge.

None of these stories is fully true. Clarke has spoken only once at a banquet, and then for a friend, and he considered himself such a failure at it that he will not likely ever try again. When he does give his time freely, it is to such events as celebrity golf tournaments, where he doesn't have to speak.

And yet, there are other sides to his image. When Flyer backup goaltender Bob Taylor and his wife lost a baby, Clarke was there with money to help, though Taylor hardly needed the money; and whenever any player has need of a car, one of Clarke's is sure to be available. Coach Fred Shero figures he gets about $1,000 a year from Clarke; this year he got a purebred Siberian husky. ("You treat us like dogs, so you might as well have one," Clarke said when he handed over the present.)

There is also the matter of his salary. Clarke, unlike most other hockey players, has no agent—he conducts all his own business. When his first Flyers contract ran out, he agreed to another with owner Ed Snider (for a rumoured $120,000 a year) and they shook hands on it. Later, before Clarke had actually signed the contract and was therefore under no legal obligation to the Flyers, the newly established Philadelphia Blazers of the World Hockey Association came along with a first offer of $1 million over five years. But Clarke honoured his handshake. Only recently, he renegotiated his contract himself, and it is now set up to pay him a certain amount over a great many years, virtually a lifetime contract.

So there are, obviously, honourable actions to consider in trying to understand Bobby Clarke. And to hear his teammates say it, you would think Clarke is nothing less than a man who fully deserves his disciples. "He's just the best captain around," says Reggie Leach, Clarke's best friend from the days when they played junior hockey together. "Yes-men are a dime a dozen," says Fred Shero of his team leader. "Clarke is the most valuable player I've ever seen in sports."

With such devotion, Clarke can well afford to be a fighter, though he's hardly tough: "I'm like a rat. I'll fight when I'm trapped. But I can't fight to begin with. I don't like guys bouncing punches off my head, so I'll fight if I have to. I've had a few draws. If I can grab his arms and hold on, I'll call it a tie."

He knows only too well he'll never lose badly, for Schultz, Kelly or some other Flyer will be there. "If he was at the bottom of a fight I'd jump in, even if it meant getting kicked out of the game," says Leach. "I wouldn't think twice about it."

And Clarke has used this moral support to prove his point until no further proof is needed. Though he has never shown any great natural talent, he has won the Hart Trophy twice as the league's most valuable player, is now a perennial all-star centre, and last year was named Canadian male athlete of the year as well as the 1975 winner of the Lou Marsh Trophy, given annually to Canada's outstanding athlete (when they phoned to inform him, Clarke hadn't a clue as to what the trophy was about).

Materially, he, his wife, Sandy (whom he began going with in Flin Flon when he was fifteen), and their two children are set for life. He is building a new home near Philadelphia, drives a Mercedes free (as a gift from Flyer owner Snider), a half-ton truck (thanks to a promotion deal with a garage), and has endorsements that include Sherwood sticks, Bauer skates and a Philadelphia clothing store that advertises "Mr. Mean Becomes Mr. Clean— Bobby Clarke in Jack Lang Clothes."

With that security, it's possible to understand why a player as celebrated as Clarke has already moved to pave his exit from hockey. Last year he went to his old Flin Flon junior coach, Pat Ginnell, who now owns the Victoria Cougars, another junior club, and he asked Ginnell if he would like him as a coach when the time comes. Right now, Clarke places that date around 1979, which would give him ten full seasons in the NHL. He may stay longer, he says, if he is still playing as well and still enjoying it. But assuming he does play only the three seasons more, they are likely to be seasons in which he is at the peak of his career.

He will leave then, or shortly after, because he has to. There will be no hanging around for Bobby Clarke. There will be no feeling sorry for him in his fading years. He was fed up with pity years ago.

Bobby Clarke retired as a Flyer in 1983–84, following a season in which he scored 17 goals and had 43 assists—a good enough season to justify another in most players' minds. But not in Clarke's. He left having scored 1,210 points in 1,144 games. He won the Hart Trophy three times as league MVP, the Selke as the league's top checker and two Stanley Cups. He served as Philadelphia's general manager for more than two decades but never won another Cup. He is today a senior vice-president with the franchise.

SKATING TO A DIFFERENT DRUMMER:
BORJE SALMING
(*The Canadian*, 1976)

Enrico Ferorelli's perfect moustache is twitching. Looking lost in soft suedes and telephoto lenses, he is pacing the corridor outside the Toronto Maple Leafs' dressing room, three fingers of his right hand anxiously rummaging through his kiss-curls. No one told him that they play only three periods in hockey, not four, and he was counting on finally catching Borje Salming in the fourth. But the game is over and he has no picture, and Enrico blows quickly through his nostrils: *What can go wrong next?*

Sports Illustrated wanted a Ferorelli portrait, not just any shot, and they flew in the freelance fashion photographer from New York to capture Salming as he'd never been caught before. First there was the morning practice: Salming refused to pose. Then there was Enrico's idea that they go to Salming's home: Salming refused. Salming simply wouldn't pose; he told Enrico to grab shots of him during the pre-game warm-up, so Enrico came and set up his lights, but every time he yelled out for Salming's attention, Salming deliberately turned away, and all too quickly the warm-up was over. Enrico tried during the game, tried his best, but never having seen a hockey game before, he kept setting up at the wrong end of the ice.

"I've never had to take this kind of crap," Enrico was saying when he realized he wasn't about to be let into the dressing room afterwards, either. "*Not even from Sophia Loren!*"

It is noon on Church Street: dark enough for headlights, overcast and pouring. It is September 22 and summer is officially due to end in four hours and forty-eight minutes, making this day a perfect rear end for a failed season. Inge Hammarstrom, the Leafs' other Swede, the collar of his ecru jacket drawn tight about his ears, emerges from the heat of the Maple Leaf open kitchen where he has downed two full courses of boiled chicken and has grown increasingly impatient with this writer who asks more questions about Hammarstrom's friend, Borje Salming, than about Hammarstrom himself. He would like to get away, but for the moment the weather has forced him to stand sheltered in the doorway, and when he speaks, his voice, already soft as fall milkweed, is barely audible above the frying sound the tires make in the rain.

"I don't know," Hammarstrom says. "I just can't explain it. Borje is different—more different than all the players I've ever known."

On the other side of Church Street on another day, a dozen youngsters gather around the Church and Wood streets entrance to Maple Leaf Gardens: again it is noon. They are waiting for the end of hockey practice, standing in the special tryst where worshippers and their gods have met for all of the Gardens' forty-five years. They are the dreamers come to touch their dream, and with the Leafs it has so often been a dream of innocence, for the team has produced some remarkably humble stars: Joe Primeau, a man so reserved and modest they called him "Gentleman Joe"; Syl Apps, who never drank or smoked or swore, went to church regularly and was named Canada's Father of the Year in 1949; Red Kelly, who, when violently aroused, might let slip a "hang it." There have been other Primeaus and Appses and Kellys, but today the kids are waiting for one Borje Salming, who can out-humble the best of them. But this latest edition of Maple Leaf innocence is not the same as the others. This one not only doesn't believe in God, but commits the far greater blasphemy of having never, ever dreamed of one day playing in the National Hockey League.

Yet this matters not to those who wait. Two girls in denim and Bay City Rollers tartan begin to squeal as they catch sight of Salming through the plate-glass doors. He is wearing new jeans and a wine-coloured Scandinavian sweater, snowflakes but no reindeer. The closer he gets to the door the more he resembles someone who has been drawn by a sixth-grader for a fall-fair competition: all straight lines and sharply mitred joints, the face too long, the teeth too straight, the shoulders too wide, the hands too low. He opens the door and steps into a wild hedge of waving books and papers, and patiently—for Salming, who usually seems petrified of adulation—he signs about half and even waits while the two girls arrange Instamatic memories of their finest moment; they cuddle up to Salming's arms as he stands ramrod straight, stiff as an unpackaged Big Jim doll. "No more," he says finally. "I have to go." Across Church Street and into one of two Volvos that are provided free for his use (the other he keeps in Sweden) and then he is gone.

"I write autographs as long as I can," he says, a day later. "I consider it a part of the job. But I don't know if I'd do anything else."

Up above Church Street, in the Maple Leaf offices, the letters are stacked eight inches thick, letters that have come to Salming over the summer, when he wasn't even in the country. He has suddenly grown as popular as Leafs captain Darryl Sittler, perhaps more popular, and Gardens publicist Stan Obodiac says the two of them may well be more popular than any Leafs of the past. Certainly they are the best paid, with Salming making more than Sittler, more also than the $200,000 a year usually referred to in the newspapers—possibly the $250,000 a year one Gardens official mentions.

Once every couple of months Salming comes and picks up his mail and answers his letters himself with an autographed picture. This type of thing he can also do, for it doesn't require that he talk to anyone; letters are private, and in his own time. It's also a pressure he can cope with; some others, such as a bad game, often cause him to sit up until dawn, unable even to escape into sleep.

"He's like so many Swedes," Hammarstrom says in the Maple Leaf open kitchen. "He gets impatient when people want his time. Even in Sweden he was known as a lazy person outside of the rink."

Salming's first reaction to an interview request is to imitate a ten-year-old whose mother has just reminded him it's time to leave for his piano lesson. He asks a member of the Gardens staff whether or not he'll be paid for the interview, which is often a European practice. But finally, and reluctantly, he does agree. Tuesday, however, he is simply too busy. The Canada Cup series has just finished and everyone wants his time. He agrees to Wednesday, refuses Wednesday, agrees to Thursday, can't be found Thursday, promises Friday, but can't make Friday because Margitta, his wife, has just gone into labour, makes Saturday definite, and that date he keeps.

Not that all the waiting was worth much. A lot of "I dunnos" and "maybes" later—around strangers he is still disturbingly insecure about his English—a session with Borje Salming adds up to little more than talk about the upcoming exhibition game against Chicago, when the two most impressive players of the Canada Cup tournament, Salming and Bobby Orr, will meet for the first time this season. Salming is often embarrassed by his popularity; Salming likes living in Toronto; Salming gets homesick around Christmas . . . Just about what you expected to hear.

To uncover anything else about him you go to other people, like Gerry McNamara, the tall, gold-toothed scout for the Maple Leafs, who discovered Salming almost by accident. It was Christmas 1972, the Leafs were having goaltending problems and general manager Jim Gregory dispatched McNamara to Sweden to check out a goalie named Curt Larsson. But when McNamara arrived Larsson was hurt and not playing, which left McNamara in Stockholm with nothing to show for the cost of his trip. Determined that he'd better at least see some hockey games, he checked the papers and found that his old senior team, the Barrie Flyers, were in Sweden playing and that night were due to play a team called Gavle Brynas in a nearby town; as well, he'd been told that Brynas, the top team in Sweden, might have some players worth looking at, so McNamara went along hoping that his old friends might cheer him up.

They couldn't, but two Brynas players did. By the end of the first period it was 5–1 for Brynas: Inge Hammarstrom had four goals and Salming had one. Salming was also doing what Swedes weren't supposed to do—fighting back. "They ran at him all night," says McNamara, "and he never gave an inch."

Nor would Salming give in to the referee. A call toward the end of the game upset Salming and he punched the referee in the head, which led to Salming's immediate expulsion from the game.

"I saw my chance and ran," says McNamara. He chased Salming all the way to the dressing room and, forcing his way in, handed the Swedish player his card.

"Do you speak English?" McNamara asked.

"A little," Salming exaggerated.

"I think you could play for the Toronto Maple Leafs in the NHL next year," McNamara said. "Would you be interested?"

"Yah."

"I'll be in touch."

The game was over and the team was coming off the ice, so McNamara left, but not before he had also given Hammarstrom a card and got roughly the same answers.

Salming heard nothing until March, when the world championships were being held in Moscow. One afternoon he was awakened in his hotel room by McNamara and the Leafs' head scout Bob Davidson knocking at the door. Hammarstrom, whose English is excellent, was also there, and translated: Yes, they would both go, but not until their season with Brynas back in Sweden was over. Two-year contracts for $60,000 each sounded pretty good to them. "They were vague about money," recalls Davidson, "but after they'd seen their lawyer they came back with much higher figures." Later in 1973, Salming's Stockholm lawyer got the defenceman a two-year contract with the Leafs worth between $60,000 and $80,000 a year. In addition, the Leafs had to pay $100,000 to the Swedish team that lost the two. So they hardly came cheap.

Salming has often said he had to have a job as a machinist just to make a living in Sweden, but now he will admit, "I've never worked a day in my life." It was not as bad for him there as he has let on, certainly. He refuses to talk money, but Anders Hedberg, the affable Swedish star with the Winnipeg Jets of the WHA, says the best players there made a good living—"enough that a real star can live on hockey alone." Playing in the world championships can be worth $1,000 to $1,500; other European tournaments are worth comparatively less. Players have all expenses covered and many receive a stipend of $45 a day in lieu of money they might have made working while tournaments were on. A win during regular-season play might be worth $75, and Hedberg says he played eighty games in his last Swedish season.

"All that money is taxable," says Hedberg. "But most of the money comes under the table." This, done to preserve the players' "amateur" standing, would include such things as a free apartment—which Salming admits he had—and such fringe benefits as cash payments for playing with a certain make of hockey stick. Ulf Nilsson, another Swede now with the Winnipeg Jets, admits he had two apartments (one he gave to his sister) and received about $3,000 a year from a stick manufacturer. Nilsson thinks Salming received much more, but Salming will say only that he had such a deal, not how much.

When Salming and Hammarstrom returned to Sweden from an investigative trip to Toronto in the spring of 1973—during which they were wooed with, among other things, a sightseeing car tour to Niagara Falls—they announced they had decided to join the Leafs, and this did not go over well with the Brynas team officials. Disgusted that their main stars had fallen to materialism, they refused to let Salming and Hammarstrom even dress with the rest of the team for fear they'd "contaminate" the others. For a month the two dressed and rested between periods in a small room by themselves.

That was the insulting end to the Salming Legend, Part I. He was twenty-two in 1973, Sweden's top hockey star. And now they were phoning him and calling him a traitor. He had been Sweden's Bobby Orr in more than hockey talent, for just as all

Canadians know the story of Parry Sound and Orr, most Swedes knew by heart how Borje Salming had come out of the wasteland of Kiruna, a city so far north that the winter sun barely manages to elbow its way along the southern ledge for a few hours each day, a city where you either stay and work the mines or you take your hockey equipment and skate to freedom.

His father had worked in the Kiruna mines until he died, when Borje was five. For the next six years, until his mother began living with another man, the family lived through hard times, poor on the money she made as a waitress. He does not clearly remember those years, so it may not have been as a waitress, but he does think he was terrible at school and wonderful at hockey, and at twenty he followed his brother, Stig, south to the city of Gavle and the great Brynas team. Where the Orr story and Salming story differ is that, unlike Boston in the sixties, Brynas awaited no saviour: they were already champions.

"There is a story told about Salming when he came to Gavle," says Peter Wannman, a Swedish journalist. "When he was due at the railway station, the town sent a delegation to greet him. They were all set up and this kid gets off in old jeans and an old jacket, with his skates slung over his shoulder, and walks right by them. That was Salming."

That shyness, says Anders Hedberg, is simply a symptom of the place he's from. "Most people from Kiruna are that way, soft-spoken and solid," says Hedberg. "Kiruna produces lots of hockey players—it's Sweden's Flin Flon—and they're all like Salming."

"He had no style as a boy," says Peter Wannman, "and now he has no style as a man. All he knows to do is play hockey."

There was some doubt of that when he arrived in Toronto. At first he didn't live up to his billing. "The guys were all suspicious," says Jim McKenny, a Leaf who has since become one of Salming's closest friends. "He was so incredibly quiet and had no English. None of the guys knew how to take him. They said he had a bad back, which is one of the best injuries to have—who can really tell? But we weren't long in realizing he has a lot of balls."

By the time Salming's first three NHL seasons were through, the people were also through with doubt. He fell in front of shots until a lung bled, revitalized the poke check and, in his second and third years, even emerged as a considerable scoring threat. With his forlorn, apron-string boy's face he became the darling of the Toronto media, even though most of the press have found him impossible to deal with; the city, having not seen such humility and shyness in many years, was amazed that Salming lasted three years and seemed to grow rather than diminish. "I'd be surprised now if anything changed his personality," says Leafs general manager Jim Gregory.

Salming was also the fondest wish come true for Toronto lawyer Bill McMurtry, whose inquiry into violence in hockey began the great hockey-violence debate of the past two years. "The thesis I always had in mind was that there are better ways of proving your courage than high-sticking and fighting," says McMurtry. "And Salming perfectly emulates that thesis. He was the greatest thing that could have happened to my report."

Naturally, one day Salming had to be tested. It has always been held true in the NHL that it is possible to be a great player and not fight, provided it was known you could fight well if necessary. Bobby Hull, Orr and Syl Apps earned their reputations that way, but Salming's fighting ability was unknown until last spring's Stanley Cup playoffs when Philadelphia Flyers rookie Mel Bridgman easily defeated Salming and received an assault charge for his troubles.

Conn Smythe, the original owner of the Maple Leafs, believes that the fight—even though Salming lost—didn't do him any harm. "Nobody's bothered him since," says Smythe. "So he won. He's like Britain—doesn't win the battles but always wins the war."

The non-violent face Salming wore in Canada was not always his choice in Sweden. Once, when his Brynas team went to play against Timra, Salming reacted to a spoken insult by attacking a

Timra player and knocking him out cold. The police had to be brought in to escort him to the dressing room and then out of the arena. "The crowd really wanted to lynch him," remembers Margitta Salming.

When they first arrived in Canada she was Margitta Wendin and, like Salming, had her problems. She'd been going with him only a year, but when he came to Canada he asked her to leave her job as a restaurant cashier to go and live with him. Their lack of a marriage licence obviously didn't suit all of the other Leafs, especially the older ones. "Nobody really said anything," she remembers, "but you could feel it. I wasn't considered one of the wives, just a girlfriend, and I felt very insecure about it." In the following summer, though, she married Salming and had a son, Anders. Salming says the child was his present to her, to make her less lonely.

Today, though, there is a second baby, a girl, Teresa, born very early Saturday morning and premature enough (five weeks) to be placed in an incubator. Salming has had very little sleep, and at the Saturday-morning practice he appears sluggish and haggard, a far cry from the day before when he was laughing and kidding on the ice, skating up to a fallen Mike Pelyk, who has recently come from the WHA, yelling "Hey, Pelyk"—the English clear and the manner easy and confident—"it's tougher in this league, you know. You'd better watch it here or even a Swede will beat you up."

Today, though, the man they all call "King" (short for "King of Sweden") is standing by the bench with his head down and calling loudly and impatiently for one of the trainers to bring him glucose tablets. (Though the image is shy and gentle, Salming can at times be curt, and has even clashed angrily with Red Kelly in the past.) He washes down a half-dozen or more and then returns to the practice, and fifteen minutes later, with manufactured energy running through him, Salming is once again, as usual, the hardest worker in the Leafs practice.

At the Saturday-evening game he is still the best Leaf, and though Chicago's Bobby Orr is obviously the main attraction of the first period, the second and third periods belong to Salming. Chicago, having taken a 1–0 lead when Salming was off for holding Orr, quickly lose it as Salming breaks in alone and takes a Darryl Sittler pass for a Leafs goal, and the inspired Leafs go on to win, with Salming setting up two more goals. Salming is chosen a game star over Orr for Round 1 of the oncoming season.

When Orr and Salming play against each other, it is a competition between Orr's anticipation and Salming's reaction, for though Orr is easily the purest thinker hockey has produced, Salming may well be the game's best reflex player. His is not as awesome a hockey talent as Orr's, but it has its own beauty, and it is little wonder that recent praise for Salming's play ranges from seventy-three-year-old King Clancy, who says Salming is the Leafs' Orr, to twelve-year-old Bjorn-Erik Eklund, who was born in Luleti, close to Salming's Kiruna, who saw first-hand Salming's greatness in the Canada Cup series and who calls Salming "the biggest hero in the whole world."

Certainly, inside the Leafs dressing room you would get that impression. An emaciated, waxen Salming sits in his athletic support and soaked T-shirt and concedes that yes, it was a very good day—a baby, a goal and a star. But he softens it by saying what people expect him to say: that Bobby Orr will win the Norris Trophy this year as the NHL's premier defenceman and that "Salming will never win it." There are smiles and shaking heads: such humility, such an innocent lie.

Outside, in the corridor, Enrico Ferorelli is still pacing, checking his schedule against his airline ticket to see if he dare stay over until Monday and still meet his deadline, wondering why Borje Salming had to happen to him.

Borje Salming played seventeen seasons, leaving the Maple Leafs in 1989 for a year with the Detroit Red Wings and then winding down his career with three seasons back in Sweden playing for Shellefteå AIK. He played a total of 1,148 NHL games, scoring 150 goals and setting up another 637. In 1996 he became the first Swede elected to the Hockey Hall of Fame. Salming successfully went into the underwear business when he returned to Sweden to live.

THE THROWBACK: BRYAN TROTTIER

(*The Canadian*, 1976)

It's a long way, and not just in miles, from the struggling Saskatchewan farm, the frozen river, and the father who pulled the rest of the family into part-time work to keep things afloat. Bryan Trottier could go home again—will, in fact, this summer— but it'll never be exactly the same. No more Rowdy, for one thing: the dog died about the same time Bryan's life changed forever. Even the farmhouse isn't the way it was, all fixed up now and proudly insured by the father for many times what it was worth when Bryan still spent winters there. And the father these days has his own brand-new four-wheel drive for the rough weather and a big Chrysler New Yorker for the good days, which now seem more numerous. Both vehicles are gifts from Bryan. Even the farm itself is no longer the same: it's a business now, a working operation with a couple hundred head of cattle, new machinery and those pesky loans cleared up. All thanks to Bryan.

It's a long way to come, and he's still not used to the change. Crossing Yonge Street, on his way to a favourite plate of chips and gravy in Toronto's stuffiest hotel, the Royal York, he finds himself looking up in awe after all those years of Prairie flatlands. "Geez, you got a lot of tall buildings here, too," he says, meaning that New York City, next door to Long Island where he's playing hockey now, doesn't yet sit well with him, though he's been there since September last.

Sometimes there's a temptation to reach out and knock the straw hat off, except he hasn't one, or at least pinch him to see if

he's real, though you already know he is, having seen him interviewed during the January NHL All-Star Game when he begged
to say a "hello to my Mom and Dad," which he did. The proof
that it was no stunt could be seen in the remodelled farmhouse in
Val Marie, Saskatchewan—about seventy-five miles directly
south of Swift Current—where his father broke down and cried
when he saw his son wave home from the television set, and his
mother and sister threw their arms about each other and bawled.

A month later, Bryan still talks about that all-star contest,
remembering who sat where in the dressing room and who said
what, and how he concentrated very hard not to talk too much or
be too loud, or come on "as an intellectual" or anything, and how
finally the pleasures rose too high and he just sat there chuckling
and shaking his head.

"The dream has not come true," he says. "I am *living* the
dream. And that's better."

He came into the National Hockey League last fall with virtually no advance publicity, picked a low twenty-second in the
1974 amateur draft when he was only seventeen and one of many
underaged players (seventeen- and eighteen-year-olds) taken in
the league's "secret draft" of that year (this was held to fight back
against the World Hockey Association teams who were already
signing the best of the young junior players, such as Mark Howe).
Fully nine underaged kids were selected before him, so it was not
as if he was anything that special in 1974; in fact, the team that
selected him, the New York Islanders, advised him to stay another
year in junior hockey, and he agreed to—thereby becoming the
only one of the secret draft picks who did not immediately turn
pro—and last year, while captaining the Lethbridge Broncos of
the Western Hockey League, he was named the league's most
valuable player.

Even so, no one anticipated what impact he would have on the
NHL when he finally did arrive. Halfway through this current
season he was already touted as a shoe-in for the rookie-of-the-year

award in what has proven to be a bumper crop of first-year players. As the season began to wind down, Trottier was seriously closing in on Marcel Dionne's rookie record of seventy-seven points, and he was somehow hanging in with the league's top ten scorers—something NHL statistician Ron Andrews says has not been done since 1951–52, the season Bernie Geoffrion came to the Montreal Canadiens.

But there was much more to Trottier's arrival than the mere coming of yet another great talent. He is, as his former junior coach Earl Ingarfield puts it, "a throwback." He has come out of the Prairies like a spring wind, and the feeling is something the long winters of expansion hockey had suppressed. With rare exception, the image of the post-1967 player has been one of an instantly rich, cocky, arrogant and conceited child, far more interested in his European cars, hair, clothes, women and fur coats than in doing anything for those less fortunate citizens who grew up listening to and watching hockey, treating it like a national heirloom.

And then, while hockey limps through its worst year yet of diluted talent and embarrassing franchises, along comes a boy from Val Marie who offers some small hope for the way hockey once was, before the Hollywood era. First of all he has a different look to him: while so many of them seem like assorted covers of *Gentleman's Quarterly* magazine, Trottier is like a kid whose mother has just sent him to the drugstore for Tampax. Painfully shy. A kid of French, Cree, Chippewa and Irish heritage who took the windfall of his contract and gave his parents all they'd ever hoped for. And for himself, when his 1966 Chevrolet half-ton blew up last fall he went out and replaced it with another '66 Chevy half-ton.

This is a kid the way Frank Boucher was a kid a half-century before Trottier. He has never smoked, has tried rye and Coke but once and didn't like it, and seldom swears. He was even living in New York a full month before he forced himself into a good clothes store and traded his Prairies fare for some very conservative big city finery. He seems too good to be true, obviously, and it is somewhat gratifying to learn he does have a flaw, however small, in that he tells white lies about his salary. What he admits to is a mere (for hockey) $55,000 a year, which is about $20,000 below the NHL average. What he really gets is in excess of $100,000 a year, and that doesn't even include the earnings from a $100,000-plus signing contract that was money up front before he ever even left the farm. He's forgiven on this point only because a lot of players like to lie about their money—but they usually go the other way. Trottier lies because it seems to genuinely embarrass him to make so much.

Actually, he was a pro of a type in his last year of junior hockey. He'd been drafted the previous spring from the Swift Current Broncos, and all that summer of 1974 he figured he'd be headed for New York come the fall. The Islanders, though, took a strange stand for a club still in the process of building a team. They told him he could have a guarantee on the contract they'd already discussed, the huge signing bonus would be put in trust, and the usual car bonus would be available, but they wanted Trottier to play one more year of junior in Lethbridge, Alberta, where the Broncos' franchise had been moved.

"Nobody needed players worse than us," says the Islanders' general manager Bill Torrey, "but he was only seventeen. We wanted to give him a chance to grow naturally. Had he come with us he might have made the team or he might have been sent down to Fort Worth. And we felt he'd be better off playing for Earl Ingarfield in Lethbridge. I think that shocked his family—Bryan was the most disappointed of all."

The agent for the contract deal was Montreal's Dave Schatia, who set new records that very year with million-dollar contracts for Greg Joly in the NHL and Pat Price in the WHA. Schatia, despite his great experience, had never met anyone quite like Trottier, whom he still calls "the apple pie, ice cream kid."

"I've handled a lot of contracts," says Schatia, "and when it came time for the car part of the deal they've wanted Maseratis,

Lamborghinis, Jaguars and Mercedes. He's the only one who ever came to me and asked for a Chrysler New Yorker."

Actually, it wasn't Trottier's choice. He'd gone first to his father and asked him what kind of car he'd always fancied, and when his father mentioned a Chrysler New Yorker Bryan made sure he got it. For himself he bought nothing. The big Chrysler became just one part of a continual effort by Trottier to pay back his father, Buzz. Growing up on his grandfather's farm, as his father did, the family ties have developed into steel girders.

Buzz Trottier taught his first son, Bryan (there are four other children), to skate on the same river he learned on, a river that spills out of a nearby reservoir and runs through the Trottier section-and-a-half, not thirty feet from the farmhouse. Bryan, as this verifiable myth goes, would be out even at forty below in the Saskatchewan winters, playing long into the night with the only two opponents he could recruit, his father and the family's black-and-white border collie, Rowdy. True to a real-life juvenile novel, Bryan even taught Rowdy how to play goal, so Bryan could practise scoring. And Rowdy proved to be a determined competitor: when he died, at age eleven in Bryan's last year of junior hockey, Rowdy hadn't a tooth left.

All along, his father tried to keep the youngster in the best equipment and with sharpened skates. To cover the costs of Bryan's hockey equipment—and also to help the floundering farm and ease the $77-a-month rent on the house he took for three winters in Swift Current so the family could be near Bryan when he played—Buzz formed his offspring into a country and western band. Bryan played bass and sang, Buzz played rhythm guitar and sister Cathy sang. They learned the latest Merle Haggard, Charley Pride and Buck Owens, and they hit the road every weekend, picking up from $6 to $40 a night in little Saskatchewan and Alberta towns, sometimes dipping down into Montana, where there was less trouble over the kids being underage.

This unusual closeness created a boy who actually listened to every word his father said. When morning hockey practices made school virtually impossible, Bryan, who was a good to very good student in grade eleven, went to his father and told him he was quitting. "My Dad really scared me. 'Well kid,' Dad says, 'now you've *got* to make it in hockey.' And I knew right then and there that I had to make it if I quit."

Other fathers naturally began coming to Buzz Trottier with tales of teenage debauchery, asking for the production secrets on Bryan Trottier, but Buzz maintained he had no clear answers: "He has never ceased amazing me. He never talked back to us, never gave us an ounce of trouble. When he joined the band they started kidding him in the bars. 'C'mon, Bryan,' they'd say, 'join us for a drink, have a double on us.' And Bryan would say, 'Sure, I'll have a double—waiter! Would you bring me two glasses of milk?'"

The way Bryan Trottier tells it, in Val Marie it was a quiet way, a sensible approach to life, and no one thought much about it. You did as you wished, and people generally knew you for what you had always been. "Out there," says Bryan, "whatever happens in the family stays in the family." But those times are over forever. Bryan Trottier has already set the media windmills in motion.

When he hit New York last fall it was a little like *Mr. Smith Goes to Washington*, updated, in a different locale, and with a game other than politics. People then saw Bryan Trottier's way as a different way, a naive approach to life. He's not religious, and it puzzles people that anyone would turn out this way without some holy commitment.

Trottier's freshness will be measured and assessed each season he remains at the top, and there are those who say he is already there to stay. It was not just the recognition in playing in the NHL All-Star Game before putting in a complete season as a professional. It was also being awarded the Calder Trophy for rookie of the year in all but actual ceremony. The natural question is: How long before the milk sours? How much attention and temptation can he stand?

"I honestly don't think pressure's a factor in his case," says the Islanders' Denis Potvin, himself a much-celebrated rookie and winner of the Calder Trophy for 1973–74. "But if it is, he's the guy to handle it."

Some people have already moved to protect him from the perils of fame getting to him too quickly. Warren Amendola, the president of Koho hockey equipment, heard in September that Trottier was still living in a hotel room, and so invited him to come and stay with him, his wife and three boys for a couple of weeks or a month, whatever it took for the young hockey player to get settled. Trottier is still there, with no thoughts of leaving, and though he likely makes at least as much as the president of a hockey equipment firm, he has yet to pay a penny in rent.

"He's a guest," says Amendola, "and he's here for as long as he wants to stay. I see myself as his American father, and I don't like to see talents like his ruined. Lots of these kids are just thrown to the wolves. The clubs can't exert the influence they used to. We treat him just like our own kids. He gets yelled at for not cleaning up his room, whatever. And Bryan's head is as big today as the day he came in with us. He has no conceit whatsoever."

As for Trottier himself, he can and will speak out in assurance that it is not an act, that the unspoiled flavour runs through to the core, and that he is not going to change despite what the cynics say. "People keep asking me about the pressure, the rookie award and things like that, but I've never fully understood the meaning of pressure. The only thing you can do is go out and do your best at everything, whether it's eating habits, hockey or just watching the way you dress."

Two-thirds of the way through this season he was still trying his best and abiding true to the outdated ideals he developed on the farm in Val Marie. After a very strong game in Toronto, during which he scored an unassisted goal by stealing the puck at centre ice and putting a hard shot through goaltender Gord McRae's glove, he was sitting shyly and totally without pretension in the dressing room.

"You played well tonight, Bryan," said a sportswriter as he walked by.

"No," replied Trottier. "The team played well tonight."

Later, one of the Islanders came around with his little nephew, chasing autographs, which is often a difficult task with hockey players who have other things, like getting dressed and out of there, on their minds. When the youngster came around to Trottier, however, the farm boy from Val Marie stood up and shook his hand.

Bryan Trottier went on to play eighteen seasons for the Islanders and the Pittsburgh Penguins. He won the Calder Trophy that season as the top rookie, then went on to win four Stanley Cups with the Islanders, two more with Pittsburgh and a seventh as an assistant coach with the Colorado Avalanche. In 1978–79, he won both the Art Ross Trophy as the league's top scorer and the Hart as its most valuable player. The following year he was awarded the Conn Smythe as the top player in the playoffs. He had one disastrous year as coach of the New York Rangers (2002) and has not been involved in coaching since.

JEAN BÉLIVEAU AT SEVENTY-FIVE

(*The Globe and Mail*, April 7, 2007)

If, as is often said, the late Robert Stanfield was the best prime minister Canada never had, then Jean Béliveau must stand as the best governor general the country missed out on.

In fact, he is late to meet me on this cold April morning not because of rain falling in needles, but because of fans stopping him as he enters the hockey rink where his retired Montreal Canadiens No. 4 hangs proudly from the rafters. Even Canadien Chris Higgins—born long after Mr. Béliveau raised a tenth Stanley Cup over his head—wants visiting family members to meet his childhood hero.

No matter where this tall, white-haired seventy-five-year-old goes, there are well-wishers. His wife, Elise, has driven him to the interview, waiting patiently, as she has since they married in 1953, while he wades through those who want to touch the hem of the hockey legend whose most lasting legacy may well be class. "I don't mind the wait," she says.

"I'm very fortunate," he adds. "Just signing my name makes people happy."

Just being Jean Béliveau seems to have the same effect. Last week, he let his name stand for a dinner that brought out a thousand of Montreal's business elite—as well as Guy Lafleur, Gordie Howe, Jean Chrétien and Prime Minister Stephen Harper. The event raised more than a million dollars for children's hospitals in the province.

All the money, he had instructed, had to go to children, just as he had insisted thirty-six years earlier when the Canadiens decided to give him a special "night" in what would be his final season. "If there's money involved," he told them, "I don't want a penny of it for myself."

That exceptional night in 1971 saw the Jean Béliveau Foundation launched with a cheque for $155,855. And every post-retirement dollar Béliveau has made from appearances and golf tournaments has gone into the fund, raising millions for a camp for disabled children near Joliette.

That summer, when he took his family to Europe, he wrote ahead and asked if they might attend the weekly public audience of Pope Paul VI. When they arrived, they were told it would be a private audience. The Pope, it turned out, wanted to meet the athlete who gave everything to needy children.

When Béliveau finally retired completely from the Canadiens in 1993, he also received an invitation to 24 Sussex Drive. The new prime minister Jean Chrétien wished to see him. Jean and Elise Béliveau drove to Ottawa knowing what was likely to happen. There had been rumours about him serving as governor general. It seemed a perfect fit. Béliveau had already led an impeccable life in the spotlight. Elise—with her French and Irish background and what granddaughter Mylène calls "an explosive personality"—would make an ideal partner. And the two were sociable, energetic and fluently bilingual. But they could not take it.

The reason was simple, but private—and it involved children.

Less than five years earlier, Jean Béliveau had arrived for work at the old Montreal Forum to find two police officers and a chaplain waiting. Montreal police officer Serge Roy—husband to the Béliveaus' daughter, Hélène, and father to their two girls, then five and three—had taken his own life at nearby Station 25. The marriage had been going through a rough stretch, but there had been no indication of the depths of the policeman's despair.

Nearly twenty years later, Elise Béliveau still has trouble speaking of that time. She waits for Jean to leave the room to accept a telephone call before even attempting. "I couldn't talk about it for a long time," she says. "I couldn't talk about it all in front of Jean. I couldn't talk about it in front of Hélène."

She had been close to her son-in-law. He had, she says, such a "beautiful smile" and always seemed happy. Jean believes it was the stress of police work that was a contributing factor, but Elise says they did not know then and do not know today why he committed suicide.

"I was mad," she says. "It never dawned on me that he would do a thing like that, and when it happened, oh my goodness . . . Nobody knows why. And you blame yourself, you say, 'How come I didn't see it?' But when you think of it, it's nobody's fault. Because the one who does it, that's what he wants. And that's it."

Serge's death also left the Béliveaus with a tough decision to make about the governor general's post. "Under normal circumstances," Jean says, "we probably would have accepted. It would have been a great honour." Instead, he could not sleep when he returned from Ottawa. He found himself sitting up Saturday morning at six o'clock, still pondering.

"What are we going to do with this?" he asked Elise when she came downstairs. She didn't know. If he wanted it, she told him, she would go. If she wanted it, he told her, he would make it happen. They did want it, but they wanted more to be there for the girls.

"You don't replace a father or a mother," Jean says. "But there are a lot of things grandparents can do. I couldn't leave them behind."

They decided they would just say they were retiring and leave it at that. If he made too much of the grandchildren and word got out, he worried it would draw attention to them they did not need. So he placed the call to say no. "He would have been fantastic," says Chrétien, who then offered the prestigious appointment to Roméo LeBlanc.

"He's always been there for us," says granddaughter Mylène Roy, now twenty-three and finishing up her fine arts degree at the University of Quebec. "He's always the same with us, no matter if we were six or seven or twenty-one, twenty-two. Always the same. Never changed. He's always so attentive in his own way. Always so patient. He's always asking this, even now: 'Is everything fine? Is there anything we can do?'"

They lived nearby, close enough that the older Béliveaus could visit regularly, be there for sports, special school events and the invariable crises of the teenage years. They established rituals such as daily telephone checks, birthdays, anniversaries and Sunday get-togethers, usually swimming in the Béliveaus' pool in good weather.

Even on the day I meet the couple, Elise Béliveau had risen early to pick up Mylène's younger sister, twenty-one-year-old

Magalie, as she came off her night shift as a nurse at a Montreal hospital. Both Mylène and Magalie are deeply appreciative for what their grandparents did. In many ways, Jean Béliveau became both father and grandfather, a rock to hold on to in a time of turbulent waters.

"He's not so much of a talker," Mylène says. "He's always there, but more in a silent way. The way people see him in public is just the way he is with his family. It's more of a . . . a presence . . ."

Whatever Jean Béliveau became in life, it began in little Victoriaville. "My childhood was in no ways remarkable," he wrote in his 1994 memoirs. "It was a typical French-Canadian Catholic upbringing, one hinged on family values, strict religious observance, hard work, conservatism, and self-discipline."

Laurette Béliveau, who died young at forty-nine, installed industrial-strength linoleum on the kitchen floor so Jean and his younger brother, Guy, could leave their skates on when they came in from the backyard rink for lunch. He still lists vegetable soup with a slice of crusty bread as a favourite meal. Arthur Béliveau drove for Shawinigan Water and Power. "A wonderful man," Elise says of him. And one with his own ideas. When scouts came calling on his talented son, he turned them away. When teams tried to sign him to contracts covering more than a season, he would tell them, "In the spring, he belongs to me."

When the budding young hockey star left for Quebec City at seventeen, Arthur drove him to the bus stop in the company truck and said, simply, "Do your best, Jean—it will be enough." It is but one of many Arthur Béliveau maxims that Jean carries to this day. Loyalty is important. You and only you will know when you have paid a debt. Your name is your greatest asset.

It was in Quebec City that young Jean developed a love for children. He was such a star, even in junior, that he was given a 1951 Nash and a $60-a-week summer job driving about as the Laval Ice Cream Man handing out ice cream bars. Elise, whom he had met on a blind date, had to drive at first and, for months after he finally got his licence, had to do the backing up for him.

Montreal was desperate for the tall youngster to come to the Canadiens, but he was not keen to leave Quebec City and Elise. When he graduated from junior hockey, he said he would thank the fans of the city by staying around another year to play for the semi-professional Aces, but ended up staying on a second season as well.

Montreal finally signed him in 1953 for the unheard-of sum of $110,000 over five years. He was twenty-two and knew it was time to move on. In retrospect, however, he believes that delaying his National Hockey League career so long is what gave him a "maturity" other young stars may have lacked. "You're eighteen years old," he says, "and you come from a small town, from a quiet but strong family. For me, Quebec was the foundation. If I was ever to build on something, it would serve me."

He came out of Quebec City a hockey star, but also committed to children's charity. His popularity had allowed the city to build a new, larger Colisée—jokingly referred to as "Chateau Béliveau"—but it also showed him another power. He had been helping a local priest, Father Bernier, by coming to an old stone shed the priest had set up as a sort of club for young people and was there the morning the floor partly caved in.

"We better do something about this," the young hockey player told the priest. And he has never looked back.

It has been a life in the spotlight, one that is usually spoken of in terms of Stanley Cups and the Hall of Fame and the many awards he won for his skill on the ice. But that is only part of it. Jean Béliveau has also served as a father figure for his granddaughters. And for young players—Guy Lafleur first and foremost among them.

There were times when he needed his own rock. Nearly seven years ago, he discovered an odd lump on his neck while shaving and underwent a gruelling radiation round that has, fortunately, left him cancer-free today. But it was tough. "If you don't have faith," Elise says, "you don't have much."

On the verge of celebrating their fifty-third wedding anniversary this June, the Béliveaus are moving out of the house in Longueuil they purchased in 1955 for $18,000. In May, they will move "down the street" to a condominium with a "fabulous" night view of Montreal—the city where, for more than half a century, his own light has shone brightest.

There are no regrets, he says. When the chance to be governor general came up, he says, they did what any grandparents would do under similar circumstances.

"But it would have been great," he says, smiling shyly. "From that little ice surface behind the house in Victoriaville to make it all the way to governor general, it would have made my life full."

"You've had a full life," Elise corrects.

"Yes," he says. "I know."

Jean Béliveau was named a Companion in the Order of Canada as well as honorary captain of the 2010 men's Olympic hockey team that went on to win the gold medal in the Vancouver Winter Games. He has had further health issues, including a small stroke in 2010 that briefly hospitalized him, but early 2011 found the Béliveaus happily living in their new apartment and enjoying his eightieth year.

PLAYING AGAINST BOBBY ORR

(Fiction: excerpted from *The Last Season*, 1983)

In hockey it is called a "rep," short, of course, for "reputation." Mine grew out of North Bay: one game, one moment, the clock stopped, the game in suspension—and yet it was this, nothing to do with what took place while clocks ran in sixty-eight other games, that put me on the all-star team with more votes than Torchy. Half as many, however, as Bobby Orr. But still, it was Orr and Batterinski, the two defensemen, whom they talked most about in Ontario junior.

Bobby Orr would get the cover of *Maclean's*. I almost got the cover of *Police Gazette* after the Billings incident. My rep was made. The *North Bay Nugget's* nickname for me, Frankenstein, spread throughout the league. I had my own posters in Kitchener; there were threats in Kingston and spray-paint messages on our bus in Sault Ste. Marie; late, frantic calls at the Demers house from squeaky young things wanting to speak to the "monster!"

They didn't know me. I didn't know myself. But I loved being talked about in the same conversations as the white brushcut from Parry Sound. Orr they spoke of as if he was the Second Coming—they sounded like Poppa praising the Madonna on the church in Warsaw; for me it was the same feeling for both Orr and the Madonna—I couldn't personally see it.

Orr had grown since I'd seen him first in Vernon, but he was still only sixteen in 1964 and seemed much too short to be compared to Harvey and Howe, as everyone was doing. He'd gone straight from bantam to junior, but Gus Demers still said he was just another in a long list of junior hockey's flashes-in-the-pan. Another Nesterenko, another Cullen.

We met Oshawa Generals in that year's playoffs, and the papers in Oshawa and Sudbury played up the Batterinski–Orr side of it. "Beauty and the Beast," the *Oshawa Times* had it. The *Star* countered with "Batterinski's Blockade," pointing out that the Hardrocks' strategy was to have Batterinski make sure Orr never got near the net, though no one ever spoke to me about it. I presume it was understood.

On March 28 we met on their home ice, the advantage going to them by virtue of a better record throughout the season. I said not a single word on the bus ride down, refusing to join Torchy in his dumb-ass Beatles songs, refusing even to get up and wade back to the can, though I'd had to go since Orillia. My purpose was to exhibit strength and I could not afford the slightest opening. I had to appear superhuman to the rest of the team: not needing words, nor food, nor bodily functions.

If I could have ridden down in the equipment box I would have, letting the trainer unfold me and tighten my skates just before the warm-up, sitting silent as a puck, resilient as my shin pads, dangerous as the blades. The ultimate equipment: me.

I maintained silence through the "Queen" and allowed myself but one chop at Frog Larocque's goal pads, then set up. Orr and I were like reflections, he standing solid and staring up at the clock from one corner, me doing the same at the other, both looking at time, both thinking of each other. We were the only ones in the arena, the crowd's noise simply the casing in which we would move, the other players simply the setting to force the crowd's focus to us. Gus Demers had advised me to level Orr early, to establish myself. Coach Therrien wanted me to wait for Orr, keep him guessing. I ignored them all. They weren't involved. Just Orr and me.

His style had changed little since bantam. Where all the other players seemed bent over, concentrating on something taking place below them, Orr still seemed to be sitting at a table as he played, eyes as alert as a poker player, not interested in his own hands or feet or where the object of the game was. I was fascinated by him and studied him intently during the five minutes I sat in the penalty box for spearing some four-eyed whiner in the first period. What made Orr effective was that he had somehow shifted the main matter of the game from the puck to him. By anticipating, he had our centres looking for him, not their wingers, and passes were directed away from him, not to someone on our team. By doing this, and by knowing this himself, he had assumed control of the Hardrocks as well as the Generals.

I stood at the penalty box door yanking while the timekeeper held for the final seconds. I had seen how to deal with Orr. If the object of the game had become him, not the puck, I would simply put Orr through his own net.

We got a penalty advantage toward the end of the period and coach sent me out to set up the power play. I was to play centre point, ready to drop quickly in toward the net rather than remaining in the usual point position along the boards and waiting for a long shot and tip-in. Therrien had devised this play, I knew, from watching Orr, though he maintained it was his own invention. I never argued. I never even spoke. I was equipment, not player, and in that way I was dependable, predictable, certain.

Torchy's play, at centre, was to shoulder the Oshawa centre out of the faceoff circle while Chancey, playing drop-back left wing, fed the puck back to me, breaking in. A basketball play, really, with me fast-breaking and Torchy pic-ing. The crowd was screaming but I couldn't hear. I was listening for Orr, hoping he might say something that would show me his flaw, hoping he might show involvement rather than disdain. But he said nothing. He stared up at the clock for escape, the numbers meaningless, the score irrelevant. He stood, stick over pads, parallel to the ice, back also parallel, eyes now staring through the scars of the ice for what might have been his own reflection. Just like me, once removed from the crowd's game, lost in his own contest.

The puck dropped and Torchy drove his shoulder so hard into the Generals' centre I heard the grunt from the blueline. Chancey was tripped as he went for the puck, but swept it as he fell. I took it on my left skate blade, kicking it forward to my stick, slowing it, timing it, raising back for a low, hard slapper from just between the circles. I could sense Orr. Not see him. I was concentrating on the puck. But I could sense him the way you know when someone is staring at you from behind. I raised the stick higher, determined to put the shot right through the bastard if necessary. I heard him go down, saw the blond brushcut spinning just outside the puck as he slid toward me, turning his pads to catch the shot. His eyes were wide open as his head passed the puck; he stared straight at it, though it could, if I shot now, rip his face right off the skull. He did not flinch; he did not even blink. He stared the way a poker player might while saying he'll hold. Orr knew precisely what my timing was before I myself knew. I saw him spin past, knew what he was doing, but could not stop; my shot crunched into his pads and away, harmlessly.

The centre Torchy had hit dove toward the puck and it bounced back at me, off my toe and up along the ankle, rolling like a ball in a magician's trick. I kicked but could not stop it. The puck trickled and suddenly was gone. I turned, practically falling. It was Orr! Somehow he'd regained his footing even faster than I and was racing off in that odd sitting motion toward our net.

I gave chase, now suddenly aware of the crowd. Their noise seemed to break through an outer, protective eardrum. There were no words, but I was suddenly filled with insult as the screams tore through me, ridiculing. It seemed instant, this change from silently raising the stick for the certain goal, the sense that I was gliding on air, suspended, controlling even the breath of this ignorant crowd. Now there was no sense of gliding or silence or control. I was flailing, chopping at a short sixteen-year-old who seemed completely oblivious to the fact that Batterinski was coming for him.

I felt my left blade slip and my legs stutter. I saw him slipping farther and farther out of reach, my strides choppy and ineffective, his brief, effortless and amazingly successful. I swung with my stick at his back, causing the noise to rise. I dug in but he was gone, a silent, blond brushcut out for a skate in an empty arena.

I dove, but it was no use. My swinging stick rattled off his ankle guards and I turned in my spill in time to see the referee's hand raise for a delayed penalty. I was already caught so I figured I might as well make it worthwhile. I regained my feet and rose just as Orr came in on Larocque, did something with his stick and shoulder that turned Frog into a life-size cardboard poster of a goaltender, and neatly tucked the puck into the corner of the net.

The crowd roared, four thousand jack-in-the-boxes suddenly sprung, all of them laughing at me. Orr raised his hands in salute and turned, just as I hit him.

It was quiet again, quiet as quickly as the noise had first burst through. I felt him against me, shorter but probably as solid. I smelled him, not skunky the way I got myself, but the smell of Juicy Fruit chewing gum. I gathered him in my arms, both of us motionless but for the soar of our skates, and I aimed him carefully and deliberately straight through the boards at the goal judge.

Orr did not even bother to look at me. It was like the theory you read about car accidents, that the best thing you can do is relax. Orr rode in my arms contentedly, acceptingly, neither angry, nor afraid, nor surprised. We moved slowly, deliberately, together. I could see the goal judge leaping, open-mouthed, back from the boards, bouncing off his cage like a gorilla being attacked by another with a chain. I saw his coffee burst through the air as we hit, the grey-brown circles slowly rising up and away and straight into his khaki coat. The boards gave; they seemed to give forever, folding back toward the goal judge, then groaning, then snapping us out and down in a heap as the referee's whistle shrieked in praise.

I landed happy, my knee rising into his leg as hard as I could manage, the soft grunt of expelled air telling me I had finally made contact with the only person in the building who would truly understand.

This excerpt from The Last Season, *my 1983 novel on hockey, was based on several true incidents. I had played against Bobby Orr, so knew firsthand that experience on the ice—though at a younger age than junior hockey. And the "Billings" incident was drawn from an actual experience when I was playing juvenile hockey and a bench-clearing brawl broke out in Bracebridge, Ontario requiring an ambulance to deal with an injured player and a police escort to get our team out of town. As much of the book is set in Finland, I was fortunate enough to travel to that country in 1981 as a member of the Toronto Maple Leaves, a recreational team that played several exhibition matches against rec teams in various Finnish centres. The Last Season has had a curious life. It was published to wonderful reviews but did not sell well. It may be that the publisher, Macmillan, brought it out on the same day as their other big hockey book of the year, Ken Dryden's The Game, which set an all-time bestselling record well in excess of 100,000 copies. The Last Season, which was paired with the Dryden book in Macmillan publicity, sold about 1 per cent that amount. It was republished in paperback several times and, in 1987, was made into a three-hour made-for-television movie by CBC. The film was directed by Alan King and starred Booth Savage as Felix Batterinski. Savage won the Gemini that year as the country's best actor. Professional hockey players who have read it love it to a point where at least two have claimed that I modelled Felix on them, and several critics have called it the best novel ever written on the game. Whether it is or not will always be debatable, but it's a great honour even to be considered.*

★ ★ ★ ★

FOUR

STARS

THE ABSURDITY OF "SID THE KID"

(*The Globe and Mail*, June 13, 2009)

DETROIT, MICHIGAN

He finished hurt, but he finished what he set out to do. What some would even say he had to do. This morning, the scraggly playoff beard will mercifully go. It's time to show equal mercy to the nickname. "Sid the Kid" no longer makes much sense.

He is only twenty-one, but Sidney Crosby, as of the lifting of the 2009 Stanley Cup following his Pittsburgh Penguins' 2–1 victory over the defending champion Detroit Red Wings, is no longer much of a "kid." He stands, instead, as the best North American, by far, in the National Hockey League and Canada's only sensible choice to lead the country back to the gold medal as captain of the Olympic team.

He is not only a player of enormous top-speed skill but one of those rare players who has no need of that number, 87, to be recognized on the ice. When not forced to conceal an injury—he was hurt last night by a second-period check from Detroit's

Johan Franzen—he moves about the rink, as nearby Windsor poet Marty Gervais once wrote,

> as swift
> and keen and graceful
> as a hawk above
> a morning meadow.

"I don't recommend anyone trying to watch the Stanley Cup final from the bench," Crosby said after his left knee was hurt.

Two years in a row Crosby has led his young teammates to the Stanley Cup final. In his fourth year in the league, he made it all the way. It took Wayne Gretzky five seasons to reach his first Cup. "That's how I want to be measured," the native of Cole Harbour, Nova Scotia, said. "The Stanley Cup. That's how you measure everyone."

If Detroit can fairly be called a "dynasty" of sorts for its four Cups since 1997, then it is fair to suggest that a new reign, or semi-reign, may be under way with the Penguins. With Crosby and lesser stars bound to long-term contracts, Pittsburgh is likely to compete seriously for some time to come. Sidney Crosby, after all, could still be a half-dozen years away from what is usually a superior player's peak. Same goes for Evgeni Malkin, Crosby's twenty-two-year-old Russian teammate, the NHL's regular-season scoring leader, the leading playoff scorer, and one of the three finalists for the Hart Trophy that goes to the league's most valuable player.

Detroit coach Mike Babcock was quoting his general manager, Ken Holland, the other day when he said Holland's "big theory is you knock on the door, you knock on the door, you knock on the door every year and eventually they open the door."

That door opened wide last night thanks to Maxime Talbot's two goals and a breathtaking night by Pittsburgh goaltender Marc-André Fleury. While it must bother Crosby that for possibly the first time in his life he has not been his team's top scorer, there is no indication that Malkin is anything but content to play second fiddle and "A" to the younger Crosby's "C." All Malkin wanted, he said this week, was to have an equivalent photograph taken to that one back in Pittsburgh's Mellon Arena that shows Mario Lemieux and Jaromir Jagr holding up the 1992 Stanley Cup.

"It's my dream," Malkin said in his halting English. "Me and Sid, just like that."

Malkin and Crosby were brilliant in Pittsburgh's conference final against Alexander Ovechkin and the Washington Capitals, a series so highly skilled and dramatic that, in many ways, it is unfortunate that it could not be a final, something that cannot happen under the current east–west division of the league.

That is not, however, to diminish the Red Wings. Thanks to the merciless checking of Henrik Zetterberg, Crosby had been held to just two assists in five Stanley Cup games at the Joe Louis Arena this year and last when the puck dropped. He should have had another during Pittsburgh's first power play, when he set up Malkin at the side of the net, only to have the puck bounce badly. He never had another chance, leaving after the Franzen check and returning in the third only to sit, grimacing, at the end of the bench.

When healthy, however, he has the gift and it is obvious in every game he plays, score or not. "I wonder about it," the poet Gervais asked,

> where they found
> that inherent
> skill that natural
> beauty that way
> about them as they
> float before a goalie
> with all the confidence
> of a magician playing
> out a sleight of hand.

No one knows where it comes from, just that few have it and a great many do not. But Crosby—speaking so quietly every day this spring from the cover of a frayed Penguins cap—has also demonstrated that, at only twenty-one, he has inherited that curious quiet mantle that is the mark of the truly great Canadian players. Jean Béliveau and Gordie Howe passed it on to Bobby Orr, and from Orr to Wayne Gretzky and Mario Lemieux. There have not been many, but it seems only appropriate that Crosby be next in line, taking it from Lemieux, the last captain to take Canada to Olympic gold, the owner of the Penguins and still Sidney Crosby's landlord.

It's time for the beard to go, time to move out. And time to leave behind "Sid the Kid." It no longer applies.

The thinking that Sidney Crosby was still far from his peak came true in 2010–11, when he set a blistering pace during the first half: 66 points in 41 games, including a 25-game scoring streak. Sadly, what might have stood as his greatest season came to a crashing halt on New Year's Day, when he was knocked to the ice in the Winter Classic and then, a few days later, hit into the boards. His season was over, another victim of concussion.

OVIE, OVIE, OVIE!
(*The Globe and Mail*, May 6, 2009)

There's nothing wrong with the ad—but perhaps the casting could be better.

The commercial is for Tim Hortons coffee, Canada's official blood, and it involves a team bus pulling over on a dark winter's evening, snow gently falling as the disappointed driver announces, "Sorry guys, looks like this is going to take a while." There are children playing shinny on a nearby frozen pond, and one of the players on the bus sees this through the window he was likely just sleeping against. He gets out with his skates and stick and goes to the pond, turning one youngster speechless with a simple, "Can I play?"

That's Sidney Crosby asking; Alexander Ovechkin wouldn't ask. He wouldn't want to lose any playing time. "Did I miss anything?" a man arriving late asks as the bus starts up again, Crosby back aboard.

Well, if he missed the first two games of the Eastern Conference semifinals, Ovechkin's Washington Capitals against Crosby's Pittsburgh Penguins, he may have missed the finest hockey exhibition that the so-called new NHL has seen. Canada's Best Player against Canada's Favourite Player. Make that the World's Favourite Player—at least in the world of imagination that is inhabited by the very young.

They could make a sweeter ad right in Ovechkin's very own neighbourhood in Arlington, Virginia, where the Washington Capitals star lives. A year ago during the playoffs, children from a nearby elementary school began leaving handwritten notes, and the odd teddy bear, on his doorstep to wish him luck.

Children can be harsh critics, as well. After one 7–1 loss to the Philadelphia Flyers this season, Ovechkin stepped out to find someone had left an egg but no note—no note required to say he had just laid one himself.

Ovechkin's popularity among children seems sure to rival that of past idols such as Wayne Gretzky and the Maurice (Rocket) Richard of Roch Carrier's "The Hockey Sweater." This is not a knock against Crosby's phenomenal skills, not in the least—he matched Ovechkin goal-for-goal Monday night as each scored a brilliant hat trick and Ovechkin's team won 4–3, giving Washington a 2–0 series lead—but it is a recognition that Ovechkin touches something that is denied most stars.

Children love his absolute joy of playing. They love the leap into the boards after every goal. They love the new hip bump with which twenty-three-year-old Ovechkin and young twenty-one-year-old Nicklas Backstrom celebrate victories. They loved Ovechkin's clown getup for the shooting competition at the All-Star Game. And they loved his stick-on-fire routine following his fiftieth goal of the season.

Don Cherry attacked Ovechkin for this on Coach's Corner, and the support for Ovechkin's bringing a little delight to the game was so overwhelming that, in subsequent weeks, Cherry backed off and even began praising the Russian star. Ovechkin is not only good for the game, he is becoming the game, just as only Gretzky has done previously.

So great has been his impact on the Capitals that his thirteen-year, $124-million contract now seems a bargain. But his impact is far beyond that, heard in every road hockey and mini-sticks game in the world. Kids simply take to him. Perhaps it is because his Stone Age features give him the look of an action figure—one whose every stride and shot is so instantly recognizable he no longer needs that number, 8, to be identified. Perhaps because he is Captain Underpants to Crosby's Curious George, somehow more modern, more mischievous, more alluring to them.

Crosby is huge in Pittsburgh—he's nearly five storeys high on a banner hanging from the new rink going up at the corner of Washington Place and Fifth Avenue—and huge in Canada, where it is hoped he will bring back Olympic gold; but his demeanour at the rink is as though he has come to a board meeting of the Toronto-Dominion Bank. Ovechkin, on the other hand, always looks like recess has just been let out.

It is hard to believe that a generation ago Russian players—then known as Soviet Union players—were routinely dismissed as "robots." It was a knock that began in the 1972 Summit Series and lasted through to glasnost. Writing in 1987, columnist John Robertson reflected the thoughts of many when he complained he was sick of hearing that "the red robots from the Soviet Union" were giving lessons "on how our game should be played."

"In a pig's ear," Robertson railed. "The so-called Soviet system so many of our hockey geniuses see fit to applaud and envy, is inseparable from the abysmal depths of human degradation inflicted upon all Soviet citizens by the intrinsically evil rulers in the Kremlin."

It was said then that what would always separate Canadian hockey players from Russian players was "heart." The sort of passion Bobby Clarke showed in 1972 when he deliberately broke Valeri Kharlamov's ankle to help his team win. Some Soviet players even acknowledged this critical difference; one player, Slava Fetisov, even called himself and his teammates "robots on ice." But then everything changed.

The wall fell and Fetisov and many of his teammates came to play in the NHL. No one ever again questioned Russian "heart" after the Russian Five—Fetisov, Igor Larionov, Slava Kozlov, Sergei Fedorov and Vladimir Konstantinov, who later lost his hockey career to a car accident—were so pivotal in bringing the Stanley Cup to the Detroit Red Wings in 1997.

Today, a dozen years later, the three finalists for hockey's main individual trophy, the Hart, are all Russian: Ovechkin, Pittsburgh's Evgeni Malkin and Pavel Datsyuk of the Detroit Red Wings. Ovechkin already won the Rocket Richard Trophy as leading goal scorer and Malkin took the Art Ross Trophy as the leading point getter. Datsyuk is also up for the Selke Trophy as the league's best checker and the Lady Byng as the league's most gentlemanly player. Most astonishing of all, however, may be that Russian Alex Kovalev of the Montreal Canadiens is one of the three finalists for the league award that goes to the most community-minded player. Robots no more.

In fact, if you had to look for a comparison for the obvious passion that Ovechkin is showing these playoffs, you could do no better than . . . Bobby Clarke. The hockey world has changed that dramatically.

Alexander Ovechkin continued to dazzle the next season, claiming the Hart Trophy as the NHL's most valuable player and winning the Rocket Richard Trophy as the league's top goal scorer, with 56 goals. His team, however, failed to advance in the playoffs, falling to the upstart Montreal Canadiens. Nor did Russia fare well at the 2010 Olympics, despite predictions that they would battle for the gold medal with Ovechkin leading. His ability to win began to be questioned and the 2010–11 NHL season saw a dramatic change in both Ovechkin, now captain, and the Washington Capitals as they changed their style of play from creative attack to responsible defence. The change of style produced no playoff success, as the talented Capitals stumbled once again.

THE THIRD EYE: DANIEL AND HENRIK SEDIN

(*The Globe and Mail*, February 5, 2010)

OTTAWA, ONTARIO

No one, not even the twins themselves, quite understands how it works—just that it usually does. Perhaps like swallows and certain other flocking birds, they have figured out how to communicate with their wings. Perhaps it is as Gordie Howe once said of a young Gretzky: "I sometimes think if you part Wayne's hair, you'll find another eye."

They are Henrik and Daniel Sedin, the identical twins of the Vancouver Canucks, two players who most nights appear to have taken hockey's dreaded "blind pass" to visionary heights. Henrik doesn't look as he whips a back pass to the tape of Daniel's stick; Daniel doesn't look as he drops a back pass to his brother Henrik, perfectly in position to rip a puck past a startled goaltender.

A year ago, this description would have ended up with Daniel shooting the puck and scoring—Henrik preferred to pass and let his younger brother, by six minutes, take the glory—but then Daniel got hurt for a while last fall and Henrik had to do it all, and did it. Heading into last evening's game in Ottawa—which the streaking Senators won 3–1 for their eleventh successive victory—Henrik stood as the leading scorer in the NHL with 25 goals and 53 assists for 78 points.

His name stood ahead of Alexander Ovechkin and Sidney Crosby, endlessly described as the two best players in the game today. Could he have possibly seen this coming when the season began? "No," Henrik laughs, "I don't think so."

But then, who saw anything coming this strange hockey season? Those writing the Ottawa Senators off in January found themselves calling the talk shows to apologize and celebrate the stunning play recently of backup goaltender Brian Elliott. Those who claimed the Vancouver Canucks were but a one-tune team— Roberto Luongo in goal—found themselves singing the praises of the twenty-nine-year-old Sedins.

In fact, it is possible that the Canucks and the Senators—with Montreal and Calgary riding that final playoff spot bubble— might be the only two Canadian teams come the post-season. Ottawa was the better team this night when Vancouver elected to start Luongo's backup Andrew Raycroft in net, but both teams now stand at a comfortable 70 points. That the Canucks lead the Northwest Division is only partly because of Luongo. The Sedin line, with Alex Burrows on right wing, Henrik at centre and Daniel at left, has slowly blossomed into the best line in the NHL. And it happened by accident.

The Sedins always played well together. While Henrik jokes that it is by "guessing" that they seem always able to find each other, the more likely reason is that they have simply played together from the first moment they skated back in Ornskoldsvik, Sweden. The longest they have ever been apart was when Daniel missed eighteen games with a broken foot earlier in the season. "He goes to where he knows I can find him," says Henrik of his brother.

"You can't teach what they're doing," says Vancouver coach Alain Vigneault. "They've been playing together for so long."

Together, yes, but not always with the right person. The twins had gone through as many partners as Tiger Woods, the line working well with Anson Carter until Carter decided he was worth more than he was, then a long series of right wingers were tried with limited success—until they turned to Alex Burrows.

"It wasn't a great coaching decision," Vigneault says. "We were going through a rough stretch and we just said, 'Why not try Burrows?'"

They play differently than any other line in the game, endlessly churning the puck around the corners until one can break out or they find a seam opening to allow a pass and one-timer.

Ottawa captain Daniel Alfredsson—a Swede and a right winger who could possibly find himself playing with the Sedins during the Olympics—thinks he knows how it works. And how it sometimes falls short, as on this night when Alfredsson set up all Ottawa goals by Jason Spezza, Milan Michalek and Chris Kelly, while only Kyle Wellwood could score for Vancouver.

"They toy with you in the sense that they play with the puck with such composure," Alfredsson says. "They find each other. They play on the outside, kind of just drag you away from the net and then they find an opening. It's hard to play against, especially now that you can't hook and hold . . . They're so good at protecting the puck, it's tough to get at them . . . You don't see them 'cause they don't have that much speed—they won't burn you wide. Their deceptiveness and vision of the ice is as good as anybody."

On most nights, as if each had a third eye.

Henrik Sedin went on to win the scoring championship that year. The following season, Daniel Sedin won the scoring championship. They became the first brothers in NHL history to win back-to-back Art Ross trophies. The Vancouver Canucks, with the Sedins at the top of their game, won the Presidents' Trophy in 2011 as the top team in the entire league. The brothers faltered, however, in the final two rounds of the playoffs, and watched their Canucks lose the Cup to the Boston Bruins in seven games.

QUICK COMING OF AGE: DREW DOUGHTY

(The Globe and Mail, November 23, 2010)

OTTAWA, ONTARIO

They are such a study in contrast.

The Los Angeles Kings are the youngest team in hockey, in first place in their division and considered a Stanley Cup contender; the Ottawa Senators are in the top four of oldest teams, hoping to rise high enough to claim a playoff position. The Kings are the model of consistency; the Senators the poster for streaking in both directions, coming into their match Monday night with Los Angeles having lost three games in a row. The Kings planned not a single change in the lineup; the Senators juggled theirs as if the players were a dropped deck of cards.

Most significant among the Senators this Monday was the decision to scratch young defenceman Erik Karlsson, a brilliant-but-spotty twenty-year-old who has fought the flu lately and played as if he had it. The Kings, on the other hand, have a young defenceman, Drew Doughty, also twenty, who has already been a finalist for the Norris Trophy, which goes to the very best defence player in the league.

It is the story of confidence—the one critical element to the game that defies all quantifying.

Doughty may well have shown this most elusive of hockey traits by age one, when his father, Paul, handed him that first mini-stick in London, Ontario, but he certainly put it on public display in junior, where he was twice named the Ontario junior league's top offensive defenceman when he played for the Guelph Storm. He was drafted second overall in 2008 (just behind Tampa Bay Lightning star Steve Stamkos) and surprised even himself by making the Kings out of that fall's rookie camp.

It may be unfair, but it is difficult to be noticed as an LA King when the time zones and media conceits so favour the East. He was named to the NHL's all-rookie team in his first year but emerged as a true NHL star on the international stage, not in California. Doughty was named top defender at the 2008 World Juniors, where his team took gold, and was dominant at the 2009 world championships in Switzerland—Doughty's play was the talk of the tournament. It led directly to him being selected, as the youngest player, to the 2010 Team Canada that won Olympic gold in Vancouver last February.

"It was huge," Doughty says of his 2009 experience in Switzerland. "The world championships helped me a ton. I went in there being the fifth or sixth 'D' and didn't really know how much I was going to play. Yzerman was there, and all the guys who'd be picking the Olympics team. So if I hadn't played as well as I had at the worlds, I don't think I would have got invited to [the Olympic] camp—and never would have made the team."

The Olympics, however, were where he fully emerged as an elite player. He was expected to serve as a seventh defenceman, but by tournament end was as much a stalwart on the Canadian defence as current Norris Trophy winner Duncan Keith.

"It did a lot," Doughty agrees. "It was finally the moment where I realized I could play with the best players in the world. I went in there not playing a lot at the start and just sort of worked my way in, and that was a huge confidence booster for me. And since then, I've just sort of stepped up my game and been playing a lot better."

That applies to lately, as well, as Doughty is coming off an injury that cost him six games and kept the risk-taking young defenceman to one goal and six assists in thirteen games. "His game is coming around," Los Angeles coach Terry Murray says. "Better things are starting to happen."

Doughty says he likes playing in LA—it was his favourite team in the years Wayne Gretzky was a King—and loves that he can live a normal life and "fly under the radar."

Perhaps somewhat during the season, but not if the Kings move on in the playoffs—and certainly not as far as Canada is concerned in international play. "He's a great hockey player," teammate Ryan Smyth says. "He has the confidence to make plays that D-men don't make on a consistent basis."

But as for passing on Smyth's long-time Captain Canada moniker, Smyth isn't ready to discuss that. "I've got a lot more years left," he laughs, "so I'm not passing anything along." Yet.

Drew Doughty was considered one of the league's premier defencemen by the end of the 2010–11 season—unusual for a twenty-one-year-old in a position where players usually mature in their late twenties and early thirties.

THE EVOLUTION OF KRIS LETANG

(*The Globe and Mail*, May 4, 2010)

PITTSBURGH, PENNSYLVANIA

There's no need for the Montreal Canadiens to scout Kris Letang to find his weak spot. Just ask him. "The one-timer," the young Pittsburgh Penguins defenceman says. "I've got to work on getting my shot away faster."

Let the improvement come next season, the Canadiens should hope, not this spring, with the Montreal–Pittsburgh best-of-seven second-round playoff series tied at one game apiece.

Letang, a twenty-three-year-old native of Montreal, has a knack for big plays, whether setting goals up or scoring them himself — usually on a one-timer as he slips in, unnoticed, from the point. In Game 1 against the Canadiens, he set up fellow defenceman Sergei Gonchar to tie the game at 1–1, and then scored the team's third goal as the Penguins romped to a 6–3 victory.

Against the Ottawa Senators in the first round, he scored the game-winner in Game 2 on a brilliant feed from Sidney Crosby, allowing the Penguins to tie the series and eventually advance to the Eastern Conference semifinals. His first NHL playoff goal came in overtime last year, against the Washington Capitals. Had Letang not scored, his team would have fallen behind three games to none — and likely none of them would now be wearing Stanley Cup rings.

He is far from the biggest name on the Penguins roster — lagging some distance back from Crosby, Evgeni Malkin, Gonchar and others — but he is seen as the understudy to Gonchar. Sort of the team's power-play quarterback in training.

Nor is Letang the biggest player on the team, generously listed at six feet and 201 pounds. Yet he can hit with the force of a rocket, despite his seeming slightness. Pittsburgh head coach Dan Bylsma thinks a hard Letang hit on rock-solid defenceman Anton Volchenkov was where the Ottawa series began turning in the Penguins' favour.

Letang is happy to think of himself as the understudy to Gonchar, knowing the injury-prone thirty-six-year-old will not be there forever. The organization basically told him that in March, when it signed Letang to a four-year contract extension, at $3.5 million a year. The lengthy deal meant Letang was now considered part of the team's core, along with Crosby, Malkin, Jordan Staal, Brooks Orpik and goaltender Marc-André Fleury.

The Penguins like Letang's play, obviously, but also his character, which was sorely tested two springs ago when his best friend, Vancouver Canucks defenceman Luc Bourdon, was killed in a motorcycle accident. The players had roomed together in their time with the Val-d'Or Foreurs in junior hockey, played on two Team Canada gold medal winners at the world junior tournament, and were planning to spend last summer working out together. Letang dealt with his grief quietly and with resolve, dedicating himself even more to the game his friend would never again play.

What Letang is, at his best, is an attacking defenceman who does not neglect his own end and does not shy away from the corners. He is such a deft, quick skater with such an accurate shot that there are times when fans in other cities will hastily check their scoresheet to see who wears No. 58.

Letang stands in awe of his team's young captain, Crosby. Not so much for the scoring statistics and the trophies, but for Crosby's remarkable ability to reinvent himself. Crosby finds his own flaws—first, lower-body strength; then, faceoffs; this past year, shooting—and sets about to correct them for the next season. In 2009–10, Crosby's fifty-one goals tied him for the league lead. "He has amazed me how he can do those things," says Letang, who intends to apply such determination to his one timers from the point.

He studies Gonchar as if No. 55 is the Bible—watching the way the veteran Russian gets away that first long pass, trying to ride the blueline on the power play the way Gonchar does, seeking to find those same narrow corridors to the net Gonchar is a master at. "It's someone I would like to be," Letang says of Gonchar's work running the power play. "I've always done that as a player, always looked for the chances to jump up into the play."

It comes by him naturally, as he was a forward up until fourteen. "It was just for fun at first," Letang says. "Coach said we needed another 'D' for a game because one of our guys was sick. I tried it and liked it. I decided myself to switch."

He had to switch heroes, as well, changing from idolizing former Pittsburgh forward (and current club co-owner) Mario Lemieux to wanting to be able to play like smooth-skating

Anaheim Ducks defenceman Scott Niedermayer. Letang is still a long way from such comparisons, but it is not entirely beyond the realm of possibility given the flashes fans have seen these past two springs.

"I'm going to expect more of it next year from the way he's played," Bylsma says. Just as the Montreal Canadiens are likely to see more of it before this year is over.

Much to the shock of the hockey world, Montreal bounced the defending Stanley Cup champions from the playoffs in 2010. Kris Letang matured into a true star in 2010–11, voted by fans to start in the All-Star Game and considered the key to Pittsburgh's vaunted power play. He had indeed replaced Sergei Gonchar, who left Pittsburgh for the Ottawa Senators and the worst year of his NHL career.

MARC SAVARD'S LONG JOURNEY
(*The Globe and Mail*, May 1, 2009)

BOSTON, MASSACHUSETTS

He is known by his number, 91, by the name on the back, Savard, and the crest on the front, Boston Bruins, but also by a tag that has proved tougher to shake off than shin-pad tape. Marc Savard, selfish, lazy, not a team player . . . coach killer.

He has heard them all. His father, Bob, a handyman in Ottawa, has heard them all, too; he even offers up "coach killer" in case it had been missed. Savard, as well as his father, would rather hear about the current Marc Savard, the slick-passing centre who regularly finishes in the top ten in NHL scoring, the admittedly once defensively deficient forward who was seen diving to block shots in Boston's Round 1 romp over the Montreal Canadiens, the late bloomer (about to turn thirty-two) who would dearly love, finally, to wear a Team Canada jersey in the coming 2010 Vancouver Olympics.

But will the reputation, however true or exaggerated, trip up the future hopes? "You get tagged with these bad raps," Savard says, while his team readies to meet the Carolina Hurricanes in an Eastern Conference semifinal, "and there's not much you can do about it. I get along great with every guy on this team. It's just something they tagged on me and it's really unfortunate. But I don't let it faze me. I just keep playing."

He has played at a remarkably high level since the 2004–05 lockout season, which allowed him time to heal (knee and concussion) and then gave him a new game that rewarded speed and skill. Small by NHL standards (five foot ten, 190 pounds), Savard has averaged more than a point a game since the Bruins signed the free agent to a four-year, $20-million contract three summers ago.

That's quite a payday for a player who was once traded by the Calgary Flames to the Atlanta Thrashers for Ruslan Zainullin, who never played a shift in the NHL. Savard had 96 points his first year with Boston and 78 last year, when he missed several games to injury. His 88 points this year (25 goals) were a major factor in Boston's surprising rise to the top of the Eastern Conference, making the once-dismissible Bruins an early favourite in the Stanley Cup playoffs.

His passing abilities are so impressive—"Some plays make you think he has a set of eyes in the back of his helmet," former Atlanta head coach Bob Hartley says—he has caused most Bruins fans to forget the playmaking centre he replaced, playoff-cursed Joe Thornton of the San Jose Sharks. "His first instinct is always to pass," says twenty-one-year-old Phil Kessel, who became Boston's top goal scorer this year with Savard on his line. "He's the kind of guy who's looking to pass, even if he's on a breakaway."

And yet, there it was once more, a player whose first instinct is always to give the puck to a teammate, being tagged as selfish.

"Somebody on TSN brought it up again," Savard says. "The same old thing that I'm a 'me-first' guy. It bothers me. But I just take it for what it's worth and just keep trying to prove every single day that that's not the way I am."

Kessel has heard the raps against his generous centre and cannot comprehend how it happened. "I don't know how he got that," he says. "Who knows?"

Bob Savard thinks it happened in Calgary. He also thinks his son had some "growing up" to do before he would become the player he is today. Others close to him agree; he had a harder time getting around himself than opposing defenders.

Marc Savard had been a remarkably gifted player from virtually the first time he set out on skates in the little backyard rink. At six, the father says, other kids in tournaments were asking for his son's autograph. He played like his idol, Wayne Gretzky, and everyone said he was a sure thing to make it. "I couldn't see it myself," the older Savard says. He had played a lot of hockey himself, but "I was a fighter, I had cement hands." He thought his son too small.

Size was a major factor. But it made the boy all the more determined. He cared nothing for school, only hockey and the chance to prove the naysayers wrong. One friend thinks this is what gave Marc Savard "a bit of a chip on his shoulder" in the early days and may have put people off. Too small, yet he played Junior B at fifteen. Too small, yet he twice won the OHL scoring championship while playing for the Oshawa Generals.

Size made him a late draft pick; the New York Rangers took him ninety-first overall in 1995. Then, the Rangers virtually gave him away to Calgary simply to move up a couple of slots in a subsequent draft. It was in Calgary, Bob Savard says, that the tagging began. Though he scored points—53 his first year, 66 his second— Marc Savard fell out of favour with coach Greg Gilbert. Gilbert stressed defensive hockey first, and defensive hockey, from childhood, was usually so far down Savard's list it didn't even have a number. "I don't know what it was," Bob Savard says. "Maybe they thought he was always looking at his stats or something."

They thought he was a "whiner," perhaps hockey's worst insult. He thought he deserved more ice time, Gilbert thought not; player blamed coach, coach blamed player. "There were some tough times for sure," Marc Savard says, "especially when I felt I could play in the league at the time. I had some tough situations there, you know, obviously the coach . . ."

Calgary dealt him to the Thrashers in 2002, where a new coach, Bob Hartley, soon arrived and immediately had a profound effect on Savard. Player and coach lived on a golf course only five houses apart, and Hartley used "idle time"—pitching golf balls (Savard is a scratch player) and playing bubble hockey in Hartley's basement—to get through to the player no one else had been able to penetrate. "If he would listen," Hartley says, "I told him I would be willing to trade quite a bit of ice time."

What Savard listened to was a series of lectures on how good he could be if he wanted to be. "'You're going to waste quite a talent,'" Hartley told him. "'Your talent is a given, but the rest of it is not a gift, you have to make a choice. You have the talent to be a star, but your worst enemy is you.' In Marc's mind, it was everybody's fault, but I give him credit. He took the plan and went with it."

The plan was simple. Work harder, check harder, be a team player. In return for a new work ethic, Hartley gave him ice time with rising stars Ilya Kovalchuk, Dany Heatley and Marian Hossa. It paid off handsomely for all. Hartley "was like a father figure to me," Savard says. "He really helped me out."

When it became clear to Savard and his agent, Ottawa-based Larry Kelly, that Atlanta wouldn't be able to afford the sort of money that might be available once the player became a free agent in 2006, the choice came down to Boston or, surprisingly, Calgary, where Savard's friend, team captain Jarome Iginla, was pressing hard for Savard to return. They chose Boston, in part because it was seen as a team on the rise, in part out of concern for Savard's experience in Calgary.

Boston coach Claude Julien has carried on where Hartley left off—exchanging ice time for a commitment by Savard to be "more accountable"—and those who may have once doubted his work ethic are now able to turn to YouTube for a clip of Savard throwing up on the bench after a shift. "He's a money player," Hartley says, "a clutch performer. Give me a minute left in a game and he'll either score the goal or set it up. I just hope he gets a shot at the [2010] Olympics."

Bob Nicholson, president of Hockey Canada, says Savard's improved play has not gone unnoticed—"he deserves to be on the radar"—but Canada is deep at centre, beginning with Sidney Crosby.

"It's a thought in the back of my mind," Savard says. "It's something I think about, for sure, but I got business here right now. I think the better our team does this year, the better the chances I'd have to play in those kinds of events."

On March 7, 2010, Marc Savard suffered a severe concussion when he was hit by Matt Cooke of the Pittsburgh Penguins. Cooke was neither penalized nor suspended for the headshot. Savard returned briefly in the playoffs—the Bruins lost to the Philadelphia Flyers—and began play again in the 2010–11 season, only to suffer a mid-season concussion in a game against the Colorado Avalanche. In February, the Bruins announced that Savard would not be returning to play for the remainder of the year.

THE PRICE IS RIGHT

(*The Globe and Mail,* April 26, 2008)

MONTREAL, QUEBEC

"Just look at that wall over there."

Carey Price is standing in front of his locker long after Game 1 has ended in his favour, well after the cameras and microphones have left the room and well beyond the call of duty for a goaltender who has just played, and won, a Stanley Cup game that went into overtime.

"It's impossible not to notice," he says, pointing to the plaque of previous Montreal Canadiens who have been awarded the Vezina Trophy as hockey's best goaltender: Patrick Roy, Ken Dryden, Gump Worsley, Jacques Plante five times in a row, Bill Durnan and a net full of other names, some faded, some forgotten.

He bends a long finger up toward the line from John McCrae's "In Flanders Fields" that graces the Canadiens' dressing room wall ("To you from failing hands we throw the torch; be yours to hold it high") and runs it across faces once distributed across the country by BeeHive Corn Syrup—the Rocket, the Pocket Rocket, Boom Boom Geoffrion, Plante—until he stops at one that it seems no twenty-year-old Aboriginal kid from the isolated northern B.C. community of Anahim Lake could possibly know.

"There's George Hainsworth," he says. George Hainsworth?

And yet—it is somehow perfect. Hainsworth, who died in 1950, is rarely remembered by those who live in the "new" NHL, yet he was the original winner of the Vezina as the league's top goaltender. He won it three years running and, along the way, established a National Hockey League record—22 shutouts in 44 games—that will never, ever be equalled. He once went for more than 4½ hours of playoff hockey without allowing a goal. He won two Stanley Cups in Montreal and lives on in the Hockey Hall of Fame.

Hainsworth is dark, calm and serious in his photograph, much as Carey Price is in real life, though the lanky Price is far taller. Hainsworth was renowned for his calm under pressure, seeming almost bored as he turned aside shots and his frantic teammates attempted to clear threatening pucks from around him. The two Montreal goaltenders are — more than eighty years apart — eerily similar.

"I'm sorry I can't put on a show like some of the other goaltenders," Hainsworth said in 1931, when he was at the peak of his game. "I can't look excited because I'm not. I can't shout at other players because that's not my style. I can't dive on easy shots and make them look hard. I guess all I can do is stop pucks."

And so it is with Carey Price. All he does is stop pucks when it seems to count most. Nothing fancy, but everything smooth and relaxed and effective, even when it sometimes appears to others that things are going terribly wrong. Thursday night he fell behind 2–0 when Philadelphia scored on one shot that Price's own defenceman tipped in and another shot where a Canadiens forward missed his check, but there was no panic. It was almost as if he knew his team would come back, and they did, winning 4–3 less than a minute into overtime on a goal by Tom Kostopoulos.

He will admit, though, to a slight case of nerves in his very first playoff game, two weeks ago against the Boston Bruins. He was, after all, the untried rookie, just as Ken Dryden was back in 1971, just as George Hainsworth was in 1926. "The first game of the playoffs is the worst," Price says. "After that, you kind of settle down."

How much he settles down and how effective his calm, positional, puck-controlling style is will largely determine how far the last-standing Canadian team goes in the 2008 Stanley Cup playoffs. As former Philadelphia Flyers coach Terry Murray once put it, "As far as you go, they're taking you." Murray found out just what that meant a decade ago when his two goaltenders, Ron Hextall and Garth Snow, came up short in the playoffs and, shortly after, Murray lost his job.

"What pitching is in a short series in baseball," Detroit general manager Jack Adams said more than a half century ago, "goaltending is in the Stanley Cup playoffs."

It is, some will even say to the detriment of the game, a position so dominant that comparing it to pitching does not always do goaltending justice. And yet, almost perversely, its value is not reflected in salary. Of the top ten salaries in the game, not one goes to a goaltender. The highest on the list, Nikolai Khabibulin, who makes $6.75 million a year with the Chicago Blackhawks, is a surprising sixteenth on the list. Price, who may one day live up to his name, makes $850,000 as a rookie.

Goaltending in today's NHL often seems even more critical to success than it was in the 1950s when Adams, and everyone else, was in awe of Terry Sawchuk leading the Red Wings to an eight-game sweep of the 1952 playoffs, four of the victories coming from Sawchuk shutouts. Since the Conn Smythe Trophy was introduced in 1965 to honour the best playoff performer, goaltenders have taken the MVP honours fourteen times. Since Patrick Roy led the Canadiens to Canada's last Stanley Cup in 1993, goalies have taken the prize five times, the most recent being Cam Ward of the Carolina Hurricanes.

Ward, in fact, is the perfect example of the surprisingly hot goaltender who, in other times, turns to ordinary, but who in one astonishing spring can decide a Cup. The story of the Stanley Cup finalists for a decade or more has, by and large, been the tale of two hot goaltenders finally meeting to decide matters.

The hope in Montreal, obviously, is that young Carey Price can be as hot as young Ken Dryden was in 1971, as hot as young Patrick Roy was in 1986. If he's not, they will not move on.

It is a remarkable pressure situation for such a young man. "The only job worse," a great Canadiens goaltender, Gump Worsley, once said, "is a javelin catcher at a track-and-field meet."

"How would you like it," Montreal's great Jacques Plante once asked, "if you were sitting in your office and you made one little mistake—suddenly, a big red light went on and eighteen thousand people jumped up and started screaming at you, calling you a bum and an imbecile and throwing garbage at you?"

Bill Durnan, yet another Montreal great in the nets, once claimed he lost seventeen pounds in a playoff game—and took early retirement from the profession just to escape the annual crush of expectation.

And yet, Carey Price hardly seems to have broken a sweat this first night of Round 2. He has showered and dressed and seems perfectly content to sit here in the dressing room until it is again time to strap on the thick white pads at his stall and head out, once again, into the pressure cooker that is the Bell Centre and the demanding Montreal fans.

Ken Dryden has a different outlook on playoff pressure. And Dryden's credentials—six Stanley Cups, two Vezina trophies, the Calder Trophy as top rookie and the Conn Smythe—are impeccable. "It's the ideal time," Dryden told me several years ago. The Stanley Cup playoffs, he felt, were "the only time when you've got absolutely everything going for you."

Dryden's well-considered theory is that a shift takes place between the regular season and the playoffs, a psychological shift among the other players on the team that gives a physical advantage to their goaltender. "In a long season," he reasoned, "what do you give up first? You're tired, you're hurt, so you give up defence—it's the first to go. In the playoffs, everyone has that extra energy. The players are all coming back. The pucks are cleared. The goalie's in the best shape of the year as far as getting help. And it affects the goalie, too. You start to take the goals very personally. Every one of them."

"That's definitely true," says Price. "The players ramp it up. They play harder in front of you, for sure. But you can look at it both ways, as other guys are going to be crashing the net and doing other things to get at you."

CBC hockey analyst Greg Millen, himself a former NHL

goaltender through fourteen seasons, says Dryden and Price have a point, that "the awareness is so high for everybody" during the playoffs that it can sometimes work to the advantage of the goaltender. "There's a lot of predictability that might not be there otherwise," he says.

Even so, Millen marvels at Price's calmness under pressure, the sense that if the twenty-year-old's blood pressure were kept on the Bell Centre scoreboard, it wouldn't even measure. "He has such a huge maturity on and off the ice," Millen says. "Way, way beyond his years. Technically, he's just so good. He has learned at a very young age that 'less is better.' It took me eight to ten years to find that out—and by then my career was almost over."

Millen's fascination with Price's technical wizardry—always in position, superb at clearing rebounds and, when necessary, handling the puck—is shared by all who watch the young phenomenon. Price, however, says he has changed his game dramatically in the past couple of years. "I was pretty wild when they drafted me," he says. "I was more of a flop-around, stop-it-any-way-you-can kind of goaltender."

He learned the position from his father, Jerry, who, rather coincidentally, was a draft pick thirty years ago of the Philadelphia Flyers his son is up against in Round 2. Father and son would often fly in Jerry's Piper Cherokee from Anahim Lake—where mother Lynda is chief of the Ulkatcho Band of the Carrier Nation—to Williams Lake so that the youngster could make practices and games in the larger centre. His father's teaching and natural ability brought early success, taking the younger Price to junior with the Tri-City Americans and then, at eighteen, he was drafted fifth overall by the Montreal Canadiens.

There were, initially, some doubts raised in Montreal about spending such a high draft pick on a goaltender when many thought the position well covered in Montreal. But soon Price was leading Canada to the world junior championship, where he was named tournament MVP, and last year he won the Calder

Cup with the Hamilton Bulldogs. After some back and forth this year, he was handed the No. 1 position with the Canadiens and told to make of it what he can.

Price credits Montreal goaltending coach Rollie Melanson with turning him into a "hybrid" of two styles, the stand-up and the butterfly. "He really evolved my game into what it is now," Price says.

What it is now is impressive, though there were two third periods in the Boston series—a 5–1 loss followed by a 5–4 loss—when doubts were flying as high as the twenty-four Stanley Cup banners in the Bell Centre. He answered that with a most impressive 5–0 shutout to win the seventh game and take Montreal's hopes to the second round, where he fell behind 2–0 early but soon had them chanting "Car-ey! Car-ey! Car-ey!" as the plucky Canadiens came back for the overtime win.

This is the age of parity in the NHL, not the age of dynasties, and Carey Price's life will never be as Dryden described his old job on the January night when they raised his No. 29 to the rafters. "Watching, waiting, not doing much of anything," Dryden joked about his lonely life in the Montreal net. "That is pretty much what the 1970s were all about—that, and a whole lot of Stanley Cups."

That situation will likely never come again, in any hockey city. Right now, Montreal would be grateful merely for a chance at a twenty-fifth Cup. And any hopes it might have rests largely on jersey No. 31, which still has a long, long way to go before it reaches any rafters anywhere.

"Every round it gets worse," Price said Wednesday of the mounting pressure on the ice, let alone what that history provides off the ice. "It doesn't bother me one bit."

The Montreal Canadiens mounted an exceptional playoff run two years later, when they defeated Alexander Ovechkin and the Washington Capitals and then Sidney Crosby and the Cup-defending Pittsburgh Penguins. They managed this with truly remarkable goaltending—but not from Carey Price. The darling of the nets now was Jaroslav Halak, who put on one of the greatest playoff performances in recent memory before the outmanned Canadiens fell to the Philadelphia Flyers in the conference final. In the summer of 2010, to great controversy, the Canadiens elected to stick with Price and traded Halak to the St. Louis Blues. Price responded with the best year of his young career, appearing in more games than any goaltender in Montreal's long history and winning more games in 2010–11 than any Canadiens goaltender since Ken Dryden.

KESLER'S THE TOTAL PACKAGE

(*The Globe and Mail*, May 5, 2011)

NASHVILLE, TENNESEE

If the Vancouver Canucks are now Canada's Team—no matter whether by choice or by default—then the main flag bearer is an American. All Ryan Kesler did to win Game 3 on Tuesday night was score the goal that put the Canucks back into the match at 1–1, set up the goal that put them ahead 2–1 and then, after the Nashville Predators had tied matters late in the third period, draw the dubious penalty in overtime that gave Vancouver a power play and score the winning goal that gave the Canucks a two-games-to-one lead in this series, which continues Thursday at Bridgestone Arena. Not a bad night's work for someone who hadn't scored at all in these Stanley Cup playoffs.

Kesler is, by his own admission, a "streaky" player. He had 41 goals in the regular season, none in the opening series against the Chicago Blackhawks, none against Nashville until he rather dramatically broke out on Tuesday. A red-hot Kesler—despite an ice-cold Henrik and a cooled-off Daniel Sedin—is a significant factor in a hockey series where the goaltending has been so sharp and the defence so suffocating that goals are as rare as Canadian teams winning Canada's most-revered trophy.

Kesler's best play Tuesday probably had nothing whatsoever to do with his own hockey stick—but rather the stick of Nashville captain Shea Weber, who was sent to the penalty box in overtime for hooking Kesler. "I've got one hand on my stick and he grabs my stick," said a bewildered Weber. "And I get a penalty?"

Wednesday afternoon, Kesler was sticking to the story: "He was hooking me." At least that's what his mouth said. Kesler's mouth is easily the least interesting part of his personality. If you wish to know what he really said, you have to listen to his eyes and that small twitch that sometimes turns up the edge of his mouth. What the eyes said was this: "Damn right I suckered him. I had my arm and elbow clamped down on his stick like a big turkey wing and the referee fell for it—Shea Weber can go cry to his Mawwwmmmie for all I care . . ."

Kesler is twenty-six years old and, while long a known force in Vancouver, is only now getting the widespread appreciation his play deserves—and as much for what he has accomplished in international play as in NHL play. He is, for the third year in a row, a finalist for the Selke Trophy as the league's top defensive forward, though there are many in Vancouver who believe he also could have been a candidate for the Hart Trophy as the most valuable player, a nomination that went to teammate Daniel Sedin, an obviously worthy candidate given that Sedin won the NHL scoring championship.

The Michigan-born Kesler may well be the best U.S.-born player in the world at the moment, given that Chicago's little Patrick Kane was a bit off this year.

It is a remarkable rise for a player who, little more than a decade ago, was cut from several elite teams he tried out for and wondered if hockey was really for him. His father, Mike, who drove eight hours from Livonia, Michigan, to watch Tuesday's

Shortly after Wayne Gretzky retired a New York Ranger, I was asked to ghostwrite his weekly newspaper column.

In Pittsburgh, even a retired Mario Lemieux on the ice is worth a ticket. The 2011 Winter Classic Alumni Game would draw thousands of fans.

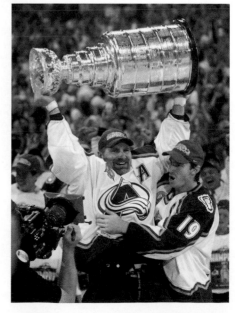

A championship is never inevitable, but with the great Ray Borque joining Joe Sakic and an all-star cast in Colorado it's hard to imagine the 2000–01 Avalanche falling short.

A young Guy Lafleur takes home the Memorial Cup as a Quebec Rampart in 1971, before becoming a part of hockey history in Montreal.

A supremely talented enigma and one of the most revered of *Les Glorieux*: Alexei Kovalev and Jean Béliveau at the Molson Centre.

In a pose his opponents have seen before and will see again, Washington Capitals' captain Alexander Ovechkin celebrates yet another goal.

Philadelphia Flyers captain Bobby Clarke chases down a man who was never easy to catch, Boston Bruins defenseman Bobby Orr.

Ryan Kesler surprised many people with his inspired play in the 2011 Stanley Cup playoffs. His disappointment was assuaged somewhat when he was awarded the Selke Trophy as the league's top defensive forward for 2010–11.

Daniel and Henrik Sedin: sharing an uncanny knack for finding one another on the ice, the Swedish twins won back-to-back scoring championships in 2009–10 and 2010–11, and powered a dominant Vancouver offence.

Brad Marchand: the Bruins rookie crashes the party—and Vancouver's hopes that the Canucks will finally bring the Stanley Cup back to Canada.

How many gold medals and Stanley Cups does Sidney Crosby need to win before we stop calling him "the Kid"?

Eccentric and beloved, before succumbing to cancer in 2003 Roger Neilson pioneered many coaching techniques considered commonplace today, including the use of game video to review plays.

Don Cherry, with straight man Ron MacLean, remains the most recognizable, popular, controversial, beloved and despised political voice in the country.

Sometimes dreams come true; sometimes they don't. Despite huge expectations, the only NHL history Alexandre Daigle made was as a cautionary tale.

Wally's Coliseum: the most
famous backyard rink in Canada
is no more.

An established great, Bob Gainey,
tries to slow down a new one,
Gretzky. Gainey would return to
Montreal as general manager in
2003, but his greatest challenges
have always come from outside
the arena.

She's been called the
Wayne Gretzky of women's
hockey, and Hayley Wickenheiser
is almost as tough to stop.

At the world junior championship, Canadian goalie Mark Visentin faced the third period from hell: a 3–0 lead, a 5–3 loss, a gold for Russia. The collapse would have ruined many teenagers, but he took the loss with courage and humility, and returned to his Niagara IceDogs to win OHL Goaltender of the Year.

Wayne Gretzky's ghost revealed: fifth from the left, back row, with the Huntsville All-Stars, Squirt, 1956–57.

game, took him on the bantam team he was coaching and kept the kid in the game.

Rather than the major-junior route chosen by most Canadian youngsters, he is a product of the U.S. National Team Development Program and Ohio State University. At eighteen, he went twenty-third overall in the NHL entry draft, far behind such today stars as Pittsburgh's Marc-André Fleury, Carolina's Eric Staal and Boston's Nathan Horton (first, second and third overall). He was not even the top American taken, chosen after Ryan Suter had gone seventh to Nashville, Zach Parise seventeenth to New Jersey and Dustin Brown thirteenth to Los Angeles.

But very quickly his career began to shine. Vancouver lent him to the U.S. team entering the 2004 world junior championship, where he scored the third-period goal against Canada that tied the gold-medal game 3–3 and led to the stunning 4–3 U.S. victory when Canada later scored on itself. It was the U.S. team's first win in the tournament. He was, as well, a key player for the Americans in the Vancouver Winter Games, scoring the first goal as the United States came back to tie the Canadians 2–2 and force overtime in the gold-medal game, a game won by Canada when Sidney Crosby scored.

He has become a major force, now widely considered one of the game's best two-way players alongside the likes of Detroit's brilliant Pavel Datsyuk. A year ago it paid off when the Canucks signed him to a six-year $30-million (U.S.) extension. No one doubts any longer whether he belongs on elite teams.

"He's a big body, works hard, good hands," says Nashville goaltender Pekka Rinne, who will have seen enough of Kesler no matter how this series ends. "Somebody you have to be aware of all the time."

"He plays at both ends of the ice," says Suter, a Nashville defenceman who is also one of Kesler's closest friends. "He's just the total package—I don't know what else to say."

Say nothing, Ryan Kesler would suggest. And let the actions speak for themselves.

In the 2011 Stanley Cup playoffs, Ryan Kesler emerged as a dominant force in post-season play. He, along with the Sedin twins, led the Canucks all the way to the Stanley Cup final, where they lost to the Boston Bruins in seven games.

★ ★ ★ ★ ★

FIVE

THE CHARACTERS

THE PRIME MINISTER OF SATURDAY NIGHT: DON CHERRY

(*Ottawa Citizen*, March 14, 1992)

It is—at least on Saturday nights throughout the winter and every night for most of each spring—the most recognizable, popular, controversial, beloved and, yes, often despised political voice in the country. It has come to Ottawa in the midst of a snowstorm, come to Ottawa to speak out and to speak loudly.

"Just shut your goddamn mouth for a minute!" Don Cherry barks from the far side of the toilet stall. "Shut up and let me talk—okay?"

"Okay," the young man by the urinals says.

The young man surely never meant it to go this far. He came in to Don Cherry's brand-new Nepean bar, had a couple, saw Cherry heading off to the washroom and figured it was as good a chance as he'd ever have to tell his buddies he'd spent the afternoon raising a few glasses with Cherry and talking about hockey—more specifically about Eric Lindros and his refusal to play for the team that drafted him, the Quebec Nordiques.

Cherry, after all, was talking hockey with everyone. For nearly three hours he had been sitting in a far corner of the restaurant and it was clear to anyone who wandered in that the last thing the host of *Hockey Night in Canada*'s Coach's Corner wished to be was inconspicuous. He had on one of those suits Nathan Detroit last wore in *Guys and Dolls.* He had his Wilfrid Laurier collars done up tight enough to choke and yet nothing, not the collar, food, autograph seekers or even the endless cups of coffee could stop the endless flow of opinion that erupts from the active volcano of Don Cherry's mouth.

"There they go!" Cherry would bark and above him, across from him, around him, television screens would fill with the video fists of Bob Probert and Keith Crowder. Every half-hour or so the same punchout, the same raw result—and yet each time the bar would stop dead and stare and shout as if the fight were live, the outcome unknown.

"Who's the toughest, Don?"

"Pretty hard to beat Probert."

"Who's your favourite player, Don?"

"Gotta go with Neely, eh?"

"Who's the best you ever saw, Don?"

"Right there." Cherry points to the screen, where Bobby Orr skates by every half-hour or so with a grace not seen since the early 1970s. "There's the best. I was behind the bench when he scored that goal, you know, and I got tingles down my back then and I still get tingles every time I see it. Never been anyone like Orr."

But now, with the coffee forcing a break in the action, the prodding has accompanied him to the washroom and Don Cherry, who is nothing if not accommodating to his fans, can take no more.

"You think Lindros should be forced to play in Quebec?" the voice barks from behind the stall door.

"Yeah, I do," the young man says.

"Well I don't. And I happen to think he's a hell of a fine young man, too."

The man is flustered. "I—"

"Shut up. I heard you out, now you listen to me. Eric Lindros is a friend of mine, okay? Where do they get off calling him a snot and a punk and a racist and a bigot? Who the hell do those politicians think they are saying he should be dropped from the Olympic team? If someone ever said those kinds of things about a Queee-bec kid they'd take him to court. Now whaddya think about that?"

"Okay, eh? I just thought I'd ask."

Moments later, Cherry is back at his coffee, stirring angrily as he recounts the story of the washroom encounter. "I tell you, the closer I get to the Quebec border, the worse it gets."

This being an inward-looking country with but two mad obsessions, hockey and politics, it had to happen that someday someone would come along to harness them together and, in doing so, create a brand-new power base. Don Cherry has become the Prime Minister of Saturday Night, a voice now so popular that hockey has become the only television sport where the audience goes up during intermissions.

In Toronto's Maple Leaf Gardens, the fans are taping up banners calling for him to take over the country as well as the intermissions. He has even become a national figure without the grace of a second language, for it is said that between periods in the province of Quebec the channels switch by the tens of thousands from the French broadcast of the game to the English—so that no one will miss the most outrageous act on Canadian television. Bashing foreigners, spoofing gays, celebrating fighting, he is so politically incorrect it is a wonder he survives on television. Yet he not only survives, he thrives, his popularity soaring by the week.

But is it an act? His close friends will say Don Cherry is, at heart, a fairly quiet fifty-six-year-old man with a gentle, sentimental streak who happens to go on instantly at the sight of a microphone or a potential fan, but none will say Cherry does not hold dear the wild opinions he serves up each Saturday night.

Thirty years ago when he was an unknown player in the American Hockey League, no one had to listen to him but his wife, Rose, who now cashes in on those dues by doing headache commercials with him. To fill in time between games Cherry would go shopping with Rose, and rail all the way home about those in the grocery line he'd seen handing over food stamps for steak when he, a working stiff, could barely afford hamburger.

If Don Cherry had never gone farther than the AHL—the scrappy defenceman did get in one game for Boston in the National Hockey League in 1955, leaving behind a career record of no goals, no assists and, more surprisingly, no penalties—no one but Rose would ever have heard about the abuse of food stamps. Nor would millions have sat by their television last winter while Cherry decided to ignore the tedious hockey game in progress and instead harangue viewers for their wimpishly feeble support for the Gulf War.

After sixteen years in the minors, he had a nickname, "Grapes," a wife he met in Hershey, Pennsylvania, a daughter, Cindy, a son, Timothy, and a lifetime supply of anecdotes—he likes to claim, for example, that Montreal once picked him up in a trade for two rolls of tape and a jockstrap. But he also came out of the AHL with a philosophical base, and it did not grow out of what he picked up on the ice and the bench, but what he picked out of books late at night when the game was still playing through his veins and he could not sleep.

He has read, he claims, every book ever written on Horatio Nelson and the Battle of Trafalgar. And since childhood he has carried with him an admiration for Nelson and Sir Francis Drake and the way in which they commanded loyalty from men. As effortlessly as he regales the crowd with tales of the AHL, Cherry can tell the stories of Trafalgar: Drake's irreverence and impatience with authority, Nelson's insistence that all the men, including his captains, write letters home before he would begin the battle. Cherry adopted this way of thinking for his own: The men around him would matter more than the men above him, loyalty would be given the highest value, and all battles were to the death.

When he became a coach this philosophy served him magnificently with his players but invariably poisoned his relations with his superiors. A league championship in the AHL brought him to the NHL as coach of the Boston Bruins, and the great Bobby Orr, who would become Cherry's closest friend.

In Boston there were enough spotlights shining down that Cherry soon found one for himself. He dressed differently—at one time in suits so tight he literally could not sit down in them—and he sure talked differently: loud, controversial and colourful. He called the game his stars played "lunch-bucket hockey" and he became a minor idol of those who believe that life, like hockey, goes to those willing to grind it out in the corners.

Cherry's coaching career in Boston and, later, Colorado, could be described as both success and failure. He won a lot, but he lost when it mattered—and never so dramatically as during the seventh game of the 1979 Stanley Cup playoffs when he sent too many Boston players onto the ice, allowing Montreal to tie the game on a power play and then win it in overtime. He was soon through in Boston. It was a mistake he admits to, but it cost him the job he adored, and more than a dozen years later he still hated to hear it brought up—which it is, constantly.

When the stumbling Colorado Rockies fired him, Cherry stumbled into a new career when Molson Breweries began lining him up for banquets. He was a hit and soon Ralph Mellanby, who was then producing *Hockey Night in Canada,* began bringing Cherry on between periods to comment and entertain. The fans instantly fell in love, but Cherry was not an easy sell in the corporate offices of the CBC, where the new commentator was instantly under fire for his characteristic mangling of the English language. Imagine the example this is setting for young viewers, they asked Mellanby, the irony never seeming to strike that while Cherry was dangling his participles the Zamboni was often icing over the blood from the previous period's fistfights. Mellanby said he would quit himself if Cherry was dumped, and Cherry soon became a Saturday night fixture.

When it comes to cleaning up hockey, the consensus among those who would act decisively is that, in Don Cherry, hockey has created its own monster. There are people at the highest levels of the game who despise Cherry's persona at the same time as they like, and protect, the man. It means they will not go public with their criticism, and it means that they have accepted that his extraordinary popularity makes him untouchable. But they still wish fate had delivered hockey's most important platform to someone with an appreciation of hockey's troubled image.

Cherry would argue that there is no image problem, and he can point to the fact that his thirty-minute videotape, *Don Cherry's Rock'em Sock'em Hockey,* has sold more than 150,000 copies, making it the top-selling video in Canada, and two more best-selling volumes have followed. There are no hot videos of Adam Oates's greatest passes.

"Isn't it ironic," Cherry says in his Nepean restaurant as Volume III of the series pounds over his head, "that when there's 17,500 at a game—fans who have all paid, incidentally—that when there's a fight there's 17,250 on their feet yelling?"

The videos and his redneck stance on hockey have made Cherry into the goons' own protector in the hockey world, and in the world of the loud bar fan it has served only to increase his popularity. There are now thirteen such restaurants. He has a successful radio show which is syndicated to a hundred stations. He makes commercials, sometimes with his British bull terrier, Blue II, and sometimes with Rose. And he now makes far more per year than the top-paid coaches in the NHL.

The wealth and the fame, however, have changed his lifestyle very little. The house in Mississauga is large but it contains the same two people each night, Cherry in the basement watching his television, Rose upstairs watching hers. He has no hobbies, plays neither golf nor tennis, takes no vacations. He has little to do with the various businesses but willingly contributes to charities, particularly the kidney foundation—Timothy was the recipient several years ago of a life-saving gift from his sister, Cindy.

Cherry gets his exercise in the basement by rowing and then turns to the fifty-two-inch screen and his satellite dish, watching a minimum of fifteen games per week, sometimes including the local minor league teams on the community cable channel. He drinks three beer a night and talks to Rose on his way to and from the refrigerator and then, later, talks to his television when the news comes on. In his basement, he is prime minister every night.

The political side of Don Cherry first began to surface at the banquets. Cherry would speak and the sessions would be thrown open to questions and soon Cherry would be discussing everything from the state of the game to the state of the country. On the hockey broadcasts he began ridiculing European hockey—"Alpo?" he once asked when the name of the Winnipeg Jets' new Finnish minor league coach came up. "Isn't that a dog food?"—and eventually his complaints about them coming over here and taking away jobs from good Canadian boys took him into the realm of immigration policy.

His comments on the infamous world junior hockey championships, after the Soviets and Canadians held one of hockey's worst brawls, took him into international affairs and, this year, his views on the Gulf War made him sound more like a war-mongering general appearing on *The Journal* than a former hockey coach appearing between periods of a hockey game. For a long time the view was that this was just Cherry. A bit humorous, a bit embarrassing, certainly not mainstream. But then, just as Cherry had predicted it would, the world began changing rather dramatically. His opinions began to sound more like the political philosophy of the Reform Party—or, as he would rather put it, the Reform Party began catching up to him. People began watching as much for the political tangents as for the hockey substance.

"He has become," says lifetime politician and hockey fan Senator Keith Davey, "the Gordon Sinclair of his generation."

And Cherry began to take his new role seriously. When Meech Lake died and few political commentators were aware of the "crankiness" that was sweeping the land, Cherry sat down and wrote Ontario premier David Peterson to let him know, "There's a tinderbox out there—and you got a match." Peterson didn't listen.

Cherry sees his role as speaking for the majority, not the minority, and says that Canada has gotten itself into such a mess because vocal minorities dominate and the silent majority does not fight back. "There's nobody out there," he says, "speaking for the people who are paying the freight, the average worker, the guys in construction and the mechanics and people like that, but me."

Cherry himself can claim he once worked in construction— between hockey jobs—and he certainly does talk the language of the construction site and the garage and the factory line, but he hardly looks working class. The love of fine clothes, he says, he got from his parents. His mother was a tailor at the Royal Military College in Kingston and his father, a big, handsome amateur baseball player, insisted on looking his best no matter what the occasion. From them he also got his passion for military history and two unshakable traits: "My mother insisted on honesty to a fault, and my father taught me to never, ever take a slight."

Both traits would make politics—certainly current Canadian politics—difficult for Cherry if he were to consider running for office, something that has often been suggested, particularly since the rise of the Reform Party, which he admits to admiring.

"I'd be torn to shreds by the media," he says. And he's probably right: Journalists who today view him as a curiosity, a once-a-week entertainment, would see him far differently if he were making his pronouncements on the floor of the House of Commons instead of behind the desk he shares with *Hockey Night in Canada*'s Ron MacLean. Cherry would, for example, want to rewrite completely the rules for collecting unemployment insurance. He would knock the turban off the Mounties. He would put an end to metric. He would bring back the lash.

"That'd put a quick end to guys beating up their wives and abusing children," he says. "And I'd volunteer to do the lashing." Cherry's approach to politics is no different from what he brings to hockey. "I react," he says. "I simply react. I was in hockey so long that's all I know how to do."

It is, he suspects, what makes him so remarkably popular with the young bar crowd, those who, like him, have never conceded there might be a bit of grey out there between what's black and what's white. "I don't know," says Cherry, "maybe my mind never got over eighteen. I relate to guys eighteen to twenty-five."

He says on national television what they say in the dressing rooms and at the bar. They don't, however, have his flair or his gift for lifting commentary off the ice so it floods the country at large. "To me," he says when considering the competitiveness of minor hockey, "that's just about the way Canada's socialism goes. Win or lose, it doesn't matter."

And from there, of course, it is a simple matter to leap straight into the future. "Change is coming," he says. "People are sick and tired of it."

He reacts. It is bar talk on the public record, the image cast of a House of Commons where they might pump fists instead of pound desks. Pure gut reaction.

"You know," he says, "we never rehearse Coach's Corner. We did it for a while but it was horseshit. Once I say something and I got to go over it again, I can't. I think about it too much. That's why I can't rehearse.

"It's a modern miracle that I'm still on the CBC."

In 2011, the CBC extended seventy-seven-year-old Don Cherry's contract through the 2011–12 season. He had long since become a Canadian icon, though an increasingly controversial one that polarized Canadians at a political and emotional level. His

Coach's Corner *had become less about hockey and more about Cherry himself and his personal causes—in particular, honouring those in military service, police officers and firefighters who had fallen in the line of duty. Seen as a clown by many, as a hero by just as many, his popularity continues unabated.*

GRATOONY:
THE IRREPRESSIBLE GILLES GRATTON
(*The Canadian*, 1977)

It is an empty sound, a hockey practice. Wood strikes rubber, rubber wood; the noise floats slowly up and fades into the rafters. Sitting alone in the stands you see the impact, wait for the sound. You watch as Johnny Bower kicks at pucks fired from the blueline by grown men old enough to be his children and cocky boys nearly young enough to be his grandsons. It takes but an instant for the puck to travel from the blueline to Bower's pads, a little longer to hear the slap followed by a muffled explosion. It rings hollow.

The Toronto Maple Leafs are working out. Bower, well into his fifties, is hanging out his life gift for all who are there to see. While many men his age have slowed to a crawl or stopped completely, Bower still has the reflexes of an active child. In the past, he was a man who won the Vezina Trophy twice as the NHL's best goaltender; in the present, he is a man who retired before expansion and the World Hockey Association came along to turn players' salaries into living cells, multiplying as we watched. When Bower retired he had no riches to fall back upon; he had to find a job. The Maple Leafs found one for him as a scout and sometime practice goaltender. Today he makes his saves in the same Maple Leaf Gardens, but the glory that once filled the air is now all in the mind.

If Bower looked behind him, back of the protective glass, he would see a young man with somewhat the air of a street punk passing by. He is Gilles Gratton, twenty-two, who plays goal for Toronto's WHA entry, the Toros, and is on the first year of a five-year contract that will pay him $645,000. The Toros practised earlier, and Gratton is on his way to the parking lot; in his pocket, fingers play against the keys to a canary yellow Porsche 911-S Targa (value: $16,670), which was provided by the Toros free of charge. Every two years he gets a new one; it's in his contract.

When Maple Leaf practice is over Johnny Bower will change into grey flannel slacks and a blue Maple Leaf blazer. The blazer is provided.

"Just look at him," Gratton says, obviously impressed with Bower's ancient abilities. "I'll never be half the goaltender he was. But I'll make more in the next five years than he made in his life. All he ever had was hockey—it was his world, man, and that's why he couldn't walk away from it. I see somebody like Bower playing and it makes me sad. He may love the sport, but it still makes me sad. For him there was nothing else . . ."

A little later the Porsche is hitting 110 with fifth gear to spare. Gratton is explaining what hockey means to him: "My ambition is to never work. That's what hockey gives me. I'll play until I stack up enough money to float for the rest of my life. Then I'm gone, man, gone. I'm a specialist of nowhere—have no and want no responsibility. Hockey gives me free time and lots of money, but I hate it. I like to win, I admit that, but I hate the pain and I hate the stupidity. The last two years I've felt like I should just say to hell with it and go back home to Montreal. Sometimes I think, 'Why am I in this rink getting pucks thrown at me when I could be home enjoying life?' And I can't answer the question, you know?"

Unlike other high-priced hockey talents, Gratton refuses to defend his salary. To him, it's a source of great amusement. "Nobody should be paid as much as I get. In real work terms I'm worth nothing. I'm not helping anyone, not making anything.

What am I doing for the world? I'm stopping rubber—what's that doing for evolution?

"The difference between me and a hockey player is this: when summer ends a hockey player gets itchy—I feel like killing myself. If I never played hockey again it wouldn't matter. A real hockey player would be broken. Me, I'd be liberated."

Actually, the differences between Gilles Gratton and a typical hockey player are far more complex than that. Most of today's players, even the most flamboyant and money-grubbing of them, could have played in other eras, providing the talent was there. Gratton could not have. Were this any other period but the mid-1970s, and had he been nursed along by anyone but gentle, sympathetic coach Billy Harris, Gratton very likely would be back in Montreal collecting welfare and slumming. ("I'll never, ever hold down a routine job," he claims.) He could never have played for those he calls "cement heads," the straight-and-narrow of hockey, the vast majority. It would have meant a major conflict of interest for him, one he could not accept. When Gratton was selected last summer for Team Canada '74 (as backup goalie to Gerry Cheevers and Don McLeod) he was taken aside by team manager Bill Hunter and asked to shave his freakish beard. "What's more important," Hunter asked, "your country or your beard?" Gratton told him—and cut it only when Billy Harris asked him to do it as a personal favour. Otherwise, his career with Team Canada '74 would have ended right there.

Ever since the two first met three years ago when Harris was putting together the now-defunct Ottawa Nationals of the WHA (they shifted to Toronto and became the Toros) and Gratton was a hotshot goaltender from the Oshawa Generals Junior A team, the two have had an understanding. Harris maintains that Gratton is treated differently for the simple reason that he *is* different, and that treating him like any other player would be a grave mistake.

"Gratton is an exceptional person," Harris says. "Not just an exceptional hockey player. He's a brilliant musician; he's as well read as anyone I know. After you've been around him a while you begin to realize that had he shown the same interest in school that he shows in, say, music, you'd be talking with a brilliant surgeon or a top criminal lawyer. His mind's that good."

While so many other players of today are busy investing their money, endorsing products, buying cattle farms, raising horses and thinking hockey, always hockey, Gratton draws astrological charts of people who interest him and writes pop music melodies that come to him. While others go to sleep at night dreaming of goals scored, fights won, and, for some of them, free women— hockey groupies—waiting outside their hotel rooms on road trips, Gratton sleeps dreaming of Spanish moors and blurred villas, of times past, uniforms and war. Sometimes he wakes screaming in pain and clammy with sweat, holding his stomach and scared for no reason.

He has dreamt again he was being stabbed.

Two mediums, at different times, have told him he was a Spanish soldier in another life, a soldier who died in combat. And sometimes during the day he gets violent pains in his stomach, always the same place, always exactly where he dreamt he was run through.

All of this, and much more, has made him hockey's most curious enigma. On an on night, he's said to be as good a goaltender as there ever has been; on an off night, as bad. Billy Harris says, "Gilles is probably the most talented goalkeeper in hockey . . . more potential than any of the young ones and the chance for the same success as Ken Dryden—if he wasn't so incredibly different." Les Binkley, the Toros' veteran backup goaltender who has played for nine teams in seven leagues in the past twenty years, agrees: "Gratton's great right now. There's just no telling what his potential is. He's great—and, boy, is he different."

So vastly different is he that Gratton, unlike most of the game's stars or future stars, could almost be considered dangerous to interview. With him there's no mumbling, no shy smiles of false modesty, overt praise for the coach and memorized catchphrases that make most players appear parodies of themselves. Gratton is Gratton: refreshing and startling. He told *This Country in the Morning* he usually wakes up horny; on a night he was selected the game star, in San Diego, he was interviewed live over the arena's public address system and told the crowd: "You have a great arena here—too bad you don't have a hockey team." He tells newspaper reporters that the game bores him, that "intelligence and hockey don't go together," that he can't concentrate, that hockey's no fun, players are paid far more than they're worth, and he's getting out.

So convincing is his threat to walk away from hockey that he actually used to terrify Harris. "Gilles was always late for practice while I coached, or, even worse, he wouldn't want to practise, and I had to tolerate it because I simply had no choice. He was the goaltender we depended on; he, more than any other person, got us into the playoffs the last two years. I always knew that if I criticized him too much there was a good chance he'd just pack his things together and never play hockey again."

Right now that's a little unlikely. Gratton genuinely wants the money so he can burn for the rest of his life. But also, even if he's not having much fun playing the game, he's having a fine time turning himself into the game's strangest sex symbol. It's not just that he likes to sign autographs "I'm easy—Gilles Gratton," but other, more kinky things. Once, at a practice last year, the gates swung open and out stepped Gratton in goalie mask and skates, nothing else, and he streaked up and down the ice for a while. In Helsinki with Team Canada '74, he was photographed by one of the wire services, in the nude and asking a female attendant about instructions for the sauna. One of his great ambitions is to pose nude in *Playgirl*.

There's a word in hockey—flake—that is about the worst condemnation a player can receive. Basically, it means wishy-washy, maybe a little garish, a trifle bizarre or eccentric, and usually with an attitude that tells the player's teammates that he really couldn't care less. Gratton loves the word ("Me? I'm a *super*flake"), but Harris maintains this is nothing but a Gratton put-on. "If he was really a flake he wouldn't have lasted," Harris's argument goes. "He's popular, and flakes aren't, but the telling thing is that when the team loses he blames himself entirely. Nobody puts as much pressure on himself to play well. And nobody wants to win as badly as Gilles."

Still, the image—as he sees it, or as others interpret it—sells well. The letters come in bundles, usually from girl fans who want to know if he's married and want him to know they're not, but will be ready in a very few years. "I'll wait, I'll wait," he keeps saying, kissing the letters before he crushes them and tosses them unanswered into the wastebasket. Some of the letters, though, he keeps. They puzzle him, especially the letters that come from the "Contessa Caserina Chloe de Climatis," who writes turgid, long letters with mythological and mystical allusions.

"I am the paramount groupie," she admits in one letter, "being a third-year university student of classics and English literature. I encountered you on the TV profile, and your discussion of women was really sublime. 'Woman for me is negative,' you said. Just remember, Gilles, a negative and a positive (which I presume you are) make electricity (and the way you've been playing lately indicates that you could do with a couple of billion volts pulsating through you). If you are a firm believer in astrology and a devotee of the occult, you surely must understand when I say that your visage is my destiny."

It is his belief in the stars that has made Gratton such a curiosity to practically everyone. In the sports world it's just not "manly" to believe in horoscopes. Gratton, consequently, has spent many hours trying to convince hockey writers that it's not simply a matter of reading his astrograph in the daily papers to determine whether he'll win or lose on a given night; rather, for him it's a dedicated and scholarly attitude toward astrology that has led him to shape his life in tune with his planetary influences. Most writers and other players, however, listen a minute, laugh knowingly inside and then walk away smirking. But some do listen. Harris did, and he too had his doubts, so he arranged on a couple of occasions to have fairly knowledgeable astrologers feel out Gratton over a couple of hours' talk, just to make sure he wasn't putting the world on. He wasn't. Less than five minutes after we met, for example, he had told me what my sign was and what traits it had assigned me.

Since Gratton spends all his spare time either studying astrology or playing music, he seldom gets out socially. He reads constantly, even on the road: on a recent trip to Cleveland, for a game he sat out, he could be seen slouched in the stands reading *The Lord of the Rings* (in French). When talking in his room—which he rents at the home of teammate Wayne Dillon's parents—he thumbs through massive textbooks on astrology, breaking away from any one point to illustrate one just past in astrological terms, then returning to the abandoned point without ever forgetting where he left off.

"See here," he says, moments after we had discussed his distaste for hockey. "I'm a Leo—right? And my sun is square to my moon. It says right here, 'Perhaps the subject is tied to a career in which he is not really interested.' Also, I've got Mars in my Fifth House, and it tells me not to gamble [this referring to our earlier contract talk] so that's why I stay out of the stock markets and keep my money in sure things. I got apartments in Montreal, and I got a $300,000 annuity that'll pay me $30,000 a year for life after I'm twenty-six. So I got no worries. I'll just float."

With all this emphasis on other-world ideas it's natural to wonder how he rationalizes spiritual beliefs with material fact. What other mystic, after all, has a $645,000 contract? Gratton's explanation is a firm belief in reincarnation; he has convinced himself he's just paying his dues in the material world. "Whatever you do in life has a reason," he says. "It's all working toward some kind of evolution. Stopping pucks in the material world might look a little ridiculous later on if I get to see what went on in all my previous lives, but that's the way it was in the material world. One of my great dreams in this life is that I hope I don't come back on earth. I hope I go on, higher—and never again as a goalkeeper. That's the way it is, man. A lot of people's ambition is to be free from the next life."

It's not surprising that the complexities of this life sometimes confuse Gratton totally; it happens, or should happen, to us all. He can't understand why people admire him for stopping pucks, something he believes is ridiculous, whereas these same people, given the chance, would despise him if he lived out his life as he properly sees it, as a do-nothing.

"It's an unbalanced world," he says. "And I'm stuck in it. Sometimes I think I've become unbalanced, too. I'll be playing a game and all of a sudden I'll just freak out. My head starts spinning faster and faster. I'm in the nets and I can't understand why I'm here at this time. What am I doing? And I look up at all those crazy animals in the crowd watching me. For what? And then I look down and see all this crazy equipment all over my body. And all those other guys—what're they fighting over a lousy piece of rubber for? So what do I do? I talk to myself. I say, out loud, 'C'mon Gilly, c'mon Grattoony, *for Chrissakes get back in the game.*'

"If only I could concentrate I'd be the best there is anywhere," he believes. "But I can't and I won't be." He used to put it down to nervousness, fighting back with three beers or a Valium just before sleep. But he stopped the beers himself, and the WHA stopped the Valium when the rules became much stricter on what the team trainer could or could not hand out. So he tried meditation, but it turned out to be a bad thing on game days. ("Made me feel like a lover boy out there.") Then he decided it was the nervousness that made him a good goaltender, and he cultivates it. He has a theory: Be nervous and irritated all winter, play well, collect the money and doze off all summer. Usually, when his mind wanders during a game, it's a safe bet that he's thinking about the off-season.

A summer for Gratton, it must be understood, is unlike summers for other players. He doesn't farm, he has no business interests ("that's my lawyer's worry"), and he doesn't even teach at hockey schools.

What he does is go back to the Highlands, his old neighbourhood in the Montreal suburb of LaSalle. He moves back in with his parents, and two houses away lives his best friend from childhood, Claude Bertrand. Two other Gratton brothers are still at home (one brother, Norm, plays for the NHL's Minnesota North Stars and there is also a sister), many other friends from past years have also stayed. It is a neighbourhood composed of a gang in their mid- and late twenties, quiet people who liked growing up there so much they've decided to put off leaving as long as possible. The ultimate neighbourhood preservation.

Come summer, Gratton lets his hair and beard grow, continues to pay himself the $150-a-week wage he receives over the winter (and saves even from that). He doesn't need much. "I spend now what I spent when I was a junior — $60 a week. I got no expenses. I don't want anything, not even a TV. Since I got the big money all I bought for myself was a $450 guitar. But I probably gave away $25,000."

He's tried to give his friend Claude Bertrand some, but it always gets turned down, even though Claude is unemployed. "I wouldn't take anything," Bertrand insists. "Nothing. Never." But they remain friends because they share a dream: one day, they'll tell you, Gilles and Claude and Claude's brother Michel will be professional musicians. All summer long, for five hours and more a day, they practice. Sometime, if the dream goes according to plan, Claude will have a little money, too. Then they can float together. Claude, understand, knows full well that Gilles will never last in hockey. They've been friends too long. "Gilles will never be a player for a team," he says. "He plays for himself. He goes his own way."

Gratton, of course, agrees, and says his time as a member of a team is running out, even though he professes great love for the Toros as a "family," not a team.

"It means far more to me to win a game of tennis in the summer than to win a hockey game in the winter," he says. "In tennis it's me alone; there's no one else to blame. Hockey, you see, has had too many things come along and take the winning out of the game. It's contracts now that decide whether you win or lose. In hockey you win even if you lose as long as you have a good contract. That's part of the reason why I'll never be the best. What's it matter? I'll play as well as I can—but it makes no difference whether I'm the best or not. My paycheque will be the same next week. And the week after that . . .

"But once my contract's up I'm gone. And once I'm gone— I mean *really* gone—I hope when they lay me in my grave there's someone there who can say Gratton never worked a day in his life. If someone can say that about me, then I'll have achieved what I set out to achieve. I've already worked out my marker:

> Here Lies King Floater
> Never Worked a Day in His Life
> But He Was Happy

Gilles Gratton did end up working—as a photographer. He left the WHA to play in the NHL for the St. Louis Blues (he walked out on the team after only six games) and the New York Rangers (forty-one games) before ending his professional career with the New Haven Nighthawks of the American Hockey League. He later lived in Europe, working as a freelance photographer. He is remembered for many things—streaking with nothing on but his mask and skates, the lion-head mask behind which he sometimes growled at opposing players, his refusal to play when the moon and stars weren't properly aligned—but also for the astonishing talent that he walked away from at twenty-five, with perhaps his best years ahead of him. One part of the story I left out to protect him was that even as he played professionally for the Toros he was coming out some nights to play as an anonymous forward in a casual beer league I played in.

NO MIDDLE GROUND: THE STRANGE CAREER OF THE GIFTED ALEXEI KOVALEV

(*The Globe and Mail*, March 22, 2008)

He has no idea what others see in him.

Mark Messier, who played with the teenage Kovalev in New York, says he is a true "thoroughbred." Wayne Gretzky, who watched the now thirty-five-year-old Russian when Kovalev's Montreal Canadiens met Gretzky's Phoenix Coyotes, says the veteran forward's play this season is at a level that deserves consideration for the Hart Memorial Trophy as the NHL's most valuable player.

"I don't know," Alexei Kovalev says.

He has no idea what it looks like, but he does have a strong sense of what it feels like when everything comes together exactly right, as it has so often this surprising season in Montreal. When he tries to explain the sensation of skating so effortlessly, it does not even require thought. He talks of that one moment of weightlessness he looks for when he pulls back on the controls of a Cessna 172 and climbs until the plane is perfectly vertical, the engine on the verge of cutting out and, just for the most fleeting of moments, the G-force lifts his body clear of the seat and he finds himself floating in space. But when he thinks of what it is like to control hockey's most potent power play, he no longer thinks of airplanes, but of helicopters.

"Manoeuvrability," he says. "I love the way you can make them go anywhere."

He has been known to rent helicopters and do nothing but 360-degree spins down the length of an open runway. He has mastered, he says, the difficult move of taking off and then backing down on precisely the same plane to land the machine on the very dime on which it took off. He is so in love with precision it is even reflected in his nickname: AK-27. He is Montreal's attack weapon, No. 27 on the back of *Les Glorieux*, who are once again glorious.

Only short months ago, the experts were saying the Canadiens would, once again, miss the playoffs. Kovalev, they said, was aging fast and slowing down, a $4.5-million disappointment last season, in which he scored only 19 goals and seemed uninterested in his team and listless in his play. The smart move would be to get rid of him. Today, Alex Kovalev is leading the team with 77 points, including 33 goals, and quarterbacks a dominating power play that has put the Canadiens in first place in the Eastern Conference before last night's games. The team is not only going to make the playoffs, but may well be Canada's best hope to win the Stanley Cup, which has not landed on this side of the border since the Canadiens won in 1993.

In this year of the Russians in the NHL—twenty-two-year-old scoring leader Alexander Ovechkin in Washington, twenty-one-year-old sophomore star Evgeni Malkin in Pittsburgh and twenty-four-year-old sniper Ilya Kovalchuk in Atlanta—the relatively elderly Kovalev often passes notice in the media. But not among those who, like Gretzky, understand the true meaning of a player deemed most valuable to his team. "He knows better than anybody what it takes," Kovalev said of the Gretzky compliment, "so it's nice to hear."

What Kovalev has managed in his fifteenth NHL season is astonishing. He has taken a line composed of himself, an aging veteran, third-year centre Tomas Plekanec and Andrei Kostitsyn, in his first full year with Montreal, and he has turned them into a line ranking with the likes of prime veterans Spezza-Alfredsson-Heatley in Ottawa and Datsyuk-Zetterberg-Holmstrom in Detroit.

But how he did it is even more amazing. He used Tiger Woods as his model.

Alexei Kovalev is stubborn. To say he follows his own mind is to understate the situation. When the native of Togliatti, Russia, arrived in New York to play for the Rangers, he thought he could decide his own ice time. When head coach Mike Keenan thought he could teach the youngster a lesson by waving him to stay on the ice at the end of another ridiculously long shift, Kovalev took it as a compliment for how well he was playing.

Slava Kovalev, Alexei's father, had been a weightlifter and wished his son to follow in his footsteps. He even installed a chinning bar on his child's bedroom door so the youngster could work out before bed and as soon as he woke up in the morning. When Alexei insisted on hockey instead of weights, his father devoted his spare time to creating the perfect hockey player, organizing a training regimen that would knock out a grown man, let alone a growing child.

But very soon it all seemed for naught. When Alexei was eight, a routine medical checkup discovered a heart abnormality, a problem with rhythm. His parents were advised to take him away from hockey and let him skate "easy" once a week, at most. "I'm not stopping," the determined eight-year-old told his mother.

He decided he would repair his own heart. He set up a strict diet of fruits and vegetables for himself, made sure he got extra sleep, drew up his own exercise program and returned to hockey. The condition, he said, still exists, "but it's not dangerous."

He was remarkably gifted as a child: bright in school, exceptionally musical and a champion swimmer. But it was hockey that he excelled at, to the point where, just as in Gretzky's case, others grew jealous of him and coaches regularly berated him for what they saw as selfish play. There were many tears, and he grew increasingly shy and quiet.

Kovalev's early experiences with coaches were not always good. One particularly tyrannical coach in Togliatti put fourteen-year-old Kovalev's team through such a gruelling workout—first running fifteen kilometres cross-country in sweltering heat—that one of his teammates and best friends dropped dead when the coach made them practise immediately after.

Last season, it seemed Kovalev had had an irreconcilable falling-out with Canadiens coach Guy Carbonneau when a Russian sports newspaper ran an interview claiming to quote Kovalev at length criticizing the Montreal coach for his defensive systems and claiming Carbonneau was anti-Russian. Kovalev, who had never before backed down from controversial statements, denied there had ever been any such interview, and no tapes were ever produced. He said it never happened, though not many then took him at his word.

Still, Kovalev could hardly blame Carbonneau for his season even if he had wished to. He played badly. He was heavy—playing at 225 pounds, when he had come into the league at 185—and he was playing a rather jazz-like Russian version of the game (he prides himself on never having a plan) that simply was not working in Montreal. "He was playing a style that had a high degree of difficulty with too low a degree of success," Montreal general manager Bob Gainey said.

Those close to the team point to a long "walk in the park"—actually a stroll along the Montreal waterfront—with Gainey early last summer as the pivotal moment that turned Kovalev's attitude around. "It's not like I stopped playing or anything," Kovalev said. "But people thought I had lost interest. Bob said that. We sat and talked. He asked me: 'What is the problem? What do you think?' Bob just let me talk. He solved the problem. I needed support and I needed people to believe that I could do the job."

Gainey, however, believes something else played a more significant role. Not only had Kovalev's NHL career taken a dive, his international career seemed at an end. Kovalev is one of the more patriotic Russian stars, having won gold in the world junior championships, gold in the Olympics in 1992 and three gold medals in world championships—the last time as the captain of the 2005 Russian team. Last spring, he wasn't even invited.

"I think it was far more these factors," Gainey said, "than it was any walk in the park with Bob Gainey. He's proud and he's resilient. He wanted to prove himself."

"I wanted to prove something," Kovalev agreed. "I couldn't do anything about what people had said about me, but I could do something at the world championships. It was my only chance. When I didn't get asked to play, that really kind of killed me. I was lost."

But then, a third factor, almost by accident, came into play. The highly sensitive Kovalev had his feelings stung by his own agent, Scott Greenspun. When Kovalev explained to Greenspun that he planned to work extra hard, get in great shape and show them that he was good as ever, Greenspun, meaning well, happened to say, "Don't forget, Alex, you were nineteen then."

"It really pissed me off," Kovalev said. "I said, 'Just watch.'"

He tore himself apart and rebuilt from scratch. He began working out almost fanatically. He lost weight and added muscle. He tracked down and found old game tapes of how he had played in his prime with the New York Rangers and the Pittsburgh Penguins and he studied the tapes, took notes and then set out to put what he had learned into practice.

If one of his sporting idols, Woods, could take apart his swing and rebuild it, then Kovalev would do the same in hockey. Not only would he adjust the way he played and fix the shape he was in, he would recast his attitude. Sullen and angry the season before—partially blaming himself for the disastrous addition of another Russian, Sergei Samsonov, to the Montreal lineup—he came into this season determined to serve as a mentor to the younger Russians in the organization: the Kostitsyn brothers, Sergei and Andrei, and defenceman Andrei Markov.

"He's cross-cultural now," Gainey said of the Russian. "He can translate those things—not necessarily words—for the others."

"The young guys see his hunger on the ice," Markov added, "and they try to do what he's doing. He's a good example."

Led by Kovalev, all the Russians—along with Plekanec, the young Czech—have been pivotal players in Montreal's impressive season of recovery. "He's like a dad to them," said Murray Wilson, the former Hab who now does colour commentary on the Montreal broadcasts. "It's like they're joined at the hip—five guys all surrounding Alexei as they walk out of the rink. He's the father image for those guys."

He also reached out to fans, at one point flying his Cessna 414 from its base airport at White Plains, New York, to a small town in the Gaspé region where the mayor, a fanatical Canadiens fan, had invited the star. He arrived with signed jerseys and sticks and stayed for days—at one point smacking up the mayor's beloved motorcycle.

But no matter, the story got out and impressed people. "There are players who come from right here in Montreal," one hockey reporter said, "who wouldn't make an effort like that." Booed in 2006–07, he became a name they chanted in 2007–08. "He has been our best player," Gainey said. "Our MVP."

When captain Saku Koivu was briefly injured, coach Guy Carbonneau took the captain's "C" and gave it to Kovalev when the team was headed to New York on a trip. Why? "He deserved it," Carbonneau said.

When Kovalev is on his game, it seems he was created solely to skate and stickhandle and shoot. "What was it they used to say about Tom Watson?" Gainey asked. "That 'his hands were made to fit a golf club.' Same for Kovalev in hockey. He looks like he was built for the game."

What he does in games often pales to the wild and inventive plays he will come up with in practice. He considers himself a freelancer, a player so creative he delights in having nothing in mind until the precise moment when something happens. He is at his happiest when he is surprising even himself. "He does things with the puck you've never seen before," Montreal's sensational rookie goaltender, Carey Price, said. "It just seems impossible what he does sometimes—but for him, it's just like walking and chewing gum."

Kovalev's centre, young Plekanec, says there have been times on the ice when he and young Kostitsyn find themselves laughing so hard at plays Kovalev has just pulled off that they forget they are part of the equation. "You just start laughing on the ice," Plekanec said. "You can't help yourself. We were playing Boston and he goes through half the team, drops his glove, leans over and picks it up—and then stickhandles through two more guys."

"You can't quit on the play, can you?" Kovalev said with a smile. "That's what I was taught. Never quit on the play. Never quit."

He didn't, and both Alexei Kovalev and the Montreal Canadiens are better for it. He talks now of playing in the next Olympics, of playing enough more years that now that he has passed a thousand NHL games, he might reach two thousand—and will be a member of the Canadiens when they bring the Stanley Cup home to its rightful resting place.

"I think anything is possible in my life," he said. "Everything comes unexpected."

Unexpected, indeed. In the summer of 2009 Kovalev became a free agent and, despite an offer from the Canadiens and even a rally by Montreal fans to keep him, he left for a sweeter deal in Ottawa, $10 million over two years. It soon turned sour. The sensitive Kovalev did not like the coach, Cory Clouston, and simply stopped trying. He "floated," uninterested, uninspired and ineffective, through most of two seasons before the Senators sloughed him off to the Pittsburgh Penguins for a conditional seventh-round draft pick. He scored in his first game and then won the game in a shootout.

THE DREAMER: ALEXANDRE DAIGLE

(*Ottawa Citizen*, December 21, 1997)

I'm different. But it's okay now—people know I'm different.
—Alexandre Daigle, December 1997

He watches it faithfully, at least once every season, and almost always alone: a Canadian kid who was once, but no longer, considered a "natural" in his country's game, stares hypnotically at an American movie on the American game, and based on a story that was written forty years before anyone in Canada had ever heard of Alexandre Daigle.

Just as other hockey players know—and love to shout out—every line of dialogue in the Paul Newman hockey movie, *Slapshot*, Alexandre Daigle can quietly recite every word that is spoken in the 1984 Robert Redford movie of Bernard Malamud's 1952 classic baseball novel, *The Natural*.

"You've got a gift, Roy," the father in the movie says as he catches a ball thrown by the young Redford. "But it's not enough—you've got to develop it. You rely too much on your gift and you'll fail."

The Natural is the story of a handsome, charismatic ball player, Roy Hobbs, who is blessed with both supernatural talent and a mystical bat called "Wonderboy." The film is a moving, exquisitely photographed account of the great American dream gone temporarily wrong: brilliance thwarted by fate, the long, difficult struggle back, the hero finally proving the doubters wrong with one dramatic, desperate, triumphant swing of the bat.

"It's a sad, sad story," says Alexandre Daigle. "Not a fun story at all—but it shows you what you can accomplish."

The book has a decidedly different ending. The final swing of the bat, just as desperate, fails to connect, the final strike followed by shame and disgrace.

"Say it ain't true, Roy." When Roy looked into the boy's eyes he wanted to say it wasn't but couldn't, and he lifted his hands to his face and wept many tears.

Like the mysterious Roy Hobbs, there are a great many things about Daigle that the fans in the stands do not know and may not understand. Roy Hobbs was advised to read Homer. Daigle has lately been reading Shakespeare and Socrates. But he will never read Bernard Malamud, not ever.

Alexandre Daigle is twenty-two years old and as of today has been paid $10,763,000 for playing slightly less than four and a half seasons in the National Hockey League. In 291 games, he scored 73 goals, which works out to $147,438.35 a goal. He has just signed—and negotiated, entirely on his own—a new one-year deal with the Senators that will kick in when his $12.25-million deal finally dies come the end of the 1997–98 season. This season as of Friday, he has scored six goals. For the 1998–99 NHL season, he will receive a raise to $2,736,000.

"You're not fascinated by the almighty dollar?" the fixer asks in the movie. "I never gave it much thought," says Roy Hobbs.

More than four years after that outrageous deal that in no small part led to the 1994 NHL owners' lockout of the players, the shortened 1994–95 season and the rookie salary cap that came of it, Alexandre Daigle is still defined by numbers with dollar signs beside them far more than by any other statistic. If people point to any of his hockey numbers, it is usually to the minus 33 he registered last season in the plus-minus rating, meaning he was on the ice for 33 more even-strength goals scored on his team than he was for goals scored by his team. It was 19 more goals against than any of his Ottawa teammates, and four more than any other player in the entire league.

One might think, then, that Daigle would like to avoid such a topic, but one would be wrong to think this. There can be no doubt that criticism stings—his closest friends have seen the tears—but Alexandre Daigle has been blessed with a public persona that renders criticism as hard to deliver as to accept.

At a charity golf tournament staged this summer by Senators coach Jacques Martin, the coach had just finished bragging to the dinner crowd about his team's improved goals-against play when a laughing Daigle took to the podium and brought down the house with an extravagant claim, saying, "I'm the guy who instituted the defensive system." "He had them in the palm of his hands," says Senators broadcaster Dean Brown, who emceed the dinner. "It was an incredible show."

It is also a travelling show. While the Senators can claim two NHL All-Stars—Alexei Yashin and Daniel Alfredsson—it is still Daigle whom the fans wait for at the hotels and outside the rinks. His is the autograph most sought, the photograph most treasured, the smile best remembered. He has what is called in the sports world "star quality," a charisma that was first noticed when he was sixteen and persists today, despite the many disappointments, despite the critics. For every boo that falls down from the stands, an electric buzz still sizzles through the rink the moment Daigle, in full stride, picks up a pass or a loose puck. Most times it doesn't work out, but on those rare occasions that it does, it seems the dream remains possible. Certainly, many continue to believe he will still come true.

The media still gather around his locker for comment. His words still matter, his enormous promise is still worthy of debate while other high draft picks have either blossomed or been dismissed. He sits facing questions and notepads with a ready smile and disarming quip, his shoulders almost always hunched into a blue, sweat-stained T-shirt.

If the cameras could catch those shoulders bare, they would find two small tattoos. On the left shoulder, a red Superman emblem: "Super-Daigle," he likes to call it. On the right, a symbol unrecognized in hockey, where the tattoo of choice is more often the Tasmanian Devil cartoon character. On Daigle's right shoulder is a looping circle, one half dark, the other half light. It is the yin and yang from classic Confucianism, the dark side and the light side of the hill of life. The contrast is deliberate: light and dark, heaven and earth, birth and death, matter and spirit. The yin and yang may appear opposite, but they are actually complementary. Each makes up for what the other lacks. To be whole, they need each other.

The contrast in Alexandre Daigle's life is growing more apparent by the year. While some of his teammates are mystified—some even miffed—by his failure to devote every moment of his life and every ounce of his energy to hockey, to make his game and profession the absolute priority, Daigle's main drive has been to gain some measure of balance in his life. His closest friend in Ottawa does not even play hockey, does not talk about the game, but is instead a twenty-eight-year-old finishing a PhD in clinical psychology at the University of Ottawa.

When Yannick Mailloux looks at his friend, Alexandre Daigle, he sees not a hockey player but *"un animal prise dans une cage"*—a caged animal. "Alex is a dreamer," says Mailloux. "Alex is like anyone else. He has dreams—even if he is playing in the NHL. We all want to become players at some time. But you know, his dreams are more real than our dreams.

"He wants more. He wants to be Alex. And Alex is different."

"Sometimes" [he said to her,] "when I walk down the street I bet people will say there goes Roy Hobbs, the best there ever was at the game."

She gazed at him with touched and troubled eyes. "Is that all?"

There are no secrets to the great Canadian dream that a young Alexandre Daigle shared with millions of others who were then very much like him: every one of them a natural, a different stick in their hands, though, sharp blades on hard ice, the rest of the known world trailing, the blade of the stick snapping, the puck soaring, the goaltender missing, the Stanley Cup rising.

"Dreams really do come true," NHL Hall-of-Famer Lanny McDonald later wrote of the first day he reported to the Toronto Maple Leafs. " . . . I'd finally made it. There I was at the Gardens, about to begin playing for the Toronto Maple Leafs, the team I had cheered for like crazy as a kid. I sat there, realizing that everything I had dreamed about had come true."

Jean-Yves Daigle shared this common Canadian dream, only his took him to the Montreal Canadiens instead of to the Toronto Maple Leafs. Like most young dreamers, Jean-Yves Daigle would eventually give up on something that just wasn't going to happen and settle down to a different life. He married Francine and began working for a Laval printing company, just outside Montreal. And the dream he simply passed down, as is done in households all over the country every single winter.

"Everyone thinks, 'My son will play in the NHL,'" says Jean-Yves Daigle today. "Every father believes that. Even when he says, 'No, no, no, it's not true.' They all think it. Believe me, I know."

He tried to interest the first son, Sebastian, and encouraged the girl who followed, Veronique, to play hockey as well. He spent hours building a backyard rink, shovelling and pounding down the snow, levelling the surface and flooding long into the night with pails of hot water and a garden hose that would stiffen the moment he laid it down. But it didn't work. Sebastian and Veronique learned to skate, but were not very interested. By the time the baby, Alexandre, was walking around and wanting to go out to play, Jean-Yves's rink was a memory. What, he had decided, was the point?

The youngest boy, however, was different. He hounded his parents and older siblings to cart him off to neighbourhood rinks and wait for him, and soon he was demanding to be signed up for hockey. Jean-Yves laughed at the youngster's first attempts to get the stick to move the puck, yet there was something different about this youngster. He could move faster than anyone else. And he also had what Jean-Yves Daigle calls *"la loie de conviction*—if you want something, if you work hard enough, it's there for you."

The father saw this enormous desire in the son, and decided to do whatever he could to help. "Every parent puts skates on their child," Jean-Yves Daigle says, "and then it starts. It's a big job, but nobody has any experience. It's like a horse race. Ten horses start out, but only one wins. Sometimes it's a photo finish, the difference between first and second, and the difference can be just a detail.

"That's why I worked for ten years on the details. Skates just right, always new laces, the right way to lace up a skate, black tape on the stick, the right sleep. It's just the details. All the boys are the same, good parents, good boys, good skaters. What's the difference, then? I work on the details."

This was not Walter Gretzky teaching passing techniques on the backyard rink. This was not the stereotypical hockey parent pounding on the glass and calling the coach at all hours of the night. This was merely Jean-Yves and Francine Daigle doing what they could do to support their child's great dream. "I never said to him to shoot for the top," says Jean-Yves Daigle. "It's attitude. And attitude is the job of the parent."

If Alexandre's team lost, Jean-Yves would say to him: "You have to think about losing. Then you go to sleep. When you wake, it's gone. When you win, when you score five or six goals, I want you to think about that very hard before you go to sleep. But tomorrow it is gone. You have to forget a bad game; you have to forget the best game."

This may seem a small point, but it was to have the most profound effect on the boy as he grew. Instead of being serious and driven, even angry, he was happy-go-lucky, easy-going, confident in himself and content. The parents never pushed, never yelled.

The one time the father did criticize the son's play—for a dumb penalty he took in junior hockey—the boy burst into tears. "When parents yell, I don't understand that," says Jean-Yves Daigle. "It is important to be positive all the time. He's a hockey player, but first of all he's a child."

The child had a gift, an extraordinary gift of speed. From the moment he was set down on the ice, he was the fastest in his age group, and soon faster than even the older players. It seemed a phenomenon, but in fact it was an oddity. Alexandre simply raced up the ice and scored, and because of his extraordinary feet, his hands—and to some extent his brain—never had to deal with the traffic and congestion of the game as other youngsters had to. The blessing of such speed was also a curse—but, of course, no one knew this at the time.

By peewee age, Alexandre Daigle was already being noticed, the thirteen-year-old who had scored 150 goals for his Laval team. By sixteen, he was Quebec junior hockey's rookie of the year. By seventeen, he was threatening Mario Lemieux's junior record of 282 points when, dramatically and unexpectedly, he was suspended by the league for a vicious cross-check on another player. The suspension cost him a chance at the scoring record but—as can only happen in hockey—it increased the interest of NHL teams in him. He was not only fast, they thought, but also believed, incorrectly, that he had North American hockey's beloved "mean streak."

It was all happening so fast, the youngster simply stepped back and let it unfold. In his heart, he had hoped to go to Michigan State on a scholarship. But the world, it seemed, wanted him to be a hockey player, not a student, and he was more than content to go along without protest. After all, he was having great fun and he was enjoying the attention. He loved the spotlight, and nowhere did it shine more brightly in Quebec than on a hockey rink. Already they were talking about the money he might make playing professional hockey. His father, however, kept telling him that there were more important things in life.

"It's just money," says Jean-Yves Daigle. "It's not the most important thing in life. The most important thing, *être heureux*—to be content."

Money, however, would soon become the story, just as it had forty years earlier for another junior phenomenon named Jean Béliveau, who had starred for the same Victoriaville team that Alexandre Daigle joined. In the days before the NHL entry draft, the gifted Béliveau had been the object of a great struggle between Quebec City and the city of Montreal. It went on for years, the Montreal Canadiens finally winning in 1953, when they lured Béliveau to the NHL with a contract unheard of in those days: $110,000 over five years. "All I did," said Montreal general manager Frank Selke, "was open the Forum vault and say, 'Help yourself, Jean.'"

Four decades later, in Quebec City, Alexandre Daigle was drafted first overall. The right to draft him became a bizarre battle between two terrible teams—the Ottawa Senators and the San Jose Sharks—to see which one could come last in order to claim what was called, in the press of the day, the Daigle Cup. And the contract he was offered—$12.25 million over five years—changed both the young man and the old game before it had run its course.

That hot and hazy June day when he was drafted, Daigle joined the silver-haired Béliveau in a horse-drawn calèche that carried them through the streets of Old Quebec. Women laid roses in their path. A young couple brought their newborn to be touched. And Béliveau, sitting in the seat opposite, was struck by both similarities and contrasts that took him back to when he was just starting out.

When Jean Béliveau was nineteen, a year older than Daigle was that sultry day in Quebec, he was equally famous, but hardly as rich. He was paid $6,000 a year to play for the Quebec Citadels, and picked up another $60 a week in the summer, driving around with a dairy cooler in the trunk of his car, looking for kids to treat to complimentary ice-cream bars.

The only pressure Jean Béliveau had back in 1953 was to play. Alexandre Daigle didn't even have to play to prove himself. His face that morning was not only on the front of *Le Soleil* and *Le Journal de Québec*, he was the cover of the *Hockey News*, a main feature in *Sports Illustrated* and the subject of a television documentary, *The Franchise Kid*. His selection, so predictable, was carried live, coast to coast. When he signed his first endorsement deal it was covered as if it were a treaty between two governments—and yet the deal, with a sports card company, struck the first sounding note in the reefs hidden ahead: Alexandre Daigle appeared on glossy trading cards in a variety of uniforms, including dressed up as a nurse.

Béliveau had always said exactly the right thing. In the '50s, the '60s, the '70s, when he had retired as gracefully as he had played. But these are the '90s, where saying the right thing is no longer desired. If Jean Béliveau had been a media darling in a time when the media tended to romance character and heroics, he was nothing compared to Daigle at a time when the media sought a different kind of character and controversy.

What is the difference between you and Eric Lindros? Daigle was asked in the city that still felt snubbed by Lindros, who had refused to sign with the Quebec City team that had drafted him two years earlier. "*I drink my beer!*" Daigle had laughed, and the world, for the moment, laughed with him. Lindros, of course, had been in court, ultimately acquitted of allegedly spitting beer over a young Ontario woman. Daigle's quick wit—even in a language he was still learning—was the hit of the day. And how does it feel to be drafted first overall? he was asked. "Nobody remembers who was picked second," he laughed. And again, everyone laughed with him.

Chris Pronger, the gawky eighteen-year-old Ontario kid who was drafted second, was asked what he thought, and Pronger stammered and blushed and eventually suggested everyone check back in five years or so. Five years later, Pronger—after his own battle with various demons—is the respected captain of the St. Louis Blues. Just turned twenty-three, he has been named to the Canadian Olympic team that will compete in Japan in February.

"I remember," Pronger said one day recently when his Blues were in Ottawa. "But there's more than just No. 2." Pronger ticks off the other graduates of that 1993 draft who have excelled, so far, beyond Daigle: the third pick, Chris Gratton, who recently signed a deal that will pay him $14.4 million to play this season for the Philadelphia Flyers; the fourth pick, Anaheim's Paul Kariya, who may well be the best player in the game today. Others might add Rob Niedermayer, who was taken fifth, Kenny Jonsson, twelfth, Adam Deadmarsh, fourteenth, Saku Koivu, twenty-first, Janne Niinimaa, thirty-sixth, Eric Daze, ninetieth. Earlier this fall, it was rumoured that Ottawa and the Chicago Blackhawks were talking about a deal: Daigle, even up, for Daze. No. 1 for No. 90.

"I guess someone is going to have to eat his words, isn't he?" smiled Pronger.

Five years after that glorious day in Quebec City, Alexandre Daigle's NHL career has been spotty, at best. His rookie year included a respectable 20 goals and 31 assists, but his play paled against that of another Ottawa rookie, Alexei Yashin, and the comparison was salted by the fact that Daigle was so overpaid and Yashin underpaid—a complaint that Yashin and his agent would soon take public. His second season was blurred by the owners' lockout, and his quite adequate 16 goals and 21 assists lost in open questioning about his desire and defensive liabilities.

What was happening was that the neglected arts of his childhood play—working in traffic, in particular—were catching up to him at the NHL level. The Ottawa coaches of the time, Rick Bowness and his assistants, E.J. McGuire and Alain Vigneault, began to wonder how much of the ice surface Daigle could see. As he ran out of ice space for the first time in his life, he seemed to lose both pucks and confidence.

It was said he showed fear on the ice, a charge he denies and says his reactions were simply a matter of not being prepared. No one had taken care of the "details." "I'm not afraid," he says. "But at first, young players don't know what to expect. After five years, if you go into Philly, you know what kind of game to expect."

Early in his third year, Daigle tried to answer his accusers by "driving hard to the net," and he ended up breaking his wrist the first time he tried the move. It caused a disastrous season—five goals in 50 games—and the naysayers and non-believers only grew. In his fourth season, he began well, but there were always unfortunate distractions. A joke about carrying a "bomb" onto a flight leaving Pittsburgh backfired badly, embarrassing both Daigle and the Senators. He ended with 26 goals and 25 assists, many of the goals spectacular, but he tailed off terribly as the Senators fought to make the playoffs, and his playoff output was embarrassing: zero goals, zero assists.

This fifth season began with enormous promise. At the urging of general manager Pierre Gauthier, he switched his sweater number from 91 to 9—Roy Hobbs's number—and got off to a quick and impressive start. In California in October, however, his elbow suddenly ballooned with infection, and the healing was slow and painful. He hurt his arm on a goalmouth scramble. His line was broken up because of ineffective play and, even though everyone else on the team stopped scoring as well, his play was always more noticed than that of the others. He, after all, was Alexandre Daigle, former No. 1 pick.

Sitting across from Daigle as that calèche rumbled through the streets of Old Quebec, Jean Béliveau could not see into the future, but he did know that this future would always be under special examination. "The hopes of several million Québécois ride with him," Béliveau said of Daigle in his 1994 autobiography.

Players who come out of such a background, said the former Canadiens captain, "have a particular cross to bear. The expectations of an entire province often go with them, and the pressure exerts itself in unusual ways."

Another Quebec teenage sensation, Marcel Dionne, had felt that pressure a generation before Daigle took it on. Now retired and an NHL Hall-of-Famer, Dionne once spoke of how deeply he grew to resent the game and his great gifts before he and some of his family moved out of province, just to avoid it. "Hockey, hockey, hockey, hockey!" said Dionne. "I was going nuts!"

Guy Lafleur felt it so profoundly in his early NHL career with the Canadiens that there were times when he would walk up to the small office that the retired Béliveau kept in the Montreal Forum, sit on Béliveau's blue, red and white chesterfield and weep.

"When you are preceded by the publicity," Béliveau said of Lafleur in a 1980 interview, "people expect so much. Sports fans are so demanding . . . I told him, 'You have a heavy load on your shoulders. I remember some nights I would score three goals and on the way out people would say I could have scored four or five. Whatever you do, people expect more. And it makes you press when you're on the ice. You want to do well to get rid of this anxiety.'"

Béliveau preached patience to Lafleur, but the people would not be patient. All he could do was sit with the troubled young Canadiens player and wait for the tears to dry. "I've always been there when he needed somebody," Béliveau said. "And he knows I'll always be there."

Alexandre Daigle has proved far more reluctant to share his moods. Toward the end of his first year, he did, however, open up to Bertrand Raymond, the respected columnist with *Le Journal de Montréal*, conceding, "I'm often depressed. Some mornings, I'm all alone with my Rice Krispies . . . I try to convince myself that I can't let the situation affect me—but, frankly, I never thought that it would be so difficult."

"Some nights I'll play well," Daigle told Raymond, "but the next game I'll be rotten." It is a pattern that has, to a large extent, persisted.

He says the criticism doesn't bother him. He says he never reads the papers. He shies away from much of his fan mail, fearing attacks, and has not once investigated the massive website on the Internet that is faithfully maintained by an avid fan in England. But still, he knows what is said.

Yannick Mailloux remembers being at work at a clinic when, at two o'clock in the morning, the telephone rang. It was Alexandre, weeping.

"I don't feel good," he told his friend.

"What happened?" demanded Mailloux.

"Nothing. I just don't feel good."

"He was melancholy," remembers Mailloux of the call. "I just talked to him for a long while and he was fine. I was there for him."

Like a good friend, Mailloux deeply resents the criticism, particularly when he feels it goes too far. "It hurts me, too," he says. "I feel they don't know him. I feel they don't have the right to judge him—but then I think, I guess they do. He's making about $3 million. They're paying $80 to watch the game. He's not scoring."

Mailloux has heard most of the stories that can circulate in a city as small as Ottawa. He knows there have been times when Alexandre Daigle has been guilty of the boorish behaviour of the young and pampered, but he has seen his friend mature in the past few years. "He's a completely different guy than he was a year and a half ago," says Mailloux. While there is no doubt Daigle indulged himself in young women who were attracted to a rich, handsome young hockey star "for a while," and that he loved to be the centre of gatherings, there has been such a change that Mailloux now calls his friend "a loner."

The bar scene has largely lost its appeal, and often now if Daigle goes out with Mailloux and Mailloux's live-in girlfriend, Julia, the three will sit and talk quietly with other friends, drinking nothing stronger than water. Just being there, however, is usually enough to strike a new story of Alexandre Daigle on the town.

"Look," says Mailloux, "with all the things Alex has had to deal with, he didn't fall into drugs or booze or anything. It would have been easy for him. But he didn't. He always stands up in front of the critics. For this, we owe him respect."

Guy Lafleur's early response to the growing pressures was to drink endless cups of coffee and chain smoke cigarettes all the day of a game, including between periods, with plenty of beer to follow after. He hid in his apartment, watching *The Three Stooges* and writing poetry. In one that he entitled "Candle," Lafleur might have been speaking for Alexandre Daigle, as well:

> By your light you make us dream
> In your glow we lose our cares
> Tell me why you don't burn always? . . .

Alexandre Daigle's response has been decidedly different. He has surrounded himself with a small circle of friends, men and women, who are intellectuals and artists. Very privately, he has sought to repair an education that ended, as so often happens in hockey, in high school. Where he once bragged he was learning English by watching *Beavis and Butt-head* cartoons on television, his television show of choice now is *Biography*. He now reads the classics—Shakespeare's *Hamlet*, *Macbeth* and *Romeo and Juliet* this past summer—and is working his way through a thick book on the great philosophers of history: Socrates, Plato . . .

"That's one of my dreams," Daigle once told Yannick Mailloux. "Having a degree in something." Three years ago, during the lockout, Daigle secretly enrolled in courses at the University of Ottawa, hoping to study administration. Had he not been advised to return to his junior hockey club in Victoriaville, he would have kept up the studies, delighting in the fact that, in the few classes he attended, no one had asked him a single hockey question. Perhaps it was because, when they went around the classroom and asked each student to talk a little about himself or herself, he told them he was a "dancer."

Harriet Bird—who shot Roy Hobbs in *The Natural*—would find a far different athlete in Alexandre Daigle, for it is he who is constantly asking the pivotal question of both the book and the movie: "Is that all?" It is for others to say he might have been better off if he had never signed that contract that branded him for life. Asked endlessly if he would do it all differently if he could, Daigle has always smiled and replied, "I would not be so foolish.

"My first contract was a big thing," he says. "But I never wished I'd never signed it. I'm twenty-two years old and I'm secure for life. In the long run, I'm a winner."

"Money," Jean-Yves Daigle had said, "is not the most important thing in life. The most important thing, *être heureux*—to be content."

Had it not been for money, Alexandre Daigle might never have found the contentment he came across almost by accident, and by paying dearly, two summers ago. He was coming off the worst season of his life. Five goals, a dozen assists, injury and ridicule. He wanted nothing to do with Ottawa, nothing to do with Quebec, nothing to do with friends or teammates or the omnipresent, inquiring media.

He flew to Los Angeles and checked into the Ritz-Carlton. He rented a car deliberately unlike his image—a green Cadillac Fleetwood. He hired a personal fitness instructor and became what he calls a "gym rat," working out obsessively. He put on muscle and weight. He went out and purchased the finest pair of Roller Blades that money could buy and put them in the trunk of the big Cadillac and began driving out to the boardwalks of Venice Beach and Marina del Ray, where he would strap them on and skate for miles in the sunshine.

When people stared at him, he felt they were looking at a different Alexandre Daigle, and he liked it. "They were looking at me," he laughs, "because I had good skates."

Not because he was the hockey player with the big contract. Not because he wasn't working out. Not because he was on the front of the sports pages. He made friends in California who knew nothing of hockey. He began to date different women. He started to see more of the actors and artists who lived there, and liked their company. And they liked him. "Alex has *entregens*," says Mailloux. "He's good with people. He's easy to approach."

He found he fit in there better than he had ever fit in anywhere before. Here were people who shared his passion for fashion—Daigle and Mailloux once made a "pilgrimage" to the Miami home of designer Gianni Versace, who was gunned down this summer in Florida—and who could talk about the things he was becoming interested in: design, museums, travel, film. He even began to fantasize of a second career: he would come back, he would take acting lessons, and one day he might even become a movie star.

"I'm fascinated by actors," Daigle admits now. He goes to movies and, on his own, studies film. He is intrigued most by those actors who take on a role completely, immersing themselves in the character they must play. "It can be a three-month project, just doing the research," he says. "Say you were going to be a policeman. You'd want to go out on patrol. You'd want to find out what it is to feel like a cop."

"In life," says Yannick Mailloux, "we all have an ideal, something we want to be. For Alex, it's not being a hockey player. He wants to be Alex. And Alex is different. And the Alex he wants to be doesn't fit the criterion of hockey player.

"He's so much more than Alex the hockey player."

There is something about this comment that does not wash well in Canada, where the value system is such that most parents would rather have their child grow up to play in the NHL than become a neurosurgeon. How could there be more, some will ask, than being drafted first overall and signing two consecutive multi-million-dollar contracts to play hockey? Because Alexandre

Daigle seems to want so much more, his own best friend has become convinced that Daigle will probably never become the player that was envisioned that June day in Quebec City when his name rang out first, and loudest, in the packed Colisée.

"I don't think so," says Yannick Mailloux. "Not because he doesn't have the talent to be a great player. He does. But it's deeper than that. If I tell you you're doing the greatest job in the world and you're getting paid a lot of money to do it, but in your mind it's not the greatest job in the world, well—if it's a problem for you, it's a problem. He wants to be so much more."

Now that Daigle has discovered that in himself, Mailloux says he will be like a "warrior" in pursuing it. He has seen it before with women; he sees it lately with learning. "Alex knows what he wants—and he knows how to get it."

As an example, he points to the highlight of Alexandre Daigle's fall, which had nothing to do with either scoring goals or winning hockey games. "I was watching the music awards on TV," says Mailloux, "and there was this guy on who looked a lot like Alex, I thought. Same style of clothes, same way of carrying himself. 'Maybe you should play an instrument,' I said to Alex. Next day I came back from school and there was a message on my answering machine. It was Alex: 'Yannick, I bought a piano—and I've already taken my first lesson!'"

"I believe we have two lives," she said.

"What do you mean?" Roy asked.

"The life we learn with—and the life we live with after that."

Alexandre Daigle never did become an NHL star. The Ottawa Senators eventually gave up waiting for him and, in 1997, traded him to the Philadelphia Flyers, where he started with a splash but soon faded. He played for the Tampa Bay Lightning and the New York Rangers before quitting the game in 2000 to seek out a career as a Hollywood film producer. In 2002 he returned to hockey, playing for the Pittsburgh Penguins and in 2003–04 probably had his best season with the Minnesota Wild, scoring twenty goals while performing as a defensively responsible forward under coach Jacques Lemaire. In 2006, with no further opportunities in the NHL, he left for the Swiss leagues, where he found success (twice winning the league championship) and, presumably, happiness.

THE POWER OF THE PEST: BRAD MARCHAND

(*The Globe and Mail*, April 23, 2011)

MONTREAL

He looks more like an extra in a theatrical production of *Oliver* than a National Hockey League player. He looks sort of, well, sneaky with those quick, darting, dark eyes and prominent nose. Listed at five-foot-nine but likely fudging, he seems tiny for hockey. Yet twenty-two-year-old rookie Brad Marchand could well be the best thing the Boston Bruins had going for them as they fought back to tie their best-of-seven playoff series with the Montreal Canadiens at two games apiece.

Even as the Bruins were losing the first two games in Boston, it was Marchand who was continually in the face of the Montreal players, Marchand who never stopped trying even when it seemed futile. Thursday night in Montreal, Marchand did the early lifting that ultimately turned the table.

Montreal was up 3–1 when he began creating problems along the boards and behind the net, his preferred work stations. First he set up defenceman Andrew Ference for a goal, then he flipped a puck from behind the net that forward Patrice Bergeron ticked in to tie the game. More than anyone else, he took the game from lost to opportunity, the Bruins winning 5–4 when Michael Ryder scored on Boston's very first shot of overtime. With just over twenty minutes, the rookie led all Boston forwards in ice time, and his three blocked shots were second only to defenceman Johnny Boychuk.

But there is much more to his game. Marchand is the sandpaper that grates, the mouth that distracts, the player even his own teammates call The Rat and, among themselves, The Little (expletive). He is to today's Bruins what Ken (The Rat) Linseman was to the Bruins of the 1980s: beloved teammate, despised opponent. Marchand takes pride in irritating the other side. "I always tried to," he says. "I wanted to. It was kind of my game. It gets me more emotionally involved, and when I do that, I play a little better."

When did this attitude begin? The Halifax native has become a "pain" to play against in his first year of the NHL, was a noticeable pain through two world junior gold-medal victories, and was known as a pain playing for three different teams in the Quebec Major Junior Hockey League. "All the way back to novice or atom," he says with a laugh. "I used to try to hit guys. I wasn't supposed to, but . . . it just kind of stuck with me."

He knows he sometimes pushes too far. As this regular season wound down, after scoring a short-handed goal against the Toronto Maple Leafs, he celebrated with an exaggerated golf swing—symbolic of the Leafs' lost season—and it cost him and his team. Not only did the riled Leafs come back and win the game in a shootout, but his coach, Claude Julien, tore a strip off him in the dressing room.

So far these playoffs, in four hard-fought games against the Canadiens, Marchand has picked up but a single minor penalty. He doesn't want to hurt his team. When they introduced him as part of the starting lineup for Boston, the Bell Centre crowd booed him louder than any other Bruin. He makes that much of an impression, just as fellow rookie P.K. Subban of Montreal gets the loudest boos in Boston and the greatest cheers at home. Both were considered candidates for rookie of the year, though neither made the final list of three. Marchand, however, outshone Boston's prize rookie and 2010's No. 2 draft pick, Tyler Seguin, this season, as Seguin has yet to dress for a postseason game.

Marchand and Subban were teammates when Canada won the world junior tournament in the Czech Republic in 2008. They're friendly but not close, perhaps because there is only room for one yappy irritant at a time on a team. "He's a good guy off the ice," Marchand says of Subban, "but everything changes when you're out there."

Even so, he acknowledges their kinship in spirit. "Some guys have it, some guys don't," Marchand says matter-of-factly. "It can work against you, though. You can get too caught up in it and then take penalties. At the same time, it's a lot of fun doing it and it can be effective."

So far, it certainly has been, without the usual negatives. He says he is aware of the costs of going too far. "I tend to get too emotional and I just kind of go," he says. "And whatever happens, happens." He was suspended in minor hockey, benched during the junior Super Series, reamed out in American Hockey League, all for acts he happily acknowledges were foolish and ill-considered. "Come playoff time," he says, "you do definitely have to watch yourself and watch how much you do, and if you cross that line. . . . You have to keep it in your head all the time."

Fortunately, he has help keeping it there: a mentor in forty-three-year-old Mark Recchi, who joined the Pittsburgh Penguins the year Marchand was born. "Any time he talks," Marchand says of Recchi, "everybody just quiets down and listens. He has an air about him. He said, 'I'll get upset with you, but it's not going to be about you missing a pass or you should have given it to me at this time or playing your position or little things like that."

Instead, Recchi "critiques" Marchand: where to go on the ice, how to behave off the ice. Marchand finds Recchi to be the equivalent of "another coach" on the ice, a father figure off. Recchi has even let him know when, during a game, it's okay "to chirp guys," meaning unleash the mouth and see if Marchand can draw someone into a penalty.

Whether the effect was all Recchi's guidance or not, Marchand had a year no one expected. Up for twenty games a year earlier, he had but one assist to show for his effort. Listening to Recchi, often playing with him, Marchand scored a remarkable 21 goals this year.

He had even told Boston general manager Peter Chiarelli that he'd reach 20 goals this year, something Chiarelli did not believe possible at the time. "I don't know if I believed it at the time," Marchand says. "I was just trying to say anything I could to get on this team.

"Thank God I did. I'd hate to have that hanging over my head."

With Brad Marchand continuing to play well, the Boston Bruins advanced to the 2011 Stanley Cup final, where they met the President's Trophy–winning Vancouver Canucks. Marchand scored nine playoff goals, a team record for rookies, two of those in the Bruins' Cup-clinching game-seven victory in Vancouver.

★ ★ ★ ★ ★ ★

SIX

BAR DEBATES

THE LIGHTNING-ROD COMMISSIONER
(*The Globe and Mail*, January 29, 2011)

NEW YORK, NEW YORK

Impossible not to think of Canada here on the fifteenth floor
of a building that sits, appropriately, on the Avenue of the
Americas.

Snowflakes the size of pucks are floating down this late January
day, turning everything from Times Square a block over to Central
Park, visible straight down Sixth Avenue, into a northern winter
delight. Canada's national game is on display everywhere—from
photographs of famous Canadian hockey players to replicas of
every name that has ever appeared on the Stanley Cup. There are
Inuit sculptures on the shelves and a coffee table that holds a handsome book on the Americans' northern neighbour that has been
signed "To a great friend of Canada—Stephen Harper."

The prime minister's great friend is none other than Gary
Bettman, commissioner of the National Hockey League these
past eighteen years and a figure who, not unlike Prime Minister

Stephen Harper, causes wildly fluctuating emotions among those he encounters. While the changes in the professional game Bettman oversees have been dramatic—new franchises created in the south, teams moved from Quebec City to Denver and from Winnipeg to Phoenix, the players locked out by the owners for the entire 2004–05 season, the game reinvented to reward skill and speed, a salary cap put in place, Gretzky and Lemieux replaced by Crosby and Ovechkin, Sidney Crosby sidelined with the game's current curse, concussion—Bettman himself seems barely to have changed at all since he took office in early 1993.

He remains, at fifty-eight, a trim, smaller man whose dark brown hair remains precisely in place as well as space. His dark suits are as much a certainty as Dick Tracy's. He speaks with hands that often pound points home with fingers. He moves with an agility fully recovered from last fall's arthroscopic surgery on his knee and, this snowy day in Manhattan, he is off to a hockey game between the New York Rangers and the Florida Panthers.

It is a see-saw game, fast and turning, the crowd in Madison Square Garden rising and falling with every goal, Florida with the lead gained and lost, then the Panthers winning on their own comeback. Fans all about leap to their feet, sag in their seats, scream and sigh as the game moves on. He watches carefully but, watching him, it would be impossible to tell what is happening on the ice or, for that matter, what is happening in his thoughts.

"I never cheer," he says. He has trained himself not to show emotion during a game. "I can't cheer. If I show emotion one way or the other, people get upset."

He does, however, from time to time attend NHL games as a "regular fan." It happens in New Jersey, close to where Bettman will sometimes take his four-year-old grandson—a Devils fan— to a match, the crowd unaware that the unshaven, sunglass- and cap-wearing man in jeans and an old sweater high-fiving with the little kid is actually the commissioner of the league.

This night, however, he is in familiar uniform: dark suit, crisp shirt, red tie. He sits where the fans sit, and when he moves through the crowds and corridors the reception is, to a Canadian, somewhat surprising. "Great job, Gary," a man cries out. A woman wants a photograph with him. "Love the product!" a man shouts as he passes by.

What would they shout in Canada? One man swilling a beer in one of the Garden corridor bars shouts sarcastically from a distance—"Where'dya play yer hockey, Gary?"—but all the rest in those most American of venues are polite and approving.

Bettman's image in the country that calls hockey its national game and treats it as national religion is, at times, as polarized as Sarah Palin's in the United States. He is blamed for everything from the demise of the Quebec Nordiques and the Winnipeg Jets to the league's endless debates on what to do about headshots, one of which is threatening the year, if not the career, of Sidney Crosby, Canada's golden Olympic hero. Bettman has been accused of denying Hamilton its chance at an NHL franchise when BlackBerry billionaire Jim Balsillie was rebuffed in attempts to take over the Pittsburgh Penguins, Nashville Predators and Phoenix Coyotes, potentially bringing an NHL franchise to Hamilton.

His applauders have been less vocal, but there are those who believe if not for Bettman, Canadian franchises might have been lost in Ottawa, Edmonton and Calgary, perhaps even Montreal and Vancouver as well. "The Canadian franchises as a group have never been stronger," he says. "Go back to the time period 1999 to 2001. There were tons of commentary, editorial articles suggesting there was only going to be one franchise [Toronto Maple Leafs] left in Canada. And that was something we could never allow happening. Canada is the heart and soul of this game, and this game is too important to Canada. If we couldn't be strong in Canada, we couldn't be strong anywhere.

"I knew that the first moment I took this job. I knew that *before* I took this job. I knew the history and the traditions and the relationship between hockey and Canada. I mean, people can talk about baseball or football in the United States [but] that pales in comparison to the strength of hockey in Canada, and the importance of hockey in Canada."

The franchises are indeed much stronger than they were a decade earlier, when it seemed only government intervention could prevent a number of the small-market northern franchises from going under. A combination of the league's Canadian team assistance plan and, most importantly of all, a quickly rising Canadian dollar to par or better with the U.S. dollar has created the reverse situation today: the Canadian teams, by and large, are the healthiest franchises.

Bettman says that the reason he and Harper, a hobby hockey historian, get on so well is that they "share an acknowledgment of the importance of the game to Canada—and the importance of Canada to the game." He stops short, however, of pledging to move the shakiest U.S. franchises to Canada should those teams fail completely. Harper, as any Canadian politician would, supports the return of the NHL to Quebec City and Winnipeg, which lost their teams in the dire financial years of the mid-1990s. Quebec fans have long hoped that the faltering Atlanta Thrashers might fly north, while Winnipeg has for some time now been perceived as the natural soft landing for the bankrupt Phoenix Coyotes, currently owned and run by the league as the search for a buyer continues. While conceding that Quebec City and Winnipeg would have priority should relocations prove the only solution, he cautions both cities not to get too excited by the prospects.

"We don't run out on markets," Bettman says of the long-standing situation in Arizona. "You only leave as an absolutely last resort. It will turn out all right, one way or the other." He remains convinced that the current negotiation will produce a new owner and a guaranteed future for the team in Phoenix. "But if it doesn't," he adds, then "we will have done everything humanly possible to make it work . . . All sports are at risk if you can't determine who can be a partner and where your franchises are located, because those are the two most important decisions that any sports league has to make."

That thinking, of course, was at the very core of Bettman's refusal to accept BlackBerry billionaire Jim Balsillie as a potential owner of several U.S. franchises, including the Coyotes. Balsillie believed that the market and, if necessary, the courts could decide who owned what where, but saw that argument derailed when the league itself elected to take up ownership of the foundering Phoenix franchise. In terms of where franchises are located, Bettman appears equally reluctant to entertain another team in Southern Ontario, despite the clear sense that the fan base is there and there are already three teams located in the Greater New York Area.

Further expansion seems unlikely under Bettman's time. "Everybody tells me we shouldn't dilute the talent base," he says. "There are also a lot of people who tell me we have more than enough talent to expand. My guess is there will never be a meeting of the minds of everybody on that subject."

He knows he will never be cheered in Canada—booing heads of sports leagues is part of fan ritual—but says the boos from the stands, not to mention the anonymous web attacks, are very much at variance with what he hears face-to-face with Canadian fans. They like "the product," as the man at the Garden shouted out. They like the "cost certainty" that came with the salary cap. They realize that the league is much healthier financially, with revenues soaring during his tenure to $2.9 billion this year from $460 million. They mostly like the new rules that opened up the game. And they like that NHLers now compete in the Olympics, of particular import to reigning gold medal winner Canada.

But he still gets it—and will get it again as these comments are dispersed. "I've developed a thick skin about it," he says. "You can't be thin-skinned and still do whatever you think is right." He is well used to the most common knock given to all in hockey who have never had their own rookie card—"Where'dya play yer hockey, Gary?"—and his answer is simple: "They don't pay me to play."

They do pay him, however, every bit as much as a top player: in the $7-million-a-year range. The multi-millionaire Gary Bettman is a far cry from the kid who used to pack a lunch, catch the subway and use his student card to land a fifty-cent by the rafters so he could watch basketball or hockey while doing his homework.

When he travels nowadays, it is with security—a reality that began during the earlier 1994 half-season lockout when player Chris Chelios angrily said Bettman should worry about his family and own well-being, as some crazed fan or a player "might take matters into their own hands."

He still ignites anger, though such veiled threats are no longer spoken. But he also inspires enough loyalty that senior staff have largely stayed with him over the years and the various league owners—traditionally individualistic and at times difficult—have stuck by him despite occasional flare-ups.

The greatest example of owner solidarity under Bettman concerns the situation in Phoenix, where the Coyotes (formerly the Winnipeg Jets) have bounced from box-office disaster to the courts to several different potential ownership deals. It was Bettman who convinced the owners that the league itself had to buy the team to prevent Balsillie from taking over the franchise and moving it.

"All sports is at risk if you can't determine who can be a partner and where your franchises are located," Bettman says, "because those are the two most important decisions that any sports league has to make."

While Bettman is master of the stock answers that usually match, word for word, what he said months earlier, he can at times become animated and spontaneous, even angry. It infuriated him that people were suggesting that it took a headshot to the likes of league superstar Sidney Crosby to cause the league to take the rising concussion issue more seriously. "I don't buy that characterization," he says. "In fact, in his case it was a collision." There was no penalty on the play when Washington's David Steckel caught Crosby's head after a whistle had blown in the outdoor Winter Classic, played New Year's Day in Pittsburgh. As such, Bettman argues, there was no criterion in place for further punishment or suspension.

"That was a consequence of a physical game," he says. "As long as body contact is encouraged, and our game is played at a high rate of speed, then you're going to have some consequence."

In his opinion, Rule 48 that the league put in place in 2010 after a series of controversial hits to the head has worked just fine. The rule banned lateral or blindside hits where the head is the primary point of contact, but stopped far short of the ban on all hits to the head, accidental or not, that other contact sports have and that a great many in hockey have called for since the Crosby injury. "We're still seeing more concussions than we'd like," the commissioner concedes.

He maintains, however, that the league's track record on dealing with concussions is good, with baseline testing of injured players beginning a decade or more ago. While further work needs to be done to increase the level of safety, the answer does not lie, he believes, in automatic and standard suspensions handed out by the league like parking tickets.

"The acts that need to be addressed by supplemental discipline are like snowflakes," he believes. "No two are alike. There are always some similarities, but the players' histories are different, the circumstances different, the nature of the incident different, the time of the game different. It's not susceptible to a template or a standardization where one size fits all."

He says he understands the criticisms and knows that this topic is volatile and emotional. The criticisms he will not accept are the personal accusations that arise with each suspension concerning the league's intentions and, at times, the impartiality of those dispensing the league's decision on justice.

"Don't challenge my integrity," he says, voice rising. "This is what we do. This is what I do and [deputy commissioner] Bill

Daly does and [league disciplinarian] Colin Campbell does. It is what we do and we do it with passion. You can't function if you blow with the wind.

"Why would you do anything but the right thing, or at least what you believe to be the right thing?"

The 2010–11 season proved to be one of Gary Bettman's most difficult years, with the Phoenix ownership situation unresolved, the Atlanta Thrashers foundering and a huge public outcry over headshots following the Sidney Crosby concussion. Bettman used the general managers' annual meeting in Florida in March to announce a five-step plan to address player safety, including a new testing protocol and steps to improve rink facilities and equipment. The league stopped short, however, of banning all hits to the head. While he may have lost some public support, he maintained the support of the owners who employ him, as they granted him a five-year contract extension. Shortly after, the Atlanta Thrashers conceded defeat and the franchise was moved to Winnipeg, striking a hard blow to Bettman's "southern footprint" strategy for NHL expansion.

"A MAN'S GAME"
(*The Globe and Mail*, February 12, 2011)

If hockey is truly "a man's game," then why are the games brought to us by Cialis and Viagra?

Erectile dysfunction appears to have become to the modern National Hockey League what Imperial Esso's "Happy Motoring" once was to the Original Six—Viagra plastered to the rink boards, Cialis wink-wink ads filling every stop in play on the television, Levitra promising you'll be ready to play should the coach tap you on the shoulder . . .

This has been another terrible week for the "man's game." Despite unprecedented criticism of professional hockey's unwillingness to address a matter that is threatening its players, the situation continues unabated: New Jersey's Anton Volchenkov suspended three games for a headshot to Zach Boychuk of the Carolina Hurricanes; Pittsburgh's Matt Cooke (hockey's serial offender) suspended four games for leaving his feet in an attempt to crush the cranium of Columbus defenceman Fedor Tyutin from behind.

It was a week in which one elite player, Marc Savard, packed it in for the season due to concussion, a week in which rumours spread concerning the game's most elite player, Sidney Crosby, possibly losing the remainder of what should have been his greatest season to concussion.

And it was a week in which one sensible player, Boston's Andrew Ference, was attacked on *Hockey Night in Canada* for daring to say a headshot delivered by teammate Daniel Paille on the Dallas Stars' Raymond Sawada was "a bad hit." A wonderful week, indeed, to head into the CBC's *Hockey Day in Canada*, in which the national game will be sentimentalized, lionized, glorified and worshipped.

It is a great game, but it surely needs some work. The problem is that headshots have become the global warming of hockey, a polarizing issue that pits the disbelievers against the believers, with no results to show for all the braying back and forth. *Hockey Night in Canada*, with its vast array of old-school thinkers, has become Fox News. The mainstream media, with their editorials demanding action against headshots, have become Al Gore. So nothing ever seems to get done.

The loudest shouting has come from the naysayers. Mike Milbury has groaned about the "pansification" of the game and dismissed those who disagree with him as "soccer moms." Don Cherry—who began his media career with *Rock'em, Sock'em* videos—blows a gasket over Ference speaking his mind, suggesting it breaks some imagined "code" of the sacred hockey dressing room.

The quieter voices are more numerous, but have gained little. The NHL did bring in a specific rule against blatant headhunting, but still lags far behind other team sports when it comes to offering protection for vulnerable brains. For weeks the debate has been about what happened to Sidney Crosby's head, whether the concussive blow was delivered, perhaps by accident, by Washington's David Steckel during the New Year's Winter Classic or by intent when Tampa Bay's Victor Hedman crushed him into the boards a few days later.

No longer. Instead of looking back, the hockey world now looks ahead: When will Sidney Crosby come back? Will he come back at all this year? He himself says he expects to, but can offer no date. "There's no timetable," he said on Thursday. "I hope I'm back."

So should the league. Crosby was in the midst of a seminal year. He was running away with the scoring race. He had just come off a twenty-five-game scoring streak when the first blow landed at the Winter Classic. His only serious rival over the past few years, Alexander Ovechkin, had been reduced to star status from superstar—of which hockey now had only one.

While hockey is a team game and golf an individual sport, comparing Sidney Crosby's impact on hockey in 2010–11 is not that much of a stretch from Tiger Woods's impact on golf in the years leading up to his self-inflicted blow to his image. When Woods departed the golf scene for a significant time, the PGA went into freefall in terms of interest and TV viewership. The falloff would not be so dramatic if Crosby were lost for the season, but it would be significant. The Crosby–Ovechkin storyline had been compelling for years; that storyline is, for the moment, lost.

It is no stretch at all, however, to compare Crosby's concussion problems to those of earlier players such as Paul Kariya and Eric Lindros. Kariya, it will be recalled, was on the cusp of

NHL superstardom when he was struck down. Lindros had reached NHL superstardom when he suffered the first of several concussions. Neither was ever to reach those heights again.

It could be, before all this is over, that Sidney Crosby's greatest contribution to the game will not be the Olympic gold medal–winning goal of a year ago, but his sad situation forcing the NHL—the braying naysayers included—to wake up to what hits to the head have done and are doing to hockey.

It's not a man's game at all. It's a child's game. And it is what has become dysfunctional.

LOST AT SEA: *HOCKEY NIGHT IN CANADA*

(*The Globe and Mail*, October 2, 2010)

"*Hockey Night in Canada* has become a program about itself." There is nothing new to this statement—apart from the fact, perhaps, that it has now been typed and printed—as it has been said now for some time by those who were once part of the CBC's flagship sports program and is often said by those still involved with it.

Think of the recent *HNIC* as the *Seinfeld* of TV sports, a program that, in the final analysis, is really about very little, at times nothing, but the characters, often outrageous, who come and go between commercials—or, in this case, between periods. If only it were as funny. It has become a program about itself, when it should be about the game.

No one—apart, perhaps, from nostalgic Toronto Maple Leafs fans—is asking the program to happily motor back to the era of Murray Westgate and Ward Cornell, but just as the iconic hockey show evolved over the years from 9 p.m. starts and the dreaded telestrator, it is time to rethink a program that is vitally important to Canadians but has clearly lost its way.

While the production values of the broadcast, including much of the play-by-play work, remain world-class, the package has become not only predictable but seems, at times, barely aware that viewers have tuned in to see a game. For some time now, the TSN package has been far more informative and, most significantly, far more on topic.

It is difficult to say what happened to such a once-venerable show, but something undeniably has over the past few years. The game invariably takes a back seat to the Don Cherry–Ron MacLean grand entry, to the ramblings of the Coach's Corner segment in the first intermission and to the views of new additions to the show who often seem so stuck in the game's past that, unbelievably, Cherry at times emerges as the voice of reason.

Cherry is a most difficult subject to address. His national popularity is undeniable, his humour, and that of his gifted partner MacLean, often quick. But he seems only vaguely interested in today's game and, despite the endless "I told you so's," has largely lost sight of how today's game is played. His sermons on kids getting themselves and their sticks out of the way of shots are now ancient strategy; today's defensive game is all about shot blocking, the goaltender often the last to see the puck. The program no longer reflects public taste when it comes to officiating. *HNIC* seems to hate the new rules, while polls have claimed 85 percent of fans embrace the crackdown on obstruction.

The listing of military and police tragedies on Coach's Corner is seen by some as an honest tribute by a sentimentalist who truly cares (my own view) and by some as a sly trick to ensure invulnerability from criticism. This facet of the show cannot possibly be addressed, deciphered and fairly dealt with in such short space, but it is still fair to say it is a reach from the show's mandate to bring the national game to a national audience.

Analysis, partly because of these heart-wrenching interludes, now falls to others. Recent additions such as Mike Milbury—Don

Cherry on training wheels—and the excitable P.J. Stock seem more out of the last century than this one. While regular panellist Pierre LeBrun brings superb reporting to the grouping—and the brief new media section offers welcome insight—too often the talk disintegrates into the tired "It's a man's game" chatter and National Hockey League Players' Association minutia rather than the striking and fundamental shifts the game has undergone since the lockout and the salary cap.

Where, many of us ask, is the analyst—imagine such articulate world players as Anders Hedberg or Igor Larionov—who can speak to the creative wonders that delight the imagination of all those youngsters who both play and dream the game: Ovechkin, Crosby, Kane . . . ? *HNIC* often doesn't even seem to like such young stars.

Where is the coaching voice—Ken Hitchcock, for example— who can articulate how it is that today's coaches seem more university lecturers than fire-and-brimstone preachers? Where is the calm voice of reason—such as my *Globe and Mail* colleague Eric Duhatschek—who is both knowledgeable and sensible and might take issue with those who, like Milbury, will speak of a head hit "as a thing of beauty?"

"If you don't like it," he once said, "change the channel." Unfortunately, we cannot. So please change the show.

In early 2011, in the midst of a public outcry against violence in hockey, Mike Milbury dramatically came out against fighting during a Hotstove *panel discussion. Milbury called for a full ban on fisticuffs and, very candidly, stated: "The only reason we have fighting in the game is because we like it."*

DEATH TO THE FOURTH LINE

(*The Globe and Mail*, October 6, 2010)

This is a perfect time to bell a hockey cat that has had far more lives than can ever be justified. The fourth line.

They try not to call them that anymore. Perhaps it's just not considered politically correct these days. Broadcasters tend to refer to the three forwards on the bottom rung of the team as "the energy line." This may be because the lesser lines, especially the fourth, tend to have the most media-friendly players on them, players sharp enough and experienced enough to know—and certainly with enough time on their hands eventually to realize, if it's not readily apparent—that their careers are as fragile as a solution to the Phoenix Coyotes.

Coaches being asked questions about their roster will say they do not have a "third" or a "fourth" line, as if they are somehow indecipherable from each other. If that were so—and it isn't—then how much better would "third" lines in NHL hockey be if the three players on it were chosen from the best of the six to eight roster spots currently available to make up the final two lines of a team?

The reality is that the typical fourth-liner in the NHL could be replaced with any one of, say, a thousand other professional hockey players around the world who had neither the contract nor the luck to land such a position. Or, if the sport would only do so, they could be replaced with . . . nothing.

If the modern exhibition season proves anything, it is that today's NHL players are in remarkable shape. They leap straight from summer into winter. And yet, as the pre-season games drag on, the central question (beyond goaltending) in the era of the salary cap almost invariably boils down to which single player, perhaps two, is going to crack the lineup—and usually so far down the lineup that those covering training camp have to check the media guide to find out where he came from and how his name is spelled.

This often amounts to more attention being paid to a player who will be on the ice for a handful of minutes or so a game than he will receive in a season of regular play. Think about it: Given that the players are in such good shape, how can it possibly be that a line that takes up three to six minutes of ice time a night is in any way a necessity? The three other lines would, and could, happily consume those rare shifts.

And even if an argument, however moot, can be made that spreading the ice time out among four lines keeps the other three lines stronger, what exactly is wrong with having periodically tired players on the ice? As the new rule on icing has shown, having a faceoff with fresh players on one side and gasping players on the side that iced the puck adds an intriguing element of possibility to games. If hockey is indeed, as they love to say, a game of mistakes, why not give us more mistakes that can become scoring opportunities?

The NHL roster is set at eighteen skaters and two goaltenders. We know from fluke experience—the Calgary Flames' problems with the salary cap and injury as the 2008–09 season wound down—that a team can get by with as few as fifteen skaters against eighteen, as the Flames actually won a couple of games with that shrunken bench. The ECHL sets rosters at a limit that eliminates the need for a fourth line. The American Hockey League had slightly smaller rosters but is at NHL numbers in order to have consistency between the mother club and the affiliate.

There are, as well, other advantages to shaving off that final line. Team payrolls would come down, in several cases by millions of dollars. The cap could be reduced, although experience tells us it would more likely result in even more money being made available to the Ilya Kovalchuks and other unrestricted free agents of the game.

Still, team costs would come down, not just in salaries, but in the care and feeding and travel of that unnecessary fourth line— perhaps even come down enough to cause a drop, however slight, in ticket prices. And finally, it would help clean up the game. Most fourth lines are merely support groups for the team enforcer. Someone has to skate out with the player on his way to the penalty box, so two healthy bodies are kept on the bench simply to skate out for the necessary faceoff before the fisticuffs begin.

All this is fanciful thinking. The National Hockey League Players' Association would never stand for the elimination of so many jobs: ninety if you simply lopped off the fourth line, but in effect far more as each team maintains plugs for their lower lines both in the press box and in the minors. If that many players retired at once, TSN would have to extend its sports panel to twice the length of an NHL bench.

However, it is a question often raised in morning-skate corridors and late-night bars. Some in the game say that the only possible modern rationale for a fourth line is to make it specialize in penalty killing, but this is a role easily transferable to other, higher lines. Recent champions—the Chicago Blackhawks, Pittsburgh Penguins, Detroit Red Wings—have all illustrated the benefit in having players who can actually play form the fourth line. But this equally argues in favour of dispensing with that fourth line in favour of creating a superior third line out of the multiple players otherwise available for two bottom lines.

Others in the game wonder if, in fact, the elimination of that fourth line would have any actual effect on the frequency of fighting in the game. "Even if they went to two lines," chuckles Jim Schoenfeld, former player and coach who is currently assistant general manager of the New York Rangers, "some team would find a way to put a tough guy on one of those two lines. And then everyone else would follow suit."

Perhaps so. Perhaps not. Either way, it all argues the same point: A fourth line is unnecessary.

PENALTIES THAT MEAN SOMETHING— NOW THERE'S A CONCEPT

(*The Globe and Mail*, March 31, 2008)

It never rains but pours. Even when we're talking about frozen water, it seems.

It was Friday evening, and a hockey-mad son and I were flicking through NHL Centre Ice in search of a match that, this time of year, can decide an entire season. It should be the best time possible for the national game. Yet never, it seemed, had the lame old joke "I went to a fight and a hockey game broke out" been more on display.

We dipped into the Thrashers–Hurricanes match and found Atlanta's Eric Boulton and Carolina's Wade Brookbank pounding on each other. We flipped to Flyers–Devils and caught Philadelphia's Randy Jones swinging away with New Jersey's Mike Mottau—the scrap barely over when the giddy announcers punched up video from a December match that showed Mottau whaling away on the New York Islanders' Mike Comrie. Over, later, to Vancouver at Minnesota and a third period with the Canucks' Jeff Cowan, Nathan McIver and Alex Burrows slugging it out with the Wild's Derek Boogaard, Brent Burns and Pierre-Marc Bouchard.

This, after a day in which the news was all about former Vancouver player Todd Bertuzzi suing former Vancouver coach Marc Crawford for allegedly ordering Bertuzzi to go out and make the Colorado Avalanche's Steve Moore "pay the price" for a previous hit on Vancouver's captain. Some "price"—Moore ended up with a broken neck from the notorious mugging and will never play again.

It was also a day in which YouTube and the sports highlight shows continually replayed the footage of junior goalie Jonathan Roy skating the length of the ice to rip the mask off another teenage goaltender and beat him into submission, to the apparent delight of his father and coach, Hockey Hall-of-Famer Patrick Roy—earning both Roys minor suspensions and causing the government of Quebec to demand that Quebec junior hockey clean up its act.

What is going on here?

The most intriguing development is the story out of Quebec, where the premier and the provincial minister of sport are telling junior hockey it must come up with a solution by June. Premier Jean Charest has further asked all other junior leagues in Canada to "undertake a reflection—and the message from Quebecers is that the moment has come to do away with fighting in junior hockey."

This has, obviously, reignited a debate that has gone on in this country longer than free trade. Hockey violence—a much broader brush than fisticuffs alone—has been tackled before by provincial governments, most particularly Ontario, with no discernible effect. It has also been debated for decades within the game itself. The great Muzz Patrick, who was Canadian heavyweight boxing champion long before a Hockey Hall-of-Famer, concluded that "fighting doesn't make any sense" more than half a century ago. In more recent times, such NHL general managers as Serge Savard ("Stop it altogether"), Glen Sather ("Our fans won't miss it") and Harry Sinden ("distasteful") have called for an end to fighting—all to no avail.

The players must have a safety valve in such a physical game, the defenders say—a preposterous position given that other games are just as physical and, besides, why is it always the same players who are blowing those valves? It's the only way we can sell the game in the United States, they say—an increasingly puzzling position given that the game, even with fights, has become a difficult sell in so many U.S. markets.

You'll never stop fighting in hockey, even the Quebec minister of sport admits. True, but you can still ban it. Fighting is not allowed in any other like sports, the critics of fighting argue, and they point to football, baseball, basketball and soccer as examples. Yet fighting does occur in football, baseball, basketball and soccer—even if not nearly so regularly as in hockey.

The difference is that these sports penalize it. Hockey, on the other hand, rewards it. There is no team punishment whatsoever for fighting in hockey—they simply pretend there is. Two players drop their gloves and pound away on each other, stopping play, and then are sent off for what is called a "major penalty." It is probably the silliest phrase in all of professional sport. There is, in fact, no penalty at all—play resumes with neither side shorthanded, as if the fights had never even happened.

Come contract time, the sluggers table those "majors" just as the skilled players table goals and assists. To use just one convenient example, Carolina's Wade Brookbank will be far more rewarded for his Friday night "major" than he will be for the single goal he has scored this season.

If, on the other hand, fighting were made a real penalty in hockey—say each team would play short-handed for the length of the penalty, as would happen if Brookbank had tripped Boulton rather than punched him—it would have the most profound effect on how the game of hockey is played. Punishment would be real and instant, rather than some later-date suspension that might or might not be handed down. Fighting would, in effect, no longer be allowed in hockey, the same as it is disallowed in all those other team sports.

It would still happen—but a lot more hockey games would break out than is currently the case.

The Quebec junior league did strike a committee to look into the issue of fighting. Instead of a full ban, however, the league chose to beef up its rules. Fighting continued.

HOW WAYNE GRETZKY RUINED HOCKEY
(Today, spring 1982)

This is the thought of a heretic, I know, but Wayne Gretzky could be the worst thing ever to happen in the National Hockey League.

The idea first came to me in the perfect place: a drafty, late-night dressing room in a small Ottawa arena. The idea—wacky as it at first sounds—struck hard, and the natural instinct was that such a notion, like some of the underwear in the place, deserved a good airing. Yet I kept it to myself. Why? Well, no one else was talking hockey. Two guys were bitching about who was supposed to have brought the beer. Someone else was recounting how some Brit thought to unfreeze his car door lock by warming it with his breath and spent the better part of an hour lip-locked to the side of his vehicle. How could hockey dare interrupt such intellectual discourse? So I let it pass.

Trouble is, no one talks true hockey anymore. All thanks to Wayne Gretzky. Last year this same Ottawa dressing room would have been full of Toronto Maple Leaf insults; this year, that sad story is about as compelling as the Canadian Constitution. Someone might have asked who'd be the best bet to build a hockey franchise around, and various names would have flown about, surely even that of Gretzky himself. Someone else might have argued that Mike Bossy is the greatest natural scorer the game has seen, and one of the old guys, surely, would have countered with Rocket Richard. But not anymore. Not since Gretzky.

No one cares anymore, see. Thanks to him, all hockey talk is suddenly completely academic. Canadian hockey has turned out to be no more mysterious a game than Rubik's cube, and now that it's been mastered, perhaps it's time to throw it out.

When Gretzky scored his 50 goals in 39 games, he settled once and for all an argument put forward by the Russians a full ten years ago: the NHL is not the be-all and end-all of hockey. Since the definitive 8–1 Soviet victory over the NHL's best in last year's Canada Cup, Gretzky has hammered away all season at the Soviet point that the top competition is not necessarily found in the NHL. Moving toward the end of the season more than 60 points ahead of any rival in the scoring race (leading, for heaven's sake, by more points than Toe Blake, Howie Morenz or Ace Bailey had in total when they won their scoring championships), Gretzky has forever removed any cause to ever again discuss hockey with friends in a heated manner.

After all, what's to compare? No Howe–Richard rivalry, no Hull–Mikita debate, no Esposito–Orr race. Wayne Gretzky himself admits he has had to turn to setting his own personal standards to pursue (100 goals this season, 200 points overall), and it has made him less like a true hockey player and more like a scratch golfer who argues he only goes out to play against the course.

One can't help but wonder where the rest of the NHL went in 1981–82. Wasn't there a big trade between Buffalo and Detroit? Didn't some Philadelphia Flyer punch a referee—grounds for a life suspension in more sensible sports—and get hit with a stunning $500 fine? Who cares?

Most of the true wonder of sports grows out of its unpredictability, and Gretzky has ruined even that. Picking up *The Globe and Mail* to read about his three goals and four assists the night before against Minnesota has become as predictable and enthralling as the morning's editorial against marketing boards.

Gretzky is simply not in the same league as the others in the league in which he plays. When Post cereals puts out its winter promotion "NHL Stars in Action" and the twenty-eight "exciting action cards" fail to include Gretzky, it is like a late-Saturday-night jukebox without Willie Nelson. Mike Bossy turned up in the box of Alpha-Bits we bought, and the kids couldn't have been less impressed. For them, hockey, a game played by six-man teams, has become a one-man sport. Nobody, not even Bossy, matters a hoot.

The only way to repair the shattered egos of the Bossys and Lafleurs and Dionnes and Clarkes is to get rid of Gretzky. Then there might be something worth arguing about once again. And it might not be that hard, either.

Gretzky is much too modest to say so publicly, but his history would seem to say he might be getting as bored of it all as we are of him. Always, right from the very first, he or his father has pushed for more competition. At fourteen, under tremendous controversy, he left Brantford for a Toronto team; at sixteen, he went to Sault Ste. Marie for Junior A; at seventeen, again under controversy, he turned professional in the World Hockey Association; and at twenty, after the merger of the two leagues, he was the only hockey player who mattered in North America. There were no more hurdles left.

Which is precisely why he should consider defecting.

And why not? The Stastny brothers left Czechoslovakia for more money. Gretzky could go the other way for more competition. He might even work his way up to playing with the likes of the great Moscow Spartak star, Sergei Shepelev, the only player ever to upstage Gretzky when he beat him out for the all-star centre position in the 1981 Canada Cup. Shepelev's five goals against Gretzky's one assist in the playoffs might have had something to do with it, or perhaps it was the way Shepelev swept around Denis Potvin and Larry Robinson as if they were practice pylons and scored—whatever, Gretzky could start low and work his way up, just as he has so many times in the past.

I've even found a team for him. It's on the Danube River in northern Yugoslavia, a town about the same size as his hometown, Brantford, called Novi Sad, where the Izokej Klub Vojvodina lost all twenty-eight of its matches last year by an average score of 17–2. It's a perfect deal. Gretzky needs a challenge and the NHL needs to get rid of him so he'll quit making them look so bad.

Then we can all get back to talkin' hockey.

I was obviously being facetious with this tongue-in-cheek piece, but it remains true that Wayne Gretzky changed hockey more than any player in history. It was his popularity in Los Angeles after the 1988 trade that led to a proliferation of franchises in the south—an event that many believe did hockey little good as it watered down the product and created a number of franchises that have not worked out or will not. When Gretzky retired in 1999, hockey slowly began returning to its senses as a largely gate-driven, northern sport, popular more in pockets of the United States than throughout the States as had been the dream in the early 1990s. The fact that Gretzky remained the world's best-known hockey player a decade after his retirement argues that this phenomenal talent, with an ability to transcend sports into celebrity, was more a blip on hockey's timeline than a permanent shift to major sports status and continued growth. He really had no peers when it came to the entire package: skill, marketability, celebrity.

RIDDLE WITHIN AN ENIGMA:
JUST HOW GOOD IS MARTIN BRODEUR?
(*The Globe and Mail*, April 30, 2009)

With the exception of horse racing, eighty seconds do not make or break a brilliant sports career. But they are bending it a bit in the case of Martin Brodeur.

In a year in which Brodeur's athletic accomplishments were roughly comparable to Secretariat's—first setting a record for total games won by an NHL goaltender, then chasing the career regular-season shutout record to within two blanks—Brodeur's dream season came to a grinding, rather humiliating halt in less than two minutes Tuesday night in front of a dumbstruck New Jersey Devils home crowd.

Right up until the 18:40 mark of the third period, it seemed entirely possible that Brodeur's amazing season might even include a record for playoff shutouts and even a Stanley Cup, his fourth during a fifteen-year career in which NBC Sports, the NHL's official U.S. network carrier, declared this winter, "It's a no-brainer — Brodeur best goalie ever."

Ever? Well, he didn't look it at times in the Devils' first-round game with the Carolina Hurricanes. It seemed a given that the Devils would be moving on to the second round when, first, Carolina's Jussi Jokinen scored on a one-timer that Brodeur couldn't cover in time. And then, with a mere 31.7 seconds to go until what appeared certain overtime, Eric Staal scored on what appeared a rather non-threatening wrist shot from the right circle — an almost identical goal to one Tuomo Ruutu scored in the opening moments of this critical game.

The Hurricanes called it a miracle. The media said it was one of the greatest comebacks of all time, but the goals were hardly deserving of such glory. It could be said, and will be said, that Brodeur could not be faulted on any of the goals, but it is equally true that goalies end up faulted on all goals. It's their job, after all, their only job, to keep pucks out. Vladislav Tretiak called goaltending the most "noble" position in all of sport. It is also the least understood — "not a job," the late Gump Worsley said, "that would interest any normal, straight-thinking human" — and, by far, the most critically examined.

Brodeur's impressive catalogue of accomplishments — Calder Trophy as rookie of the year, four Vezinas as the league's top goaltender, Olympic gold medal, World Cup championship, numerous all-star game appearances — always comes with an asterisk in any discussion concerning the best ever. His great fortune and misfortune as a goaltender is to have played all his career with the same team, the Devils, a franchise so dominated by the defence-first, -second and -third philosophy of general manager Lou Lamoriello that it would be easier, some nights, to do play-by-play on paint drying.

One could well relate to Hurricanes owner Peter Karmanos when, during Game 6, the cameras settled on him in the middle of an enormous yawn. Under such coaches as Jacques Lemaire, Claude Julien and, now, Brent Sutter, the suffocating style of the Devils has at times been said to be the real secret to Brodeur's numbers, at least as much as his own impressive abilities.

Hockey fans passionately debate Brodeur's status compared to Patrick Roy, whose regular-season total of 551 wins he passed this season, and Terry Sawchuk, who still holds, if only barely, the career record of 103 shutouts. Both were brilliant in their day, though fewer and fewer even recall Sawchuk's day. The brilliant goaltender died in 1970 following a scuffle with a teammate; he was just forty. His finest moment came in 1952, when he led the Detroit Red Wings to the Stanley Cup in the bare minimum eight games required, allowing a total of five goals and getting four of the wins with shutouts.

But others will argue for any number of stars from the distant and not-so-distant past, including the eccentric Dominik Hasek, who arrived in the NHL well into his career and who won six Vezinas and was twice chosen league most valuable player, an honour that has never gone to Brodeur. Nor has Brodeur ever won the Conn Smythe Trophy, which goes annually to the MVP of the playoffs.

Jacques Plante, Bernie Parent, Johnny Bower, Glenn Hall, Grant Fuhr, Billy Smith, Ken Dryden, Tony Esposito, Worsley, Tretiak . . . the list of the best ever is as long as fans wish to make it. So passionate are some to knock down competitors for the title there is even a website out there called brodeurisafraud.blogspot. com. On the other hand, the *New York Post* calls him "the Gretzky of Goalies" now.

Because of the sheer numbers, it usually comes down to Brodeur against Roy and Sawchuk, with both certain to trail the thirty-seven-year-old Brodeur—who still has three years left on his contract—before this is over. Roy was the mercurial Montreal

Canadiens star who delivered improbable Stanley Cups in 1986 and 1993 but who was testy, self-centred and, usually, a pain to deal with. Sawchuk was legendary for his sourness, his untimely death in a fight with a teammate at a team gathering as telling as anything that can be said about him.

"Toss a cup of rice at Terry and he'd catch it all," Randall Maggs quotes Ted Lindsay as saying in Maggs's powerful *Night Work: The Sawchuk Poems.* "But he could be one son of a bitch, and kept the others on edge."

Brodeur, on the other hand, is hockey's most easygoing, approachable goaltender, a rarity in that he happily talks on game days, and a media favourite in that he will still talk, even after a bitter loss. In that, he is likely the best ever.

But as for this year's performance settling any debate once and for all, forget it. That argument is less about best ever than it is forever.

On December 30, 2009, Martin Brodeur shut out the Pittsburgh Penguins 2–0 for his 105th career shutout, setting a new all-time professional hockey record. On April 6, 2010, he recorded his 110th career shutout and his 600th career win by defeating the Atlanta Thrashers 3–0. The New Jersey Devils, under new head coach John MacLean, launched 2010–11 disastrously, in dead-last place by Christmas. Brodeur was among several players taking blame for subpar play. After MacLean was replaced by Jacques Lemaire (back on the Devils bench for the third time), the team began a rise through the standings that very nearly took them into the playoffs. Brodeur played well in the new year, but his overall statistics remained disappointing. In May 2011 he turned thirty-nine.

NICKNAMES
(The Globe and Mail, December 11, 2010)

He declines to speak on the matter, it being a personal and rather sensitive issue. But Ron Hainsey, fine stay-at-home defenceman with the Atlanta Thrashers, has a problem with today's NHL—he can't get a nickname.

He cannot because, under current hockey nickname protocol, he already comes with one, there being no known diminutive for Hainsey and tacking on the *de rigueur* "y" or "ie" on Hainsey sounds, well, just a bit goofy. And so, Hainsey must live with the fact that he alone is nicknameless on a team that boasts a "Stewie" (Anthony Stewart), a "Laddy" (Andrew Ladd), a "Burmy" (Alexander Burmistrov), an "Eags" (Ben Eager), a "Kaner" (Evander Kane), a "Sopes" (Brent Sopel), a "Litts" (Bryan Little), a "Bolts" (Eric Boulton) and so on and so on down through the roster.

In modern hockey, if you know the last name, you can guess the nickname. "There's no creativity," moans Steve (Stumpy) Thomas, one of the last of the truly great hockey nicknames.

Thomas, now forty-seven, works as a player development consultant with the Tampa Bay Lightning following a shining twenty-year NHL career that included stints with a half-dozen teams including the Chicago Blackhawks and Toronto Maple Leafs. Thomas got his famous moniker when the Leafs called him up from the St. Catharines Saints during the 1984–85 season. He made the mistake of walking through the Leafs' dressing room in his undershorts and veteran Bill Derlago took one look at the short, stocky Thomas and announced to the rest of the team that the new rookie "looks just like a stump."

"I have never been able to shake it," Thomas says with a laugh. He immediately began answering to Stumpy fully aware that if he fought it, "they'd just come up with something more dastardly."

Thomas now works for a team where one of the game's most exciting new stars, Steven Stamkos, answers to "Stammer" and sometimes to "Hammer." The Lightning's other star, Martin St. Louis, is—prepare for it—"Louie." The lack of creativity Thomas mentions is endemic to hockey circles. Sidney Crosby remains "Sid the Kid" even as he enters veteran status. Alexander Ovechkin is "Ovie." Patrick Kane is a "Kaner," too.

Here, the modern Ottawa Senators are "Alfie" and "Spez" and "Kovie," a far, far cry from the Sens of old: "One-Eyed" Frank McGee, Frank (The Pembroke Peach) Nighbor, "Fearless" Frank Finnigan (also known as "The Shawville Express"), Fred (Cyclone) Taylor, Reginald (Hooley) Smith . . . Goaltender Percy LeSueur of the old Senators was dubbed "Peerless Percy" by Malcolm Brice, the sports editor of the old *Ottawa Free Press*, and it seems most of the great nicknames came about that way; the gift, desired or not, from the local sports press.

The great Montreal tradition of nicknames—Maurice (Rocket) Richard, Bernie (Boom Boom) Geoffrion, Jean (Le Gros Bill) Béliveau—all came from reporters. The last brilliant Montreal moniker came courtesy of *Sports Illustrated*'s Michael Farber, who was working for the Montreal *Gazette* when he happened to cover a game between the Habs and Leafs in Toronto. Goaltender André Racicot let in a goal on the first shot, the third shot and then a long shot, all early. Farber tabbed him "Red Light" and the name stuck.

Reporters weren't always particularly original—any player with Native heritage became "Chief," all Campbells became "Soupy"—but they were far superior to most of what passes today for clever.

Hockey had such a rich history of nicknames that it is hard to believe it was only a few years back that fans cheered or booed "Terrible" Ted Lindsay, "Fats" (Alex Delvecchio), "Moose" (Elmer Vasko), "The Entertainer" (Eddie Shack), "Shaky" (Mike Walton), "The Golden Jet" (Bobby Hull), "The Big M" and "Little M" (Frank and Peter Mahovlich), "The Roadrunner" (Yvan Cournoyer), "Suitcase" (Gary Smith), "The Hammer" (Dave Schultz), "Battleship" (Bob Kelly), "Knuckles" (Chris

Nilan), "The Grim Reaper" (Stu Grimson), "The Rat" (Ken Linseman), "Cementhead" (Dave Semenko) and on and on and on. There was a time when even the coaches had brilliant tags: George (Punch) Imlach, Clarence (Hap) Day, Hector (Toe) Blake, Fred (The Fog) Shero.

There are today precious few left—Teemu (The Finnish Flash) Selanne is forty but still playing for the Anaheim Ducks, goaltender Nikolai Khabibulin is at times still "The Bulin Wall" for the Edmonton Oilers—but none ever again to compare to Frank (Ulcers) McCool or Lionel (Big Train) Conacher.

There is hope, though, however faint. Christian, the son of "Stumpy" Thomas, is playing for the Oshawa Generals of the OHL, pegged to one day follow his father into the NHL. That would be Christian (Stumpy) Thomas.

"He's got it now," the original says with a smile.

NET ANALYSIS: ECCENTRICITY OR GENIUS?

(*Ottawa Citizen*, November 30, 1996)

Goalies used to be dismissed as eccentrics and buffoons, clowns of the crease. Now they're hired as analysts. What happened?

It is noon at the Corel Centre, and Curtis Joseph, the star goaltender of the Edmonton Oilers, and Jim Ralph, the retired goaltender turned broadcaster, are sitting in a tight corner of the visitors' dressing room, speaking in a language only fellow goaltenders will understand.

"We got a great scam going," says Joseph, laughing.

"One of these days people are going to cotton on," adds Ralph, chuckling. "And then it's all over for all of us."

But it will not be for a long time. For whatever reasons—and there more reasons than there are goaltending styles—the goaltender seems to have evolved to a higher evolutionary plane than other hockey players. They are presumed by the media to be smart and are quoted widely. They retire and move, seemingly effortlessly, into broadcasting positions until it seems, sometimes, as if the entire world of hockey analysis belongs to old goalies.

Ralph, who hosts the Molstar broadcasts of Ottawa Senators games, is but one of several. Former NHL goaltender John Davidson, who does colour on New York Rangers telecasts, is the most widely recognized on-air hockey personality in the United States. Greg Millen, who played for six different teams, now seems to work for as many broadcast outlets, from *Hockey Night in Canada* to the NHL's own cybercasts. Former Chicago goaltender Darren Pang works extensively for ESPN and other American broadcasters. John Garrett, who played for Hartford, Quebec and Vancouver over a six-year NHL career, is a mainstay of the *HNIC* Western broadcasts. Brian Hayward, who played eleven years in the NHL, was a surprising and refreshing counter to Don Cherry this past spring during the CBC's telecasts of the 1996 Stanley Cup playoffs.

It didn't used to be this way. The current image of the NHL goaltender as articulate, glib, informed, analytical and smart is in sharp contrast to all the notions that preceded this recent development. In past generations, goaltenders used to be known for everything but. They had spectacular nicknames: Frank (Ulcers) McCool, Tiny Thompson, Frankie (Mr. Zero) Brimsek. They got caught up in silly stunts: Toronto's Turk Broda sitting Buddha-like on a weighing scale. They were renowned for their eccentricity: Jacques Plante knit his own underwear; Gary (Suitcase) Smith insisted on showering between periods.

There was Gump Worsley, with his Yogi Berra demeanour and ability to supply the game-stopping quote. (Asked which team gave him the most trouble, the New York goalie didn't bat an eyelash as he answered "the Rangers.") There was Johnny Bower, going on national television to sing "Honky, The Christmas

Goose." There was Gilles Gratton, streaking about the ice during practice with nothing on but his goalie's mask and once telling reporters that his injury was so old it dated from the Spanish Inquisition, when he was caught in battle in a previous life.

Now goalies are erudite, quotable, admirable, sensible, poised. What on earth happened? "Everyone was a buffoon back then, kind of," says Ken Dryden, the former Montreal Canadiens' goaltender who is now an admired author and social commentator. "Nobody used to talk. The interviews we used to hear on radio and TV were all pretty bad."

Dryden points specifically to the cast-in-concrete image of the late Jacques Plante as a raving eccentric, when he was known by his cohorts as one of the game's brightest thinkers. The beginning of the change in perception dates, in no small part, from the publication of Dryden's seminal book *The Game* in 1983. Here was an athlete not only writing entirely by himself, but writing magnificently, showing an understanding of the game—and the position— not previously available.

"Because the demands on a goalie are mostly mental," Dryden wrote,

> it means that for a goalie the biggest enemy is himself. Not a quirk of size or style. Him. The stress and anxiety he feels when he plays, the fear of failing, the fear of being embarrassed, the fear of being physically hurt, all the symptoms of his position, in constant ebb and flow, but never disappearing. The successful goalie understands these neuroses, accepts them, and puts them under control. The unsuccessful goalie is distracted by them, his mind in knots, his body quickly following.

Dryden, in fact, was a trailblazer for those netminders who would later move on to broadcasting careers. The U.S. network ABC hired him to work the Olympics, and the fact that he fit in quickly and easily is, he says, readily understandable: in a way, they've already done it.

"In the post-game," Dryden says from his home in Toronto, "you go to the scorer and the scored-upon. You go to the scorer maybe every second night or so. But you go to the scored-upon every night. When you're a goalie, you get practised at being able to talk about it." That goaltenders would end up as analysts and colour commentators seems, to Dryden, only a natural progression: "The broadcast booth in baseball is filled with pitchers and catchers. In football, it's the quarterback. These are the people who see the whole game."

"Basically," says Greg Millen, "there are three things that come into play. One, when you're a goaltender, you're a focal point, so you're used to dealing with the media on a daily basis. Second, your personality is such that you chose to be a goaltender because you wanted to be the centre of attention. And third, the game is always in front of you. A big part of being a goaltender is the ability to anticipate, to read how a play is going to happen. Fans can see how a play can happen. They want to know why it happens."

"It's because of what you see," says Jim Ralph. "You see the whole game. And you spend a lot of time sitting around watching the game."

Ralph believes a number of factors come into play. Goaltenders shout at their defence to do certain things, meaning they have to anticipate flow and solutions. Goaltenders share "scouting reports" on shooters. Goaltenders spend enormous time "visualizing" how a game will be played. All that and this, he smiles: "We think we are smarter."

Ralph, like the others, says the goaltender's personality cannot be underestimated. "It's what Dryden was getting at in his book: Does the personality get attracted to the position or does the position form the personality?"

"Goalies are different," was what Dryden wrote.

Whether it's because the position attracts certain personality types, or only permits certain ones to succeed; whether the experience is so intense and fundamental that it transforms its practitioners to type, I don't know the answer. But whatever it is, the differences between "players" and "goalies" are manifest and real, transcending as they do even culture and sport.

Make no mistake: they are different. Goaltenders form almost a secret society within the hockey world, so caught up in their own world that they have virtually created a second one for themselves on the Internet, where sites for "hockey goaltenders" number close to nine thousand and where the discussions about personality and preparedness can sometimes reach into the mystical.

"Our position," says goaltending instructor Paul Fricker, who calls himself "The Goalie Doctor" on the World Wide Web,

is truly played against ourselves, rather than the other team. The players on the other team are just there to give us or deny us what we need from playing goal. A real goalie (regardless of the stock answers we hear in the newspapers and on the TV) plays for one reason: to be the star, the centre of attention. In another word, ego. We all play goal to fulfill our need to be wanted, appreciated, needed, etc.

A hockey goaltender, Dryden wrote back in 1983,

is more introverted than his teammates, more serious ... more sensitive and moody ("ghoulies"), more insecure.... [A] team allows a goalie to sit by himself on planes or buses, to disappear on road trips, to reappear and say nothing for long periods of time, to have a single room when everyone else has roommates. . . . What these qualities suggest is a certain character of mind, a mind that need not be nimble or dexterous, for the demands of the job are not complex, but a mind emotionally disciplined, one able to be focussed and directed, a mind under control.

Used to the pressure of their position, they find the pressure of the camera and deadlines relatively simple. "If you lose," Frank (Ulcers) McCool, who played in the War years, once said, "the fans blame the goalie and the reporters take up the cry. After a while, the other players believe what they read and the goalie feels like it's one man against the world . . . Pretty soon, the goalie feels like an outcast."

But no longer. Today they are the first ones the media goes to for an explanation of what happened, and perhaps because of this increasingly cozy relationship, the first ones the media managers go to when an opening arises in the hockey broadcast industry.

One almost certain to head there some day is Boston's Bill Ranford, who says, "I'd love to do that when I'm done playing." His reasons are much the same as the others'—a chance to stay with the game, a second career, a natural outlet for his easygoing, articulate nature—but he inadvertently lets slip one of the best-kept goaltender-broadcaster secrets.

"Goalies figure they're always the scapegoat for all the times the team blew a game. This is their chance to get back."

By 2011, the proliferation of goaltenders as analysts and panellists was even greater, though former enforcers and fourth-liners were giving goalies a good run for the money in the broadcast world. It continued to baffle as to why there were so few highly skilled former skaters in the booths—and no European-trained players whatsoever, despite the fact that many of the most interesting hockey thoughts expressed in the English language were coming from those speaking it as a second or third language.

THE MONOTONOUS SAFETY OF CLICHÉS
(The Globe and Mail, May 21, 2007)

I have been rendered unconscious. It has now been more than a month since the Stanley Cup playoffs began and we have yet to hear an original thought.

"Is the first goal important?" the media want to know. Presumably, in a game in which a 1–0 score is not at all unusual, it is.

"Your best players have to be your best players," the coaches tell us and, presumably, if they weren't they wouldn't be.

"So long as we stick to our game plan we'll be all right," the players say. I have long given up the obvious follow-up to that comment—"And what, pray, is that game plan?"—because, well, they don't know, but it sure sounds good.

Hockey is a terribly simple game complicated by error, and in this way it largely defies analysis beyond "stuff happens." A "game plan," fancy as it might sound, amounts to the team deciding to send one player or two players into forecheck. The rest is all speed and skill and pucks flipping like coins—luck, more than anything, determining the heads and tails of an outcome involving two largely equal opponents. But the games—and even more so, the days between games—demand words. The media insists; the water cooler demands.

"We just want to take it one game at a time," the players say, although with June fast coming on we sure do wish there was an alternative.

"We don't want to get too high or too low," players say after wins as well as losses, though the post-series dressing rooms suggest it is impossible to get any higher or lower.

"It is what it is," someone will say and someone else will nod, though no one has a clue what this phrase means.

"Talk to us about . . . ," someone will say, inserting whatever fits at the end of the sentence—a particular player, the power play—and essentially conceding that there is, in fact, no question to ask when there is really no answer to be given. The old clichés persist: we have to bring our "A" game . . . we had our chances . . . we out-chanced them . . . they'll have to regroup . . . we need to play desperate . . . we have to stay focused . . . obviously . . .

There are also new clichés being born before our very ears: Players checking successfully now have "quick sticks," as if the sticks—not the players—have somehow taken over the task; fourth lines are now called "energy lines" so as not to hurt the feelings of those players who simply are not good enough; goaltenders now stay in "the paint" instead of in the crease; long breakout passes—hardly a new invention—are now called "stretch passes"; and digging in the corners now involves something called the "half-boards."

All this, of course, is in the sportswriter's attempt—and I myself am guilty—to make more of an extremely simple game ("He shoots, he scores") than should be necessary. Yet what makes it necessary is that sports channels now have as many panels as Ottawa and Washington politics and the demands of the media, particularly between games, are so immense that "filler" is required both in content and conversation.

It has reached the point this year where several times I have heard the word "plethora" applied to hockey—a word that had those of us covering the 1979 federal election rolling our eyes every time Joe Clark hauled it out. I still have no idea what it means.

Ken Dryden, who has experience in both hockey and politics, says it is perfectly understandable that clichés and catchwords and catchphrases should dominate in both cultures. There is great safety in saying nothing, great danger in actually saying something. "It's why athletes sound dumb and why politicians sound dumb," Dryden said over lunch at last December's Liberal leadership convention. "There's not much upside, and a very big downside."

Clichés, says Dryden, are controlled. "They're sort of acceptable—and they don't lead to something else that may get you into trouble."

Trouble is when a coach might accidentally use the word "choke" even if casually discussing a lunch that didn't go down particularly well. Trouble is one player on one side daring to suggest the goaltender on the other can be had.

Trouble is a politician admitting a mistake rather than accusing the opposition of being on "a fishing expedition." It's why politicians promise their campaigns will "focus on the issues" and then focus on nothing but personality. It's why they promise "change" but shy away from "reform."

It's why they speak inanely of "going forward" without the foggiest notion in which direction forward lies. It's why "at the end of the day" the late-night news is almost invariably no news at all.

It's why, after years of covering both sports and politics, I've come to think the main difference between the two worlds is that politicians don't have numbers on their backs.

No question about it.

New phrases continue to take on new life until they have long since been beaten to death by tongues. The current fad in the hockey world is to say "moving forward" at least once a sentence. As if there were any other direction to go . . .

SUPERSTITION: THE ULTIMATE INTANGIBLE
(*The Globe and Mail*, April 14, 2007)

He probably has no idea what he is sitting on. But if Sidney Crosby were to stand up and raise the plywood seat in the locker stall he has been assigned in the Scotiabank Place visitors' dressing room, he would find something remarkable. At the very bottom, below all the extra pads and tape and assorted hockey detritus, he would see that someone has taken a Sharpie pen and written: "Wayne Gretzky sat in this stall during his final game in Canada, April 15, 1999."

And it is here that Sidney Crosby sat for his very first National Hockey League playoff game in Canada, April 11, 2007.

Some kid, likely here for a minor-hockey tournament, has scribbled his own name in red ink over the makeshift plaque. His first name is Michael. His last name is Crosby. Coincidence? A sign? Who would dare say on Friday the thirteenth, the day before Crosby's young Pittsburgh Penguins attempt to even their Eastern Conference playoff series against the more experienced Ottawa Senators.

One game into the series and already superstition is at play. The Senators have declared nearly half of their far-larger dressing room off-limits to all, whether media or players. No one, absolutely no one, is allowed to tread over the huge Senators logo on the carpet.

The Penguins have their own eccentricities. The team began its stay in Ottawa by posting all the news clippings of the day on the wall back of the workbench—stories of the miracle year this team has had, stories of the amazing young stars such as nineteen-year-old Crosby, eighteen-year-old Jordan Staal and twenty-year-old Evgeni Malkin.

The morning after the Penguins fell 6–3 to the Senators in a game that was nothing short of embarrassing for the young stars, the clippings wall had vanished. And already, only one game into the post-season, the playoff beards are sprouting. Crosby says he hopes his amounts at least to a moustache by the time the end comes, whenever it comes. Young Ottawa defenceman Anton Volchenkov rubs his face and shakes his head in disappointment: "I'm trying, but that's it."

"You noticed!" twenty-four-year-old Colby Armstrong, Crosby's winger and close friend, shouts in triumph as a reporter remarks on the tiny stubble forming below the player's chin. "This is my first playoff beard. I've never had one before. I've only got a few hairs coming up, but there's a couple there that I'm just going to let go."

It is a time for insanity, but not time yet for the depths to which the madness of superstition can sometimes sink and will very likely sink somewhere, on some team, before the four long rounds of the Stanley Cup playoffs are through.

The first time the Senators reached post-season play back in 1997, they threw their faith not in their coaches, not in the crowd, not in their goaltender—but in a tiny wooden Buddha that forward Tom Chorske had picked up in a San Francisco souvenir shot. "Buddha Power" became the clarion call of those young Senators, the equipment manager charged with making sure Chorske carried the tiny statue around in his shaving kit as the inexperienced team took the Buffalo Sabres to seven games before losing the final match in overtime.

The following year, when the Senators reached the second round, they transferred their faith over to the dyed platinum-blond hair of goaltender Damian Rhodes, and rode this strange talisman for eleven games before losing to the Washington Capitals.

The modern Senators may never have gone that far in the play-offs, but they have proved to be one of the more superstitious groups over the years. They once began playing with Lego parts in the dressing room in the belief it would make them all better team-builders. They have in the past switched to their third jerseys for road games in the hopes that a change of cloth would bring them better fortune. The coaching staff once tried to bring an end to a regular-season slump by holding a seance in the train-ers' room, complete with candles to help them call on the ghosts of One-Eyed Frank McGee, King Clancy, and Fearless Frank Finnigan. It didn't work. One goaltender—and we shall spare him the humiliation of using his name—refused to change his underwear during one playoff run that, perhaps fortunately, came to a quicker-than-expected end.

The greatest Senators superstition came about by accident. Forward Bruce Gardiner was once in such a terrible scoring slump that he dramatically marched his stick into the washroom and tried to flush the blade down the toilet. When he went back out on the ice and quickly scored a goal—and began scoring fairly regularly for a while—he never began a game without first going to the toilet. The stick flush has to rank among the great hockey superstitions of all time, right up there with the Philadelphia Flyers bringing in Kate Smith to sing "God Bless America" instead of the national anthem before must-win games. When Smith died in 1986, the team still brought her back—in video form singing from the scoreboard screen.

Back in 1952, a local seafood merchant carried an octopus into a Detroit Red Wings playoff game and tossed it onto the ice from the stands. He said the sea creature's eight arms stood for the eight victories then required to win the Stanley Cup. The tradition somehow survived expansion and the octopus, despite the sixteen victories now required to claim the Cup, remained an annual tradition.

Making sense is not a requirement in hockey superstitions, despite the reaction of the Pittsburgh reporter who took one look at Ottawa's carpet logo and rather appropriately growled: "If they don't want anyone to step on it, why didn't they put it on the wall?"

Former NHL head coach Fred Shero used to carry rosary beads during games, though he was not a Roman Catholic. Former Toronto Maple Leafs coach Red Kelly once convinced his players they would perform better with "pyramid power" and began placing small pyramids beneath the bench. Punch Imlach, another Leafs coach, once wore a hideous sports jacket throughout the 1967 playoffs and believed if he ever failed to wear it, the Leafs would lose. They won that year—but have not since. Perhaps now it is the curse of the ugly jacket.

We have barely touched on goaltenders: the late Jacques Plante claiming he played better in underwear he himself had knitted, Patrick Roy talking to his posts and refusing to skate over any of the lines on the ice . . .

But if the Hockey Hall of Fame ever devotes a section to hockey superstitions, it will star a non-goaltender, Phil Esposito. The former Boston Bruins star used to flip out if someone accidentally crossed sticks in the dressing room. He had to wear an old turtleneck, inside out, every game. He would not stay in a hotel room that had the number 13 anywhere on the door. His game gum had to come from a brand-new pack. During the anthem he had to say the Lord's Prayer, as well as several Hail Marys. He once had so many lucky charms and rabbits' feet and four-leaf clover key chains hanging in his locker he had trouble finding his equipment.

The team that would be represented in that special section would be the Edmonton Oilers of the glory years back in the mid- to late 1980s. Gretzky was among the worst, always dressing in precisely the same order from shin pads to gloves. He had the equipment manager carry a supply of baby powder, which he would sprinkle on his taped sticks to "soften" the passes. He had to deliberately miss the net to the right in the warm-up and after the warm-up, have a Diet Coke, a glass of ice water, a Gatorade and a second Diet Coke before he was ready to play.

The Oilers would stand and "boo" the other team's starting lineup as head coach Glen Sather read out the names. They had to slam the butt ends of their sticks into a steel door that led to the video room as they passed it on the way to the ice. Equipment handlers Barry Stafford and Lyle (Sparky) Kulchisky used to have icemaker Trent Evans give them a bottle filled with water taken from the snow scraped off the Edmonton ice, and before playoff road games they would sprinkle some of this "holy water" on the ice surface of the enemy rink.

Five Stanley Cups later, who could argue? And Evans, remember, was the icemaker who buried the "Lucky Loonie" at centre ice in Salt Lake City at the 2002 Olympics, thereby initiating one of the game's most enduring superstitions.

Most of today's players have their own, though some are reluctant to speak of personal superstitions. "I have lots," Ottawa fifty-goal-scorer Dany Heatley said, "but none I'm going to let you know about."

"I have habits but no superstitions," Ottawa captain Daniel Alfredsson said. "If I feel I'm getting superstitious, I'll change. So I guess I'm superstitious about not getting superstitious."

Armstrong, on the other hand, has them and has no fear of talking about them. When the players leave the dressing room, he says, he can't move until Penguins teammate Ryan Whitney gets to where Armstrong stands waiting. "We don't even do anything," Armstrong said with a laugh. "I just wait for him. That's all. That's it. It's stupid."

Maybe so—but just maybe as well . . .

THE CASE AGAINST DECEMBER BABIES

(*Ottawa Citizen*, December 26, 1990)

This column must be written, but it is hoped that, at least until January 1, its contents will be banned from the nation's maternity wards.

The idea of some highly ambitious hockey nut sitting around with the paper while he waits for the doctor to announce "It's a boy!" is just too much to bear. If he reads what Roger Barnsley has to say, he'll find out he completely blew it. The chances of having a November or December baby boy make the National Hockey League aren't all that much better than the chances of having a November or December girl make it.

In fact, according to Barnsley, the most important contribution Canadian parents can make to their child's hockey career has nothing to do with the top line of skates, the best equipment or even power-skating classes.

It's to mess around on April Fool's Day and pray for a New Year's Day baby.

Dr. Roger Barnsley is the dean of education at St. Mary's University in Halifax, and he's been fascinated by the relationship between date of birth and performance since that evening in 1983 when he talked his wife, Paula, into going off to a Broncos junior game while both were at the University of Lethbridge. Growing rather bored with the game, Paula Barnsley began reading the program for something to do, and it struck her as curious that the vast majority of the players from both teams had been born in the early months of the year. The Barnsleys' own two sons, both born late in the year, were involved in hockey but hardly succeeding, and it struck the mother, a psychologist, and the father, an educator, that there just might be a connection here.

There was. It has now been five years since the Barnsleys and Dr. Gus Thompson published their first scientific paper on the phenomenon. Their hunch is now irrefutable fact: approximately four times as many junior and professional hockey players are born in the first quarter of each year than in the last quarter.

Just for the record, Wayne Gretzky's birthday is fast approaching: January 26. In the years since, the Barnsley-Thompson argument has been further refined. By studying minor hockey they have been able to demonstrate how those children born in the early months of the hockey year (beginning January 1) are the ones who remain as participants, while those born in later months tend to be the ones who drop out.

It is highly disturbing news for all parents, for Roger Barnsley has grown increasingly fascinated with the thought that his "relative age effect" may be showing up in another childhood endeavour that also uses January 1 as the cut-off date. School. In fact, the longer Barnsley looks at school, the more it takes on all the obvious flaws of the minor hockey system. Schools stream children according to ability—or apparent ability. Both have tier levels tied to advancement.

Here's how he sees it working: children are judged less bright when the reason they are progressing more slowly is that they are younger, and so they end up in the slow kids' class where no one expects much of them, whereas older, more developmentally advanced children are put into the bright kids' class, where they receive praise and are expected to do well.

Barnsley has been thinking of solutions. In hockey, he talks about altering the cut-off dates each year and working in new measures like height and weight. In school he pines for the one-room "open" classroom that showed a far greater tolerance for differences among students. But don't look for changes to come quickly. Hockey, in fact, has gotten worse since Paula Barnsley opened her Broncos program back in 1983. And schools are only now becoming aware of how long a year is to a six-year-old.

In fact, maybe this column should be kept from everyone— not just hockey loonies—who find themselves racing off to the maternity wards so late in the year. They obviously don't understand the first thing about family planning in the newly competitive world.

★ ★ ★ ★ ★ ★ ★

SEVEN

BEHIND THE BENCH

THE COURAGE OF ROGER NEILSON

(*The Globe and Mail*, May 10, 2003)

OTTAWA, ONTARIO

There were no white towels waving over Rideau Hall yester-day. But it would have been a lovely touch—considering that they are playing for Lord Stanley's Cup these days and the man who raised the first white towel in a playoff game was inside being honoured.

Perhaps the towels were missing because they weren't quite sure it was really Roger Neilson at the door. He was, after all, wearing a pressed dark suit rather than his usual rumpled jacket and no socks, with only an outrageous starburst of a necktie to identify hockey's most eccentric and innovative coach.

Now, however, there will be something to distract the eye from his legendary ties—the Order of Canada pin.

The sixty-eight-year-old Neilson was presented with the honour yesterday by Governor General Adrienne Clarkson, 110 years after Governor General Lord Stanley's famous trophy was first presented to the best hockey team of the day—and the day before Neilson's own Ottawa Senators, the only Canadian team remaining, open the third round of the Stanley Cup playoffs.

The ceremony was witnessed by a few of Neilson's closest friends. The lifelong bachelor, who has been battling cancer for the past three years, claims to have no known living relatives—unaware, perhaps, that he is considered family by everyone who has ever played for him, coached with him, attended his hockey schools or simply bumped into him in a hockey rink or, for that matter, even in one of the absent-minded driver's multiple fender-benders.

The official ceremony had to be rescheduled after Neilson was felled by a bout of pneumonia that struck after a late January trip to South Florida for the National Hockey League's All-Star weekend. Already weakened from treatment for the two cancers he suffers from, melanoma and multiple myeloma, Neilson had run into travel delays that exhausted him and allowed him to spend only the first period behind the bench as he and fellow Ottawa assistant coaches Perry Pearn and Don Jackson coached the Eastern Conference YoungStars to an 8–3 victory over the West.

"I only watched a few minutes," Neilson joked at the time. "Too much offence."

Neilson was honoured with the Order for his dedication to the game—he began coaching at age seventeen and has held head-coach positions with eight NHL teams, including the Toronto Maple Leafs and Vancouver Canucks—but it is his commitment to defence that has earned him special status in the hockey world. He was the NHL coach who perfected the infamous "neutral-zone trap," mastering it while building the expansion Florida Panthers into a team that would go to the Stanley Cup final the year after he was fired—the only firing, he says, that caught him completely by surprise.

"The trap," Neilson once said, "is the most misunderstood

system in sports. It's just positional play where you try and stop the other team from getting over centre."

A former goaltender, Neilson became a master innovator in a game that prefers tradition. He once put a defenceman in net for a penalty shot (now illegal) and is responsible for more rule changes in hockey than anyone alive. He was first to use video equipment—picking up the nickname Captain Video—and "breaking down tape" is now considered an essential coaching technique.

Neilson is famous in hockey circles for using his dogs to illustrate plays. While coaching in the junior leagues, he would bring his mongrel, Jacques, out onto the ice to demonstrate to young defencemen the futility of chasing behind the net to get to a puck handler. Dog and coach were so close that when Jacques grew feeble, Neilson took to pushing him about in a supermarket buggy.

Eccentricity has also long been a trademark. Ottawa Senators staff joke about how he can get lost driving from home to rink and shake their heads over the number of parking-lot dents he has caused—always, incidentally, owning up. He says he "hates ties" but began wearing cheap $2 and $3 ones bought from New York street vendors to show up a colleague who was regularly spending $175 on his neckwear, and the cheap tie habit eventually stuck fast.

As for the white towel, the game's recognized symbol of home fan support began when Neilson, upset with the officiating in the 1982 Stanley Cup final between his Vancouver Canucks and the New York Islanders, draped a towel over a stick and raised it in surrender. Since then, the white towel has come to represent the direct opposite of surrender in hockey.

Neilson was struck by cancer three years ago while coaching the Philadelphia Flyers. He fought back with medical treatment, his own deep religious convictions and the friendship of the sporting world. At one point, Tour de France cycling champion

Lance Armstrong, himself a cancer survivor, called to tell Neilson that the best approach was to "get back to work."

The long-time coach would never have it any other way. In a touching gesture, Senators head coach Jacques Martin stepped aside so that Neilson could coach his thousandth NHL game. Last fall, Neilson was named to the Hockey Hall of Fame. And last week, after a very tough spring, Neilson returned to the road, accompanying his team to Philadelphia, where the Senators defeated the Flyers to move on, for the first time, to the conference finals. "His goal when he started therapy in December was to return to coaching in the playoffs," said Roy Mlakar, the Senators' president and a close Neilson friend. "He accomplished that goal."

At November's Hall of Fame induction, Neilson brought down the house with jokes about former Leafs owner Harold Ballard, but also choked up when he realized how deeply appreciated he was by his hockey family.

"It's been a great ride," he said. And, mercifully, it's still going.

Roger Neilson died on June 21, 2003. He had just turned sixty-nine. His funeral in Peterborough was a huge affair attended by much of the hockey world. Following his passing, the Ottawa Senators Foundation announced it would build Roger's House/La maison de Roger, a pediatric palliative care facility at the Children's Hospital of Eastern Ontario. Roger's House has since become one of Ottawa's most cherished charities. Wayne Scanlan of the Ottawa Citizen *published a best-selling biography,* Roger's World, *in 2004.*

COACH OF THE YEAR,
FIRINGS OF THE YEAR: TED NOLAN

(*The Globe and Mail*, December 8, 2007)

UNIONDALE, NEW YORK

M aybe he was just going through menopause.

At least, that's how Sandra Nolan tried to laugh it away when her husband began complaining these past few weeks of hot flashes and headaches and suddenly finding himself soaked in clammy sweat. It could not, surely, have to do with stress. Compared to what Ted Nolan had been through in the forty-nine years that led up to this inexplicable condition, his current job as head coach of the New York Islanders was a glide on thick, smooth ice.

He had fought through poverty, the tenth of twelve children growing up on the Garden River reserve near Sault Ste. Marie, Ontario, in a small house with no electricity and no running water. So obsessed was he with hockey that he would build fires around the well to free up the frozen pump, then carry pail after pail of water to his little rink back of the house. When he and younger brother Steve first joined up to play organized hockey in a nearby community, they had to play on different lines so they could share the only stick, helmet and pair of gloves the Nolan kids owned.

He battled racism, heading off to Kenora, Ontario, for junior hockey and a daily regimen of fighting, both at school and on the hockey rink. Nolan was skilled, but it was toughness that gave him seventy-eight games in the National Hockey League before he turned to the yo-yo life of professional coaching. Up against racism as a child, he found he was up against it still as a man. At his most recent previous job, as coach of the Moncton Wildcats of the Quebec Major Junior Hockey League, he had to deal with war whoops, tomahawk chops and pretend arrows in certain rinks.

Luckily, he says with a weary smile, he knows no French so never really understood what he was being called.

He was only fourteen when his father, Stan, died of heart failure. A decade later, his mother, Rose, was killed by a drunk driver. He lost a sister to liver disease, uncles to alcoholism.

So where was the stress here on Long Island? Here he was in Gatsby country, the world where F. Scott Fitzgerald once pointed out the obvious—"The very rich are different from you and me"—and he was doing well both in the bank and on the ice. The Islanders, dismissed little more than a year ago as a Three Stooges comedy on ice, were now surprisingly respectable.

They had made the playoffs last year and were off to a fine start this season. And they were doing it with so many Canadian Aboriginals—Nolan an Ojibwa from Garden River, assistant coach John Chabot an Algonquin from Quebec's Kitigan Zibi, player Chris Simon an Ojibwa from Wawa, Ontario, and even director of player development Bryan Trottier, a Métis from Val Marie, Saskatchewan—that there were regular jokes among them about taking back Manhattan whenever the Islanders went up against the nearby New York Rangers.

Nolan's greatest delight this season was in bringing in his long-time friend Chabot to help with the coaching. Chabot too had come from rural poverty—his first skates were so large he had to wear six socks—but had grown up off reserve, as his father, eager to give his eight children a better opportunity, joined the armed forces.

While Nolan had been hit with racism at every turn, Chabot had been only vaguely aware of a difference when he was young. "I couldn't play with some of the other kids," he recalled. "Their parents wouldn't allow it." Chabot had been a supremely talented young player who had limited success in the NHL, played in Europe and gained a reputation as a "teacher" as a junior coach in Quebec.

Things were going so well for Nolan on Long Island, in fact, that cold sweats and hot flashes seemed an impossibility in a man renowned for his ability to remain calm under fire. And then, a few days ago, it was all explained. A toxic mould had invaded a new luxury complex in nearby Westbury. About four hundred apartments were affected, including the one being rented by Ted and Sandra Nolan.

When the coach arrived for practice, he had just been handed an eviction notice, and he was smiling. "I've just become a homeless person," he said.

It would not be the first time Ted Nolan has been tossed out in the cold, or, in the case of the NHL, the wilderness. Ten years ago, Nolan seemed at the peak of a soaring coaching career. He had retired as a player and gone to coach the Sault Ste. Marie Greyhounds of the OHL, where he first met, and changed the life of, Chris Simon. After winning junior hockey's Memorial Cup, Nolan became an assistant coach with the NHL's Hartford Whalers, soon moving to head coach with the Buffalo Sabres.

He took a team of low expectations and turned them into a playoff contender. He was chosen as the NHL coach of the year for 1996 and received the Jack Adams Award. The last time Nolan saw his award, it was in a cardboard box that he threw down the basement steps. He has never looked at it since.

Whatever happened in Buffalo, it still eats at Nolan. He had great success there, but it was said he warred with fickle goaltender Dominik Hasek. It was said he backstabbed general manager John Muckler, who was fired not long before Nolan was offered a gratuitous one-year contract and, insulted, decided to walk. It was said he was even showing up drunk for practice.

What was the point of denial, even if he doesn't touch alcohol? There are no gloves to drop when you fight a stereotype. For a decade, Nolan was essentially "blackballed" from the NHL, regularly dismissed as "a GM killer."

"I tried everything," he said. He sent resumés out that were not acknowledged. He called, but calls were not returned. His name would come up whenever a coach was fired, but calls never followed. It reached a point where he thought he should ask the media just to let his name disappear.

"It's one of the great mysteries," he said. "I still don't know what happened. But I'm a strong, strong believer that things happen for a reason, and when I look back on it and look at everything that came out of it, I now think that it was the best thing that could have happened."

It took him a long time, however, to come around to this way of thinking. He spent the first two years in what he calls "a real dark period" of anger and blame. "I lost my drive," he said. "I always believed if you worked hard, you would be rewarded, but . . ." His voice trailed off. " For a long period of time . . . I quit."

Two people were there to change Ted Nolan's life, one in his home and one in a movie. At home was Sandra, the pretty teenager he'd first seen walking across the parking lot outside the Sault Ste. Marie rink, the mother of Brandon and Jordan, who are today both promising young players. "She was always, always there," he said.

The other was the Will Smith film *Ali*. Nolan was smitten with the boxer's stubborn determination not to change who he was, regardless of the pressures put on him. He left the movie steeled to remain exactly the person he had been before the nightmare of Buffalo descended. And if the consequence was no more hockey, so be it.

"There's an Ojibwa word that means 'now,'" he said. "I learned to really appreciate every day. There's an old song that says yesterday is history, tomorrow's a mystery, today is the present, that's why they call it a gift."

Finally rising from that dark period, Nolan began devoting more and more time to his heritage. He got involved with hockey tournaments for Native youth and operated a hockey school that included sessions on nutrition and spiritualism as well as skating and stickhandling. He began working with the Assembly of First Nations on various projects, including the Make Poverty History campaign.

Hockey, he said, gives Native youth "an outlet. It makes you forget about your personal problems for a couple of hours."

"We want to try and make a difference," said Chabot, who has joined Nolan in various projects designed to build self-esteem among young Canadian Aboriginals. "Hockey gives us a segue into their lives."

Nolan also poured his energies into a project he started years ago in the hopes of honouring the memory of his mother. "It took me ten years before I could even talk about her death," he said, still clearly fragile from the memory.

Rose Nolan had raised the dozen children on her own after the death of her husband, who was thirty-nine. She had turned Ted into a fancy dancer and a traditional drummer, taking him off to powwows in summer and getting him to hockey in winter. She was the one who kept him going in the game when he thought he could fight the racism no longer. The day he fled his first professional camp in Detroit, she turned her back on him when he came through the door, and she refused to speak until he went back, which he did, though he admits he cried himself to sleep for weeks.

It began with a golf tournament—a sport he didn't even know how to play—and is now the Ted Nolan Foundation, which hands out bursaries. For the past dozen years, an average of five young Native women a year have gone on to postsecondary education through the Rose Nolan Memorial Scholarship Fund. "If I can make a difference," he said, "I will."

Nolan had turned so completely to Native issues—even toying with the idea of entering politics—that the call back to coaching caught him off guard. It was Moncton on the line, requesting a meeting he wasn't at all sure about. Sandra encouraged him to go, and seven minutes after he sat down, he was on the telephone telling her to start packing. "It had nothing to do with getting her to Long Island," he said.

Success in Moncton, however, combined with disaster in Long Island—bad trades, fired coaches and changed general managers—led to eccentric Islanders owner Charles Wang deciding to hire his own coach. Wang went to former Islanders all-star Pat LaFontaine for advice, and LaFontaine, who also had a Buffalo connection, immediately recommended Nolan. Nolan believes he would never have been hired if there had been a GM in place.

Wang then hired and dropped a new GM before promoting backup goaltender Garth Snow to the job. When Snow surprised the league by signing goaltender Rick DiPietro to an unheard-of fifteen-year, $67.5-million deal, the rest of the NHL howled with laughter.

Fifteen months later, the Islanders are the ones smiling. It was Nolan who suggested the Islanders honour legendary coach Al Arbour by bringing Arbour back to coach his fifteen hundredth game, and Nolan who insisted on moving himself into Arbour's old windowless office. The team made the playoffs last season and is challenging again this season, hoping to regain a swagger not seen on Long Island since the Arbour years.

Chris Simon says the essential difference has been Nolan. "If there's one word that describes Ted," Simon said, "it's leadership."

Simon likely knows better than anyone. The relationship between the two goes back to Sault Ste. Marie, when Nolan was coaching. He persuaded the teenager to quit drinking before he ruined his life and any chance of a hockey career. "He was 247 pounds and had all kinds of off-ice problems," Nolan remembered.

"He pretty much told me his opinion of the life line that I was going along," said Simon, who added he has never touched alcohol since and has played nearly eight hundred NHL games. "With Ted," Simon said, "it was never only about hockey."

It is a familiar refrain among the players. Mike Comrie, who arrived this fall as a free agent, says he had always heard "what a great players' coach he is. Well, it's true. The first thing he thinks about is the player. You get so you almost don't want to let him down. He wants you to have a life off the ice. He brings every-thing back to a life lesson."

"Hockey's only two hours a day," Nolan said. "There's a big life out there."

Ted Nolan was fired, again, in July 2008. The Islanders had missed the playoffs and were, it turned out, on a downward spiral that has continued. Nolan has never returned to the NHL. Instead, his time is devoted to the Ted Nolan Foundation and the training of future Aboriginal leaders and the education of Native women. His foundation is now partnered with the Tim Horton Children's Foundation, sending fifty Aboriginal children a year off to summer camps. Ted and Sandra Nolan's sons have both been drafted by NHL teams, Brandon by the Vancouver Canucks and Jordan by the Los Angeles Kings.

THE NOT-SO-GLORY DAYS

(*The Globe and Mail*, November 11, 2010)

OTTAWA, ONTARIO

Here is where it all began, where it all came crashing down, and where Thursday evening—should they happen to win together again—the celebration of the improbable will take place over a quiet beer and a few chuckles. Alain Vigneault, coach of the Vancouver Canucks, would have his three hundredth win.

Fifteen years ago, he believed he'd never see his first.

It was another mid-November back in 1995, and Vigneault had his first NHL job as assistant to Rick Bowness, coach of the hapless Ottawa Senators, which were then mired in an eight-game losing string after standing dead last in the NHL the previous three seasons. There was no surprise when the axe fell. More relief than anything else that, finally, it was over.

The Vigneault–Bowness combination is one of the more intriguing marriages in all of hockey. Bowness was named the Senators' first coach in 1992 and interviewed Vigneault, a local junior coach who had taken his Hull Olympiques to the Memorial Cup, merely "out of courtesy."

But he took on Vigneault because the young coach had been "so impressive" in the interview. He also had a great sense of humour and Bowness, fully aware of what he was taking on, felt that would be as important as knowing how to run a power play.

The Senators—given what the Tampa Bay Lightning's Phil Esposito called "snow in winter" in the interleague draft—were dreadful. They lost seventy games that first year, including forty-one successive road games. They held a rookie camp in which the leading scorer turned out to be writing a first-person column for the local *Sun* newspaper. They had a break-in during which the thieves made off with everything but the game tapes—"Burglars with taste," remarked E.J. McGuire, the other assistant coach. They made the ESPN highlights only once, when a player fell down the stairs at the old Chicago Stadium. *Sports Illustrated* claimed they were "the worst team" in sports franchise history.

By the time the coaches were fired they had been through the wars together. They had dealt with Alexandre Daigle's nurse's uniform, Alexei Yashin's salary holdouts and, at one point, a goaltender who skated over to the bench in the middle of a game and told them he had just had a heart attack.

"It was tough on you," Bowness remembers. "Losing just beats the living crap out of you when it's night after night. It takes its toll."

"Those years were real challenging and real tough on a personal level and a professional level," Vigneault says. "You go through those times where you know even if you're putting your best foot forward you have no chance of winning."

But they learned from their mistakes and discovered, as well, how compatible they were behind the bench. Bowness moved on to coach the New York Islanders and then went off to help Wayne Gretzky coach the Phoenix Coyotes, and he tried, unsuccessfully, to get Vigneault to join. Vigneault went back to junior, then to the minors and at thirty-nine was named head coach of the Montreal Canadiens, where he unsuccessfully tried to talk Bowness into signing on.

Finally, after Vigneault had been fired in Montreal, he landed in Vancouver and immediately went after Bowness again—this time succeeding. Only this time their roles would be reversed: Vigneault as head coach, Bowness as associate.

"I was just a kid when I went to work for Rick," Vigneault says. "He's helped me out a lot more than I was able to help him back then. Now, mind you, I could say that he could have had Scotty Bowman coaching that team and it wouldn't have mattered that much."

Fifteen years on, it's working fine. Vigneault, now forty-nine, was named NHL coach of the year in 2007 and says he couldn't have done it without Bowness, now fifty-five, from whom he learned so much so many years ago.

"I learned about challenging yourself," Vigneault says, "about trying to stay positive, trying to keep moving forward, trying to work with guys to make sure their spirits aren't too down. Players aren't stupid, either—they know when they look at the lineup on both sides that they don't stand much of a chance."

Bowness today says he couldn't have done better than hire the local kid he thought he was seeing as a courtesy only. They've been lucky to have each other, and lucky to have survived to enjoy, finally, some success together.

"Every day in this league is a good day," Bowness says. "I tell the players, 'Count your blessings—you're lucky to be here.'"

In the spring of 2011, the Vancouver Canucks, coached by Alan Vigneault and Rick Bowness, won the Presidents' Trophy as the top team in the entire NHL and reached the Stanley Cup final. Their personal triumph was saddened, however, by the tragic death of E.J. McGuire, who had become the head of NHL's Central Scouting Bureau. McGuire, fifty-eight, died of a swift-moving cancer the week the NHL's regular season ended. The three had remained close friends since their days together in Ottawa.

COACH GRETZKY

(*The Globe and Mail*, December 10, 2005)

SCOTTSDALE, ARIZONA

Here, at the luxurious Resort Suites, with palm trees swaying in the background and steaks thicker than hockey pucks sizzling on the barbecue, four full teams of dreamers are gathered to raise an opening-night glass to Wayne Gretzky Fantasy Camp IV. For a mere $9,999—a portion of which goes to charity—men who are plumbers and dentists and real-estate dealers in their regular lives will, for five days, live a grown-up version of Wayne Gretzky pajamas and Wayne Gretzky wallpaper. They will play a round-robin tournament—no hitting, no slapshots—of beer-league-level hockey, each team sprinkled with retired stars such as Hall-of-Famer Paul Coffey, Rick Tocchet, Kirk Muller and the Courtnall brothers, Russ and Geoff. The paying players are guaranteed one game with Gretzky himself, as well as an autographed picture of the hockey wannabe standing with the one so many believe to be the greatest ever to play the game.

And some dreams cannot be bought—at any price.

Take Wayne Gretzky's, for example. He sits at the head of the room as the cigars are being handed out. He is dressed, as always, like someone out of *GQ*, impeccable in a tight, thin leather jacket, dark turtleneck, pants and shoes. He is rich beyond belief. He can drive a Bentley one day, a Hummer the next. He has a solid marriage to a Hollywood actress and five children who are as polite as they are blond. He looks younger than the forty-five years he will turn next month. His face is unlined and, remarkably for a hockey player, unscarred.

He is so famous that even now, into the seventh season of his retirement as the National Hockey League's all-time leading scorer, winner of four Stanley Cups, holder of a stunning sixty-one NHL records, small boys who never saw him play will stand outside the rink hoping for a signature from the man even they call "The Great One." He will park in a reserved space that no one else will dare take because of its instant identification with the number he once wore: 99. And when they announce the starting lineups at the game to be played the following evening, the home crowd will cheer loudest not for any of the players, but for the rookie Phoenix Coyotes coach, Wayne Gretzky.

And yet, on this night, when the old stories flow and the cigars glow, the rookie coach is no different from the plumber from New York or the dentist from Ontario. He is dreaming, dreaming, dreaming of playing in the NHL.

Paul Coffey stands at the back of the room and still cannot believe that his great friend, his former teammate on those glorious Edmonton Oilers Stanley Cup teams, has done what no one ever expected and what Gretzky himself once said he would never, ever do.

"I knew something was up when he went quiet," Coffey says. "I sent him an e-mail and he never answered back. All I said was, 'Coaching, are you nuts?' Then I pushed down on the question-mark key—until it had filled the whole screen."

"I know, I know," he says, smiling sheepishly.

—

Wayne Gretzky is standing at the edge of the Coyotes' dressing room in the Glendale Arena, which is on the other side of Phoenix from Scottsdale. He is trying to deal with the demands of five-year-old Tristan—"*Tie my shoe! Tie my shoe!*"—and the question that has trailed him ever since he announced this summer that he was returning to the ice surface, albeit not to play.

He is acutely aware of the sports theory that holds the truly great cannot coach. Rocket Richard was such a bust with the Quebec Nordiques that he quit less than two weeks into the job. Bobby Orr couldn't take being an assistant coach in Chicago. Brad Park failed in Detroit. Basketball's Wilt Chamberlain, football's Bart Starr, baseball's Ted Williams—all brilliant players who found managing lesser mortals too much to bear.

Gretzky himself once believed this. Five years ago, in a column he wrote for the *National Post* following his retirement—a column I was then assigned to help out on—he said that, even though he might one day return in some capacity to the game, "it couldn't possibly be coaching."

At that time, he bought into the rule of thumb that successful coaches are the Freddie Sheros, not the Rocket Richards. The examples of fine players who make fine coaches—Larry Robinson in New Jersey, Jacques Lemaire in Minnesota—are rare enough; there is, unless Wayne Gretzky proves the theorists wrong, no modern example of a brilliant player succeeding on the other side of the bench. "Most successful coaches," he continued in his column, "are either guys who had their careers cut short, like Scotty Bowman, or guys who—he's going to kill me for this—weren't on the ice all that much, so they could do a lot of watching and studying, like my old friend Glen Sather," mastermind behind the Edmonton dynasty of the 1980s.

He couldn't see the likes of Paul Coffey or Mark Messier going into coaching and trying to deal with players who wouldn't work as hard as they had and can't "see the game the same way that they do."

Somewhere along the line, he had a change of heart. First, he came back to hockey far sooner after retiring than he had intended. A year after his last game as a player in April 1999, he joined Phoenix as managing partner in charge of all hockey operations. The opportunity was simply too good to turn down.

The Coyotes had been the Winnipeg Jets, allowed by the NHL to move south in 1996 after years of losing money. Relocation seemed a ready solution, especially in wealthy Phoenix, but it has not been as simple as it seemed. Plans for a new arena based on a real-estate development in Scottsdale fell apart, forcing the franchise to scramble to avoid being moved again, this time to Portland, Oregon.

Owner Steve Ellman, a real-estate developer, knew the Gretzky name had a currency not even the banks could match, and so he offered the recent retiree a chance to become part owner. It is not known how much Gretzky paid—friends suggest nothing—nor how much of the convoluted hockey and real-estate deal he has, though a rumour in Phoenix says 18 percent. Whatever the stake, if everything Ellman has planned comes off, he will profit massively.

It was the Gretzky cachet that helped to land a new land deal in Glendale. Ellman was able to persuade the rundown suburb to put up three-quarters of the $240 million needed to build the rink, which opened two years ago. It was to be part of his Westgate City Center, a 223-acre retail, entertainment, office, hotel and residential complex, but the development has not gone quite according to plan (he recently paid a $1-million fine to the city for missed deadlines). However, with the National Football League's Arizona Cardinals now building a new stadium beside the rink, the project's future appears far more certain, eventually.

There also have been struggles on the ice. The Coyotes have missed the playoffs three of their past four seasons. Worse, the team last won a series as the Jets. The star players of recent years— Keith Tkachuk, Jeremy Roenick, goaltender Nikolai Khabibulin— have all moved on to richer contracts elsewhere. Phoenix took on an expensive new star back in 2004, veteran sharpshooter Brett Hull, but last season's long lockout, his age (forty-one) and weight problems, and the league's new rules that reward speed all contrived to create a situation where Hull voluntarily, and wisely, retired with the new season barely under way.

That left Gretzky taking over a team without its expensive stars, but with a struggling power play, a defence prone to panic and a desperate need for a goaltender who could replace Khabibulin. Hardly an ideal situation for a man who had never coached anything but his son's softball team.

And yet, this week, after a run of seven victories in their past ten games, Phoenix moved into eighth place in the Western Conference. If the playoffs began now, the Coyotes—who were not considered any threat at all—would be there. Gretzky says, correctly, that much of the credit must go to the play of goaltender Curtis Joseph, the thirty-eight-year-old free agent the Coyotes picked up this summer. But hockey is a team game, from goaltender to scorer to behind the bench—and significant credit must go to the novice coach as well as the veteran goaltender.

It's still too soon to say that he has proved himself, but Gretzky has answered some of the questions about why a man who has never failed—he became a national figure at ten, after scoring 378 goals for the Nadrofsky Steelers—would take on such a fickle job that it even carries its own defeatist mantra: Coaches are hired to be fired.

Why, then, would he do it? Why go back to the grind of eighty-two games a year, perhaps a hundred if exhibition and playoffs are included? Why take on the stress, the travel, the media bombardment? Surely not for a coach's million-dollar salary when he could easily pick up several times that by doing a few more commercials. Or, as Paul Coffey so accurately put it: "???????????????"

One popular theory holds that, just as Mario Lemieux went back to help save his NHL franchise in Pittsburgh, Gretzky turned to coaching in order to fill seats. The mere announcement that he would be taking the reins sent season-ticket sales soaring 30 percent.

"Wayne Gretzky is still the only face of hockey in the United States," says Rick Bowness, the Coyotes' acting coach before this season. "In fact, he's still the face of hockey in Canada. Just watch what the cameras do when Canada wins the Olympic gold or the World Cup. They don't go to the players on the ice. They go straight to Gretzky—that's where the passion is."

And it was passion, not economics, that eventually brought him down from the luxury seats to the coach's bench. Both he and Mike Barnett—his long-time agent and now the Coyotes' general manager—deny that there was any intention to "prop up the franchise" by having him on the bench. He is there to be noticed, they say—but by the players far more than by the fans.

He started dealing with players not in Phoenix, but with the Olympic program, serving as the Canadian team's executive director for the Salt Lake City Games in 2002 and leading Canada to its first hockey gold medal in fifty years. However, he had already found that he missed playing more than he ever would have imagined. Hockey history is littered with sad tales of greats who stayed too long and left wearing uniforms they should never be remembered for: Guy Lafleur went out a Nordique, Bobby Hull a Hartford Whaler, Marcel Dionne in the minors.

But he, like Jean Béliveau, had left while still able to perform at a very high level, and he hadn't forgotten what Gordie Howe, who unretired and kept playing until he was fifty-two, once told him: "Be careful not to leave the thing you love too soon."

Wondering if perhaps he had, he started taking advantage of the ice access he enjoyed as managing partner of the Coyotes. As he got back into shape, he lost sight of the fact that he had retired at thirty-eight, which is when most superior players do, or at least should, bow out, and he began to dream the impossible. "You think you can still play," he now says. "We all do. I would skate on the ice and practise with the guys periodically and do some of the drills." There were times when he was convinced he could still do it, that a comeback was possible. "I felt like it. I really believed."

But was it the right thing? He compares his moment of reckoning to the amateur players who went out for the CBC-TV reality series *Making the Cut*, only to discover that reality was being not quite good enough. He even found the odd person showing up at his fantasy camps was faster than he was. He also worried that he might be playing a game in his mind that no longer existed. Players had become bigger, stronger and vastly more mobile. Even in his prime, he figures, he couldn't dominate today's hockey as he did yesterday's. "I would have been hit a lot more. It wouldn't have been as easy for me to freelance out there. I was smart enough to realize I had to retire."

Coaching, however, was an option, even if he had ruled it out. He wasn't still playing, but he knew the NHL inside out, perhaps as well as anyone. "He's a total hockey junkie," says Russ Courtnall, a former teammate and long-time friend. "I've never known a guy to watch so much hockey. He knows everything about every player."

The itch to get closer to the ice really took hold during the 2004 World Cup. He had been coaching his son's ball team in the summer and had delighted in discovering hidden skills in youngsters and in devising strategy for the team. When the World Cup camp began, he was again executive director of the Canadian team, but found himself increasingly interested in how a professional coaching staff prepared, a side of the game he had never paid much attention to before. He was impressed by the thoroughness—but found the emotional side of coaching fascinating.

"They really enjoyed being on the bench," he says of head coach Pat Quinn and assistants Ken Hitchcock, Jacques Martin and Marc Habscheid. "As much as the players loved playing, they really loved coaching that team. I saw the energy they had, and the excitement they had getting ready for each and every game."

He decided to confide in Habscheid that he was thinking about coaching himself, and says his former Oilers teammate "told me I'd really enjoy it and have a lot of fun doing it."

Much to his surprise, Janet Gretzky thought the same. The family was living outside Los Angeles and growing—Paulina, seventeen, an aspiring singer, Ty, fifteen, Trevor, thirteen, Tristan, five, and Emma, three—but Phoenix was close enough for commuting and easy visits and, besides, she knew that one day he would want to get more involved in the franchise.

The real deciding factor came during the owners' lockout that followed the World Cup and shut down NHL hockey for a complete year. He had his promotional work, but it was hardly full-time. He was, in fact, spending most of his time golfing or just hanging about the house. Janet grew tired of hearing the sounds of endless "classic" NHL games coming from the television, and finally her visiting mother actually told The Great One: "You've got to get up and go to work—you've got to do something."

He began to try out the coaching notion on a wider field. During a chance meeting at the Kentucky Derby, basketball coach Pat Riley suggested that he would like it, and Janet says she was "120 percent" behind the move. They began to discuss the logistics of keeping two homes going. Ty, the eldest boy, also could move to Phoenix to pursue his own high-school hockey ambitions as well as work, part-time, in the Coyotes' dressing room.

The marriage, she says, would survive fine. "We've been together almost twenty years, and we're pretty sure how we feel about each other."

He talked it over with NHL commissioner Gary Bettman, who was very enthusiastic but had one request: Don't say anything until the lockout is resolved. He wanted something that would, Gretzky says, "put hockey on the front pages" once again before the games actually started up. By coincidence, or perhaps by design, the day his decision to coach was made public, the league announced that Vancouver Canucks player Todd Bertuzzi, who had been suspended indefinitely for a brutal attack on an opponent at the end of the 2003–04 season, would be reinstated. Gretzky's return to the game got greater play than Bertuzzi's return, much to the delight of the league.

Two games into his new life, Gretzky was on the phone to track down Courtnall on the golf course. "'Russ, I love it, I absolutely love it!'" Courtnall remembers him shouting. "How can you not be happy for someone who's doing something he loves?"

And yet, it was not his first love, nor his first choice. He would rather have played. "I'm not going to lie," he says. "I wish I could still play, but I know I can't. Brainwise, I probably could—physically, I probably couldn't. But I loved it so much. I endlessly wish I could have played."

He is still the most unprepossessing figure on the ice. Here at the Coyotes' practice facility in Scottsdale, he is barely noticeable as they skate about, a slim figure in a track suit with a thick black toque pulled so tight that only his eyes, mouth and the familiar Gretzky nose are visible. When he blows the whistle, the result is so feeble it seems he ran out of wind just tying up his skates.

And yet, when he speaks—or sometimes shouts—they listen.

Mike Ricci, a fifteen-year veteran who came to Phoenix from the San Jose Sharks, says that, increasingly, the team has come to see the man with the whistle as their coach, rather than as Wayne Gretzky. "He's very talkative, very active. He's very intense—and we feed off that."

Darren Pang, a former NHL goalie who is now the Coyotes' television play-by-play analyst, says the rookie coach has hardly been the soft touch others perhaps expected. After two dismal performances, he put his players through a gruesome forty-five-minute "bag skate"—no pucks, full out. He essentially forced Brett Hull, a close friend, to retire by cutting his ice time to the point of embarrassment. Other old friends were cut even earlier, at training camp, and later he scratched veteran Sean O'Donnell for a game and publicly criticized the highly talented but under-producing Ladislav Nagy, who responded by becoming the team's leading scorer.

"Gretzky didn't need this," Pang says. "His life was fulfilled without coaching. So why would you put yourself in a position to fail unless you had total belief that you would ultimately succeed?"

"He commands respect," Curtis Joseph adds. "Everybody listens and they don't question." Joseph has been on teams whose coaches and players snipe at each other and players often tune out coaches who have lost their respect. "I don't see that happening here," he says.

Coyotes vice-president Cliff Fletcher, now into his fiftieth year of professional hockey management, says it is absurd for people to say that coaching didn't work out for Rocket Richard so it won't work out for Wayne Gretzky. "Look," he says, "I knew the Rocket. He was one of the most capable athletes I ever met in my life. He just did it on pure power and talent. When he coached, he couldn't understand how nobody could do what he told them to do. He was such an impatient man. Wayne is so patient.

"There's always the exception to any rule. He was the thinking man's player on the ice—always half a step ahead of everyone else. He has such an extreme knowledge of the game that that is what makes him different."

Darryl Sutter, coach and general manager of the Calgary Flames, says that there is another fundamental difference between Gretzky coaching in 2005 and, say, Rocket Richard going behind the bench in 1972. Staff.

"Everybody goes on about how tough it is to coach," he explains, "but it's about trying to get the right staff. It's technical and it's staff—any area you need can be covered off in that. I knew right away he'd be fine as a coach. He surrounded himself with the right staff. He has the technician in Barry Smith. He has a former player who has the respect of the players in Rick Tocchet. He has a guy who's familiar with the organization in Rick Bowness."

According to Sutter, who took his surprising Flames to the Stanley Cup final in 2004, "it's not as complicated as everyone thinks." A successful coach can either be a teacher or a leader, and "Wayne is a great leader," he says. "One thing that is different about him is that he wasn't a big guy and he wasn't the most talented player, but he was the most insightful player there was."

With his vast experience, Bowness was a natural to keep on. Tocchet and goaltending coach Grant Fuhr, meanwhile, were old acquaintances, leading some to separate those who were "FOG"—Friends of Gretzky—from those who were not. Smith he did not know, and hired only after a suggestion from legendary coach Scotty Bowman. Having spent a dozen years as Bowman's assistant in Detroit, Pittsburgh and Buffalo, Smith was negotiating with a Russian elite team and could hardly believe he was getting the Gretzky call: "I wanted to work with him in the worst way."

According to Smith, "we're coaching by committee" while the new kid is "learning the intricacies"—and no one, he adds, could have picked a more difficult year to launch a coaching career. With the new rules, the game is being played entirely differently, with special teams counting for more than ever and defensive strategies still in their infancy. "The first couple of games were tough. I'll bet he didn't sleep."

Smith and Bowness say they are surprised by how much he listens and how easily he hands over responsibility. Delegating, Gretzky says, is something he learned from Glen Sather, who was coach and general manager of the Oilers as well as the team's president. Sather's assistants "weren't just assistant coaches, getting the pucks out of the corners for the next drill. They often ran the practices. They ran the drills . . . He did it, not because it was a new way to go. He did it out of necessity. There is no way I could coach right now if I didn't have the help I'm getting."

What, then, does he bring to the bench? According to Smith,

it's the very thing that made Scotty Bowman the best coach in NHL history: "a burning desire to win." It is this desire, this insistent itch to perform at the very top of one's abilities, that social commentator Malcolm Gladwell examined in an article published by *The New Yorker* just three months after Gretzky retired.

Gladwell, who grew up in Canada, compared the skills of the hockey genius with those of Charlie Wilson, a brilliant brain surgeon still demanding and driven as he headed toward seventy, and Yo-Yo Ma, the internationally renowned cellist. He termed the trio "physical geniuses," a motor equivalent of exceptional IQ, and found that they themselves were often not even aware of what gave them such control over what they were doing. "It's sort of an invisible hand," the surgeon suggested. "It begins almost to seem mystical."

Such exceptional people, Gladwell suggested, "are driven to greatness because they have found something so compelling that they cannot put it aside." After more than three incredibly successful decades in the game, Wayne Gretzky found that he just could not put it aside.

"When you're part of the ownership group," he explains one afternoon after the team's practice, "you don't really have a say in the game itself. It's out of your hands. When you become a coach, you become a 'player' again.

"It's not as good—but it's the closest thing. I'm a realist. It's the closest I can get to playing."

Shortly after this article appeared, Wayne Gretzky left the coach's bench on a leave of absence to spend time with his ill mother, Phyllis, who died of lung cancer shortly before Christmas. He returned to coach a team finding little success on the ice and financial horrors off of it. The franchise struggled and in the spring of 2009 filed for Chapter 11 bankruptcy. With ownership in turmoil—Research In Motion's Jim Balsillie failing in his bid to buy the team and move it, the NHL ultimately taking ownership while searching for an owner who would keep the team there—Gretzky found himself a creditor. He stepped down as coach before the 2009–10 season began. In his four-year coaching career, his team failed to make the playoffs.

★ ★ ★ ★ ★ ★ ★ ★

EIGHT

THE ELEMENTS

"GOOD, WARM, FUZZY MEMORIES"

(*The Globe and Mail*, November 24, 2003)

EDMONTON, ALBERTA

It was supposed to be, as Mark Messier said, a weekend of getting "back to the roots of hockey."

In a way it was; in a way it wasn't. I certainly do not remember any of us running naked but for a T-shirt and single sock down on the old beaver pond and then sliding like a pink-skinned otter over the McDonald's sponsor sign. Come to think of it, I don't recall any sponsors. Nor, for that matter, anyone ever stopping to watch—let alone 57,167 spectators who arrived Saturday afternoon at Commonwealth Stadium looking more like they were a Michelin Man convention than a hockey crowd.

I do, however, remember playing shinny at −16.8°C. And bad ice that was more unpredictable than a penalty shot.

The old-timers played and they shovelled their own snow off—"Losers have to do the ice," Messier joked as his old Oilers took a 1–0 lead at the half—and they wore toques and balaclavas and, after a while, as much steam was coming off their heads as out of their mouths.

"I don't know if you can ever duplicate it," Wayne Gretzky said after the old Oilers had defeated the old Montreal Canadiens 2–0 in thirty minutes of pond hockey. "It's kind of like the '72 series—you can never go back and try and do it again."

Such comparison requires a bit of a stretch. The country did not go into a state of apoplexy when it was half over, as they did in 1972; here at the half they lined up for the washrooms. There was no Phil Esposito rant to rally the home side as there was in '72. There were no-last minute dramatics by Paul Henderson. In fact, few dramatics at all apart from the introductions, as is usually the case in old-timers' games. Neither Gretzky nor Messier got a shot on net. Guy Lafleur got one shot, but didn't score. The winning goal was scored by Ken Linseman, a hall-of-fame pest, the insurance goal by Marty McSorley, a hall-of-fame enforcer.

And yet, just as strong emotion was the overriding memory of '72, it was here, as well, even if the feelings were quite, quite different. There was a remarkable charm to the Heritage Classic— "good, warm, fuzzy memories," said former Edmonton star Paul Coffey—and it could not have come at a better time for the league that pulled off this risky extravaganza.

It has not been a good season for the NHL. When the story isn't labour gloom, it has been product gloom, professional hockey caught in a dual crisis of finance and entertainment. Star players who have not been dumping on the game (Joe Thornton, Brett Hull) have been so down in the dumps themselves (Jaromir Jagr) that it has become a game without star quality. What the old-timers—who most assuredly have kept much of their star quality—and the Heritage Classic reminded people of is that the original purpose of the Canadian game was always fun, something that Thornton, for example, feels is rather sadly absent from today's trapping and dumping, clutching and holding.

The old players may have lacked speed, but they carried pucks rather than dumped them. They tried plays rather than avoid them. They played real shifts that left them tired rather than miniature shifts that, in today's hockey, are intended only to leave them blameless. "Guys who played the game," said Montreal coach Jacques Demers, "the way it's supposed to be played."

They also smiled and laughed on the ice the way youngsters have for as long as there has been ice and a way to slide on it faster than even an intrepid streaker. "We really felt like we were ten years old," laughed Lafleur, "with the legs of a fifty-year-old!"

There were a few lovely moments in the game—a flashing glove save by Edmonton goaltender Grant Fuhr, a lovely rush by the still smooth skating Coffey—but the moments to treasure were the Aurèle Joliat toques on the heads, the introductions and the undeniable first star of the game: the 57,167 fans with their puffed-out coats and their hot chocolate and Baileys.

Whether it was the bitter cold or the inspiration of the old-timers, the players in the second game, the real game, played increasingly more efficiently than usual. The colder it got, the quicker it got and the better it got—until a game broke out that has rarely been seen indoors this year, including a winning goal in Montreal's 4–3 victory by Richard Zednik of a type we had come to believe was played out only in children's imaginations and outdoor rinks.

The NHL should consider not heating its northern rinks if this is the result. But since that isn't likely to happen, let us hope that the lesson learned here is that the time has come to invite the fun back indoors.

What began in Edmonton is now a fixture in the NHL, with New Year's Day Winter Classic games having been held in Buffalo, Chicago, Boston and Pittsburgh and a second Heritage Classic game held in 2011 in Calgary. The Winter Classic has been a marketing and publicity bonanza for the league, though it is also the event at which Sidney Crosby suffered the concussion that led to hockey's great debate of the 2010–11 season.

JOY OF ROAD HOCKEY
(*Today's Parent*, September 2003)

I have heard all the arguments.

I have listened to the claims that the Greeks were playing something much like it as far back as 500 BC. I have stood on an upper floor of Vienna's Kunsthistorisches art museum and stared hard at *Hunters in the Snow*, which Pieter Bruegel painted in 1565, and I have seen, beyond any doubt, that there are two youngsters in the background playing a game any Canadian would instantly recognize. I have seen the literary evidence that Thomas Chandler Haliburton was writing as far back as 1810 about kids "hollerin' and whoopin' like mad with pleasure" as they cuffed something back and forth with sticks on a frozen pond near Windsor, Nova Scotia, and I have even argued with a farmer and a doctor who live there over precisely which pond it was. I have listened to the claims of Montreal that the first game was played there in on March 3, 1875, listened as well to the claims that the game originated in the small Ontario city of Kingston sometime in 1886 — and I have only one response to all of these claims on the Cradle of Hockey.

Not even close.

You want to see where hockey was invented, let me take you to Huntsville, Ontario, on a late February afternoon in the deep winter of 1957–58, and let us head for Dufferin Street high on the reservoir hill where the town ploughs have left a wide, flattened surface and high banks, where the light from the single street lamp at the corner of Dufferin and Mary is enough, and let us listen to the one call that is as much a part of Canadian winter as the call of the loon is to summer: "*Caaaarrr!*"

With luck, it will be Mulhern — or, as we all know him, "Uncle Danny," though he has no known relatives — and he will guide his brown Buick so the tires straddle the goalposts that we have chopped out of the hard snow and carefully placed in the centre of the road, two at one end, two at the other, each pair separated by the measure of a handy Hespeler Green Flash.

"*Caaaarrr!*"

The teams endlessly vary, the sides made up by various techniques including tossing all the sticks in the centre and having one kid, eyes shut, disperse them one at a time in opposite directions, or merely letting two big guys, or two of the little guys, stand as captains and let them choose up—everyone perfectly aware of who will be chosen first, and who, unfortunately, will go last. It is, more often than not, big guys versus little guys, the big guys—older brother Jim, Eric Wilston, Stew Wieler, Don Cockram—more skilled but fewer in number than the troop that makes up the little guys: me, Don Wilston, Brent and Ron Munroe, Ted Harman and, of course, Eric Ruby, the only person on reservoir hill who actually *wants* to play net. The road is on a slight decline, so ends are switched when the first team reaches five goals. Games are over at ten goals, with new teams instantly reassembled with the shout "*Game on!*" starting the match that will carry on until mothers grow cranky calling us in for supper.

There are few rules to this game. No slashing. No cross-checking. No "golf" shots. No sticks so worn down—"toothpicks," we call them—that they become a danger to the eyes. Wilston's big German shepherd, Rick, can watch but not play. And whoever shoots the ball down past Mary Street, chases it.

There is one other rule particular only to Dufferin Street and not likely found on any of the thousands of similar road hockey shrines across this country: No chasing the tennis balls into Mrs. Wieler's raspberry patch. In return for this sacred regulation, she agrees to tap an extra sugar maple each March and grants the road hockey player exclusive rights to the sap—God's Gatorade—as spring brings a sad end to one more glorious season of Dufferin Street glory.

I am in my fifties now and will still play at the drop of a snowflake. For decades, our large extended family would gather each year back in that same Central Canadian small town and play the Christmas Classic—a road hockey game featuring as many cousins as there were sticks to go around. There is no record of the scores, but an annual documentation by photograph: new players growing, several of them young women, old players' hairlines receding and bellies widening. Some players eventually retired and a couple, sadly, were lost forever. A few years ago, the Christmas Classic came to an unwanted end when the wonderful old woman who put on the Christmas dinner passed away; but both classics, grandmother and game, will live forever in the hearts of those who were privileged to know them.

A back street in Huntsville in the 1950s, a side street in Brandon in the 1930s, a dead-end street in Dartmouth in the 1960s—all have an equal claim to the game that has likely meant more to young Canadians than any other, in any form. I remember one spring day in New York when Wayne Gretzky, watching the Zamboni flood the ice before a Rangers practice, idly chatted with a couple of long-time sportswriters about the curse of over-organized hockey. He did not become a player, he told us, through highly structured fifty-minute ice times, but "in my own backyard, in the driveway—even in the basement" of the Gretzky home on Varadi Avenue in Brantford, Ontario.

He was speaking of the unrecognized beauty of the many variations on pickup hockey: the opportunity to dream, to seek magic, to fail and fail again until, one time, the impossible works. "Every time we teach a child something," the renowned Swiss psychologist Jean Piaget once said, "we keep him from inventing it himself."

In recent years, Canada has been plagued with stories of adults seeking to outlaw this activity one court complainant in Hamilton called "totally uncivilized." It has happened in Miramichi, New Brunswick, in Nepean, Ontario, in Port Coquitlam, British Columbia, and will happen again, elsewhere, before this coming winter is out. Neighbours will complain, the police will be called and, all too often, the issue will be settled in court—usually, mercifully, tossed out by a judge with enough common sense to realize there are better uses for the law than putting a damper on modern-day children "hollerin' and whoopin' like mad with pleasure."

"The way children are interrupted in their play by adults is brutal," Margaret Flinsch, the great American pioneer in early childhood studies, said in an interview a few years ago. "Play is trying out—experimenting. It's not a joke. Children don't play for fun. They play for real, and adults don't understand that; they laugh at what children do. To children, play is very serious."

Many would agree. Some would even argue that there are hidden values in such games. "Road hockey is part of Canada," says a man who successfully led a citizens' revolt to strike down a bylaw in Listowel, Ontario. "If anything, I think it teaches the kids to be even more *aware* of traffic."

"Like fishing or golf," *Globe and Mail* sports columnist Stephen Brunt has written, "it is a game ordered not so much by officials enforcing a code of conduct, but by self-imposed etiquette. To keep playing, rather than taking your stick and going home at the first slight, requires learning how to function cooperatively with others and acknowledge a few simple rights and wrongs."

And to acknowledge as well, this Dufferin Street alumnus would suggest, that there is something pure and sweet about road hockey that is worth preserving by action if not by law. A game that is forever being invented is one that should go on as long as there are players wanting to play.

Road hockey continues to survive, even to the point of serving as a photo opportunity during the 2011 federal election for Prime Minister Stephen Harper.

WALLY'S COLISEUM:
THE MELTING OF THE GRETZKY BACKYARD

(*The Globe and Mail*, December 22, 2007)

BRANTFORD, ONTARIO

Late fall, and tears are falling on the most famous backyard in all of Canada. Great, fat, warm raindrops plunk onto the cover of the swimming pool that sits where, in other Novembers in another century, a father would be laying down the first ice and a small, blond boy would be sitting, fully dressed in his hockey equipment, waiting for the signal to begin the season that once so defined this country.

Wally's Coliseum is no more.

The backyard rink that Walter Gretzky so lovingly built here in Brantford—using a lawn sprinkler for the base ice, then painstakingly building the "glass" skating surface with a slow-flowing hose—is now a fenced-in swimming pool.

It was here where three-year-old Wayne Gretzky took his first turns and first falls. It was on Wally's Coliseum that the ten-year-old who scored 378 goals for the Brantford Nadrofsky Steelers—who was a national figure by the age of eleven, who went on to hold or share sixty-one National Hockey League records—learned the game he would eventually transform.

Wayne Gretzky became that sensation not through structured fifty-minute practice sessions, but, as he has said, "right in my own backyard," doing whatever he felt like doing. Out here, there was only one rule to the game: Get your homework done first. Walter Gretzky, standing in the light rain with a hand on the pool fence, shakes his head at the memory of his first son's dedication. "He would be out here hour after hour," Gretzky remembers, "twisting in and out between pylons we made from Javex bottles. He used to tie a can off a string and hang it in the net and see how many times he could hit it. He used to pay kids a nickel or a dime to play goalie for him."

And he kept at it. Gretzky laughs his crinkly, eyes-closed chuckle as he recalls the night he got so caught up watching television that he forgot all about the little boy in the backyard. And how Phyllis Gretzky came storming downstairs in her night-gown screaming that it was five minutes to midnight on a school night and the boy was still out there twisting among the make-shift pylons: "What are the neighbours going to think?"

But things change. Gretzky is sixty-nine now, so remarkably recovered from a 1991 aneurysm that a movie, *Waking Up Wally,* was made of his story. The five Gretzky kids who learned to skate on this rink—Wayne, Keith, Glen, Brent and sister Kim—are all grown up now. And the "long, long seasons" of Roch Carrier's childhood are all but gone. "You can't make a rink like this anymore because the winters aren't cold enough," Gretzky says. "If you're lucky, you might have two weeks, maybe three weeks. But you can't get three or four weeks in a row of cold. You get one day cold, next day warm. You can't get a rink going."

In the 1960s, 1970s and 1980s, the family skated in the backyard of the home where Walter Gretzky still lives—sadly, Phyllis lost her long battle against lung cancer two years ago—and skated, as well, at the old Gretzky family farm at nearby Canning, where Kim and her young family live today. It was at that farm, at a 1957 wiener roast, that eighteen-year-old Walter first met fifteen-year-old Phyllis. Gretzky recalls that, as a boy, he could skate for miles on the Nith River, which flows by that old farm—"skate until you hit rapids," he laughs—but lately the river rarely freezes over. And even when it does, you wouldn't dare risk stepping out on it.

"Winters are warmer now," he says. "There's no ice."

There is, of course, still ice—and still backyard rinks in many regions of Canada—but winter is not what it once was, with rare exceptions. And most assuredly, in Southwestern Ontario, not what it was back in 1932 when not only was the ice thick on the

Nith, but Niagara Falls froze solid. In many parts of this vast country these days, Quebec songwriter Gilles Vigneault's famous line, "*Mon pays . . . c'est l'hiver*," seems increasingly out of line. My country is not winter—at least not winter as it used to be.

The new Dominion that British prime minister William Gladstone once dismissed as the land "of perpetual ice and snow" was at one time so sensitive about its bitterly cold winters that the federal government banned the words "frost" and "cold" from brochures aimed at prospective immigrants—allowing only the word "buoyant" to be used when describing the Canadian off-season. Today, *buoyant* rather accurately describes the weather in many of the more populated parts of the country.

Besides Wally's Coliseum, Canada has produced several back-yard rinks that are frozen forever in the imagination: Roch Carrier's churchyard rink from "The Hockey Sweater"; the little rink in Floral, Saskatchewan, where Gordie Howe took his first turns in an old pair of skates a neighbour had dropped off; the rink by the barn in Viking, Alberta, that turned six Sutter brothers into NHLers; the big rink on the sod farm in Thunder Bay that produced the four promising Staal brothers . . .

It is difficult to find a Canadian hockey player who does not wax nostalgically about what those little rinks meant to them as youngsters. "The rink was my getaway, my little bit of heaven," Eric Lindros wrote in his autobiography of the backyard rink his father, Carl, built each winter in London, Ontario. "If ever I had a problem in school I would get out onto the rink and blow it off. Being on the rink was the best time of day."

The most famous natural-ice surfaces in Canada produced NHL players. The most famous one in the United States produced a collection of essays—Jack Falla's *Home Ice: Reflections on Backyard Rinks and Frozen Ponds*. Falla, who has written for *Sports Illustrated*, has kept a rink going behind his Natick, Massachusetts, home every winter since 1982. He put up plywood boards and lined the rink—about a third the size of an NHL ice surface—with clear plastic sheeting, then waited for the first cold front before heading out with the hose.

It was, he says, an education by trial and error—too much water created ice that wasn't strong enough to support an adult skater—but eventually he became a local ice master. The Falla rink, which he calls the Bacon Street Omni, became a fixture in Natick and in an increasing number of publications where Falla would wax poetic about its glories. When he put those essays into a collection, Bobby Orr offered to write the foreword, saying the backyard rink was, in his opinion, "the heart and soul of hockey."

Now, Falla, at sixty-four, finds himself at the cusp of his twenty-fifth consecutive season as icemaker and Omni manager. The kids have grown up and started their own families. He has debated "retirement," but each fall some bug grabs him, the way a spring bug grabs golfers the moment they first see grass. "For me," he says, "it really is part of the rhythm of the year."

He knows, however, that it is not the same. For most of the 1980s and 1990s, the rink was in place by the third week of December and ran, with slight thaw setbacks, through the rest of winter. Since the turn of the century, he has had ice before Christmas only twice. Last year, the first skate of the season, the latest ever, was January 21. He shut things down on February 10, his earliest closing date ever.

In the best years, sixty or more people would be on the Bacon Street Omni. Last year, only sixteen people went for a skate. "I know from twenty-four years' experience that we have fewer skateable days now than we did when I started the rink," Falla says. "But even if I knew we'd have skateable ice for only one weekend, I'd still put up the rink. Bottom line on a backyard rink—or at least on my backyard rink—is that it connects me with the people I love."

Despite the constant talk of global warming, he once again had his boards up in early November, waiting for the first cold front to announce the start of the 2007–08 skating season. No fancy refrigeration units and imbedded piping for Falla, who frowns on what he sees as little more than an artificial-ice indoor arena without the roof and walls. "Maintaining and building it is half the fun," he says. As for those elaborate ice surfaces, he wonders aloud: "Aren't you getting awfully close to tennis?"

Falla's motivation has never been to produce future hockey stars—though the game is regularly played on the Omni—but to provide some alternative activity for an already active family. "Some people see their rinks as a springboard for getting ahead in the game," he says, "but my rink was never just for that. It was to give my overscheduled kids some time on their own."

His reward, he says, came only this past year when he happened to overhear his son, Brian, now thirty-six, talking about the Omni to a visitor. "It's my father's legacy," Brian said. It was, Jack Falla says, the only thanks he ever needed to hear.

With the warm autumn rain still falling outside, two of Walter Gretzky's less-famous sons—Keith, forty, and Glen, thirty-eight—sit around talking about their father's legacy and their own recollections of Wally's Coliseum. They talk about the floodlights their dad would string above the ice, how he would so carefully mould the banks so they froze hard and could serve as boards. They laugh about the wood-framed nets he built. But mostly they talk about the ice.

"Great ice," Glen says. "Absolutely great."

"Glass ice," Walter adds. "Not bumpy at all."

"I remember the shovelling," Keith laughs. "We were the ones who had to shovel it off. We used to have snowbanks higher than the fences."

But no longer. The snow comes and goes these days, banks rise and fall. It is, of course, still possible to build outdoor rinks and, in deepest winter, even possible to hold outdoor shinny tournaments in various parts of North America. But all bets are off when it comes to sustaining an outdoor rink from first cold snap to final thaw in a country where, for the most part, the mercury in outdoor thermometers now dances as much as it shrinks.

Walter Gretzky's own memories include the precise point in the yard, pool included, where he established his rink each winter. He recalls the best years and the funny moments, like the time he asked Phyllis to drop in to Canadian Tire to pick up a new lawn sprinkler in ten-below weather and they treated her like "she was crazy."

The clarity of Gretzky's recollection here is significant, as his memory was largely deleted the fall day in 1991 when he was painting out at the farm and suddenly went dizzy. In one of fate's more cruel moments, the most famous hockey father in the world lost his entire remembrance of his famous son's hockey life. He lost each one of the four Stanley Cups in Edmonton; he lost the NHL records, the all-star games, the Canada Cups; he even lost the infamous 1988 trade to Los Angeles.

"It's like I was asleep for ten years," he once told me. "It's all kind of like a dream."

The neurosurgeon who saved him after the aneurysm, Dr. Rocco de Villiers, told him that he would one day come to remember those things "that really mattered" to him. At one point, purely as an experiment, the doctor played a small game to demonstrate how Gretzky's memory could suddenly jump back without him having to wander aimlessly inside his own head in search of it.

Dr. de Villiers told Gretzky that each time he clapped his hands, Gretzky had to tell him the first memory that came to mind.

Clap! He remembered being in church the day of his mother's funeral.

Clap! He remembered one of the hymns sung at his father's funeral.

Clap! He remembered the length of the train—"about three and a half miles long," he giggled—on Janet Jones's wedding dress the summer day in 1988 she and Wayne married in Edmonton.

The doctor was impressed. "Religion must be very important to you," he said. "All your important memories involve church in some way or another."

Here in Brantford on this rainy late-fall day, no clapping is required. Gretzky remembers every possible detail of the back-yard rink, the other place of worship for his family. A precious memory, as clear and solid as that "glass ice" that is, sadly, becoming mostly memory for the country itself.

Jack Falla died of a heart attack in September 2008. He was sixty-two years old. Walter Gretzky, at seventy-two, remains as active as ever, though he still misses that backyard rink.

★ ★ ★ ★ ★ ★ ★ ★ ★

NINE

ANGUISH

THE HOLE IN BOB GAINEY'S HEART

(*The Globe and Mail*, May 3, 2007)

It was a Friday night, sure, but he was early to bed, as usual. There was a game to think about—the Buffalo Sabres, the National Hockey League's best team, in town to play his Montreal Canadiens—and Bob Gainey wanted to get an early start on Saturday.

At almost the same time that the Canadiens general manager turned out the lights in his downtown condominium, his daughter Laura stepped out on the deck of the *Picton Castle* as the ship hit heavy waters about a thousand kilometres off the coast of Cape Cod.

She shouldn't have been there. She should have been down below, in her own bed. But she was twenty-five years old, she was living her dream and, as her father often said, she liked to "live on the edge." Where this sailing gene came from, no one knew. She had been born in Montreal and grown up in Minnesota and Texas, but now she was so in love with sailing she had a tall ship tattooed on her left shoulder and liked nothing in the world better than climbing eight storeys up the mast, unfurling the royal and watching it catch the wind. The royal is a small sail that puffs out majestically, triumphantly, and is used only in light, favourable winds.

This was no night for such a sail. The gale-force wind was at fifty-five knots, the waves slamming into the fifty-five-metre-long barque and the ship tossing heavily. She'd been told to stay below, like most of the other young and less-experienced sailors. She went out on deck without a life jacket. She did not use a safety tether. Perhaps she simply wanted to see the ship battle the storm for herself. We will never know. One wave, some say a "rogue" wave, seemed to reach up and simply slap her off the deck.

Gone, in an instant, with reports of one quick, small cry for help.

No one could see anything, not with the early December dark, not with the sheered water flying in the wind, not for the exploding crashes against the hull. Those who saw her vanish could only throw flotation devices after her and pray that Laura, a fine swimmer, would be able to find one of them in time.

Bob Gainey awoke at 4:30 a.m. A fastidious, meticulous man, he busied himself with some paperwork and then, nearing 6 a.m., he checked his BlackBerry. "I had three messages," he remembers. "Three consecutive messages that came in around 11:30, 11:35, 11:45 and said 'Please call.' I didn't need to make the call to know there was a problem. I knew there was a problem. I just didn't know how bad the problem was."

Life was never supposed to be like this for a hockey hero. As West Coast humorist Eric Nicol once so charmingly put it, "For any God-fearing young Canadian, the ultimate reward is to be chosen for the NHL All-Star Game. If he later goes to Heaven, that is so much gravy."

Bob Gainey played in four National Hockey League All-Star games. He once told his road hockey and rink-rat buddies back in Peterborough, Ontario, that he was going to grow up to become captain of the Montreal Canadiens, and he did, for half of the sixteen years he played in Montreal. He won five Stanley Cups. He won the Conn Smythe Trophy as the most valuable player in the playoffs. He was so brilliant defensively that his abilities inspired the league to create a new trophy, the Frank Selke, to honour the checking forward—and he promptly won it the first four years. When he retired, he was elected to the Hockey Hall of Fame. He had been a lock for years.

Now fifty-two, Bob Gainey had a work ethic as a player so strong that former Montreal goaltender Ken Dryden, himself a Hall-of-Famer, called his old teammate and still-close friend "the playing conscience of the team." When Gainey became captain, he thought the captain of the Montreal Canadiens should be able to speak the language of the team's fans, so he taught himself French, practising with his francophone teammates and reading grammar books on team flights while others played hearts and slept.

He came by such extreme dedication honestly. George Gainey had served in the war and, for four decades, walked daily to his factory job at Quaker Oats. When Bob Gainey became captain of the Canadiens, he insisted on living close enough to the old Montreal Forum that he could walk. When he became general manager many years later, he moved close enough to the Bell Centre that he can still walk to work. George Gainey shovelled his own driveway; Bob Gainey shovelled his, and when Montreal city crews came along trying to do the local captain a favour, he would shoo them away. George Gainey was a humble man who never talked about himself or his war. Bob Gainey does not hang his career on the walls, nor is he comfortable talking about it. "My father," says twenty-nine-year-old Anna Gainey, Laura's older sister, "is a very private man."

George and Anne Gainey had five children and Bob, the youngest, was the hockey star. He was also an altar boy in a very Catholic family. His mother once told the *Dallas Morning News* that her son, then working for the Dallas Stars hockey club, had once come down with a mysterious limp that was cured through nine days of prayer and devotion. She wondered if perhaps it was a "miracle."

Whatever it was, he returned to play and went on to star for the Peterborough Petes, the local junior hockey club. Bright— some say one of hockey's brightest minds—he showed no head for school, failed once and struggled to finish high school. He was also so painfully shy it took ages for the local hockey star to ask out Cathy Collins, a pretty usherette at the hockey rink. Cathy was the fifteenth of nineteen children in another Catholic family, as outgoing as he was reserved, and soon they were together forever. Only Bob Gainey had no idea then how short forever can sometimes be.

"Life," former NHL coach Fred Shero used to say, "is just a place where we spend time between games. Hockey is where we live, where we can best meet and overcome pain and wrong and death."

It is, unfortunately, just a little more complicated than that. Life between games meant four children coming along in fairly quick succession—Anna, Stephen, Laura and Colleen, the baby. Life meant retirement and then a happy year in France, where he played and coached and worked on his French and the children all became fluent themselves. Life meant coming back to the NHL to take a job with the Minnesota North Stars and moving the family to the United States. And life meant the first of two telephone calls that no one—whether starring on the ice or face-less in the crowd—should ever have to go through.

The North Stars were in Winnipeg playing the Jets when, after the morning skate, Gainey received a message to call home. He did and five-year-old Colleen answered. *Daddy! Daddy!* she cried. *"Mommy's on the floor in the bathroom—she's not moving!"*

It was a brain tumour. Cathy Gainey had massive surgery and, over the coming months and years, gruelling radiation, chemo-therapy, good news, bad news, more surgery and, ultimately, impossible news. She fought it for five years; she moved her family when the North Stars left Minnesota for Dallas. She was ever optimistic even when she knew. She was only thirty-nine years old when the cancer won.

The two older children were off at school and, of course, dramatically affected, but the two younger, Laura and Colleen, were traumatized. It is too simple to say they felt anger and abandonment, but that is what is said because no one can possibly know and the young often cannot say. Little Colleen fell into depression and spent time in a clinic. Laura, ten when her mother died, also fought depression and, early into her teens, fell into drugs and bad company in Dallas.

It was a tough, almost impossible time to be a single father with a public and demanding job. On this warm spring day in 2007, less than five months after Laura's own death, Bob Gainey permits himself a small, sad smile: "It wasn't the first time I'd had a phone call about Laura at four o'clock in the morning." He intervened. At one point, he and two of his assistant coaches physically removed Laura from a house. Finally, she was put in a rehabilitation clinic in Topeka, Kansas, stayed nine months— "most kids stay just thirty days," he says—and came out clean and ready to try, at least, a new start.

Ed Arnold, managing editor of the *Peterborough Examiner* and a long-time family friend, learned that Laura was showing interest in photography and had her come to this small city in Central Ontario and cover briefly for a vacationing photographer. First day on the job, she learned of a hostage-taking situation and, somehow, walked through the police lines to take a dramatic photograph of the incident. Her father laughs to remember her first day's work ending up on the front page. "She was a tough, kind of no-fear, straight-ahead young woman," he says.

Laura moved back to Canada and tried her hand at art, at working with children, at environmental studies and then, on sister Anna's suggestion, signed up to train on one of the tall ships. She instantly fell in love with sailing. She found her legs at sea.

She seemed to want so much out of life so quickly that her father often wondered what was driving her. Cathy's death from brain cancer was not the first in her large family, and the concern is that there might be some genetic connection. "Laura was kind of a risk-taker," Bob Gainey says, "thinking that she might not have all that much time. I don't know how big of a play it had in how much she wanted to grab out of life and how quickly, but it had some."

After that first voyage, she returned home, dropped her bags at the front door and announced, "I want to go back." She finally did, joining the *Picton Castle* for what would turn out to be such a fateful voyage. "She kind of reached a point," says her father, "where she decided if she was going to scratch that itch, she had to get back on the ship."

There was no smooth sailing from the rehab centre in Kansas to the dark and windy night of December 8 off Cape Cod, but she was getting there. "She went through different stages," he says, "and she was still in a growth stage at twenty-five." What she was, her siblings knew, was happy at last. They could read it in her e-mails. They heard it from the friends she made in the crew. She was also good at sailing, so good that the accident should never have happened. But for whatever reason, she had to see for herself that night and paid a price youthful curiosity should never pay.

They began to search the following day. At this point, all that was known in Canada was that a crew member had been washed overboard. A woman, and Canadian. The story didn't even make the front pages. It was only as the weekend closed that word came that the young woman was the daughter of a Canadian hockey legend. And suddenly it was front-page.

They were hopeful at first, of course. "You grasp onto what-ever amount of hope there is for a period of time," Bob Gainey remembers, "and then you expand it."

"You instantly think the worst," says Anna Gainey. "There were twenty-two-foot seas that night and gale-force winds. You like to think it was quick, and peaceful. But then you start to backtrack. You think twenty-four hours, thirty-six hours, forty-eight hours, always hoping for something."

The United States Coast Guard searched and Canada also got involved. A friendly congressman from Texas got the Coast Guard to extend the search for a day, but finally the young captain in charge of search and rescue, a man who had not once previously let pessimism seep into his announcements, said they could only "send out one more plane—and when that's done we have to pull our resources."

By now, they knew. There would be no miracle. This was not some mysterious limp that went away while the family prayed. This was hard fact: no Laura, no body, no hope.

Bob Gainey says he likes to think he has some spirituality in him, but not the sort of faith that helps others get through such tragedy. "Some people," he says, "can find enormous strength in that area, but I don't. You don't turn away from the possibility, but . . ."

Coming from Central Ontario and working in Montreal, Minneapolis and Dallas, Gainey had no sense of the sea and did not even comprehend the sheer vastness of it—and the impossibility of finding anything—until he flew over the site himself on a clear day. "It wasn't in my wheelhouse that there was danger involved here," he says, shaking his head. But when he thought about the conditions that night—wind howling, waves sheering off, salt water blinding—he understood how instantly disaster could strike.

But what did it mean? It was only in talking to close friends from the Maritimes that he began to understand. "They all know someone who has been lost at sea," he says. "They know what it means." The best answer came from Anna, who told her father: "If Laura's wishes had been known, and if her body had been found, she probably would have been put back into the sea."

But still he had to deal with it. Somehow. His inclination might be to go it alone, but his friends and the Canadiens organization weren't about to let him. It had no sooner happened than the Gaineys were swamped with support. Even in the weeks when, he freely admits, he became "disengaged" from his work with the hockey club, others moved in to fill the space he left.

He considered briefly that he should step aside, that he had been rendered useless, but he couldn't see how that would accomplish anything. Besides, none of his trusted friends or colleagues had even raised the possibility. Instead, they thought he should get busy and keep busy. And, given his background, he agreed with them. He would carry on.

Bob Gainey, in the opinion of long-time Montreal *Gazette* sportswriter Red Fisher, "played through more pain, I think, than any athlete I have ever known." But this pain didn't go away with icing. This wasn't something surgery and rest could alleviate.

Gainey, who winces visibly when recognized in the streets and approached by fans, was troubled by this growing sense that so many people were feeling sorry for him. He wasn't the only person on earth working his way through tragic circumstances, but at times it sure felt like it.

"I was talking to Ken [Dryden] at one point," he remembers, "and he said, 'You know, Bob, people all across the country are thinking of you.' I said, 'Well, I wish they'd stop.'"

"There's a piece of me," Gainey says on this damp spring day, "that would like to turn out the lights and deal with it on my own."

But he knew he couldn't do that. His children wouldn't let him. His friends wouldn't let him. His country wouldn't let him. The name was too familiar, the story too compelling. "You can do that," he adds, "or you can decide to stay and turn on that light and get underneath it and take that situation and turn it in another direction."

Not long after a very tough Christmas, the remaining family members—Bob, Anna, twenty-eight-year-old Stephen and Colleen, now twenty-two—gathered at the Stoney Lake cottage near Peterborough that has become the Gainey home, even though they are there only on holidays and rarely all together. "We sort of huddled together to try and find some ways that would be positive of going forward with this," he says. A board of marine inquiry, carried out by officials from the Cook Islands, the South Pacific country where the *Picton Castle* is registered, continues.

After Cathy's death, Bob had established, with the help of Ed Arnold, a small foundation in Peterborough that helped children in need with their education. Cathy had been acutely aware of how limited their own education was and had pushed her children to excel where their parents had not. There might, he thought, be something more they could now do in memory of both mother and daughter.

"This is our story," he says, "and it got lots of public attention. Lots of people have these stories and obviously don't get the public attention, yet they have to deal with the same things."

After the loss of Laura, he had been inundated with letters and calls from parents who had lost their own children. A young man lost on a river in Northern Quebec. A young woman lost while kayaking in Europe. So many lost to a variety of accidents. All those families were trying to work through, on their own, what the Gaineys were having such trouble getting through with help.

"There was an opportunity here," says Anna, who first talked about setting up something that might help others in similar circumstances. Anna, who had previously worked for the Liberal Party in Ottawa, would go to Montreal and work full-time on this project that is still very much in the formative stages. There were already donations flowing in from the Canadiens and other organizations, including the Ottawa Senators. They set up a website (www.gaineyfoundation.com) and, over the coming months, hope to stage fundraisers for the charity.

Something happened in those days they gathered at the lake and decided to begin looking forward with hope rather than backwards with all hope lost. "We've been close all along," says

Anna, "and we became closer after we lost our mother. But now, after losing Laura, we've gone beyond close. I don't know how to say it, but we have.

"In a way, you know, we're very lucky."

Bob Gainey's No. 23 jersey was retired by the Canadiens in February 2008. More than halfway through the 2008–09 season, he fired coach Guy Carbonneau and stepped behind the bench himself before turning over the head coach job to Jacques Martin in the summer of 2009. On February 8, 2010, he resigned as general manager for "personal reasons." No one had to ask what they were. He wished to spend more time with family and would stay on as a special adviser to the hockey club. He worked with Anna on the foundation, which has become a great success, particularly in the Peterborough area. The investigation into Laura's death continued, with the Gainey family calling for greater safety precautions on such vessels. In early 2009, he became a grandfather when Anna gave birth to Jackson Robert Pittfield.

LESSONS FROM SWIFT CURRENT

(*The Globe and Mail*, February 2, 2008)

SWIFT CURRENT, SASKATCHEWAN

There is no memorial to mark where it happened on that windy, wintry day so long ago now—though the small yellow road sign with the red thermometer dipping below freezing and the fishtailing car says why it happened.

It is possible to stand on the very first turn in the Trans-Canada Highway heading east out of town and see, on a clear day when the snow isn't blowing, the welcome sign to little Swift Current: "Where life makes sense."

Too often, death makes none.

They learned all about death here in Swift Current twenty-one years ago when the bus carrying the local heroes, the Broncos of the Western Hockey League, caught black ice and whipping wind in the wrong combination coming out of that very first curve, flew off the Trans-Canada and crashed, leaving four young hockey players lifeless. And they learned it again twenty-one days ago when, four provinces and two time zones away, a van carrying the Phantoms, a high-school basketball team from Bathurst, New Brunswick, slid in bad weather into a transport trailer, killing seven players and the coach's wife.

"It hit home, that's for sure," says Joe Sakic, the Broncos star who survived that long-ago crash and went on to a spectacular career with the Quebec Nordiques and the Colorado Avalanche of the National Hockey League.

Even today it is difficult for Sakic to talk about that moment, something he has only agreed to do with the thought that there might be lessons for the Bathurst players who survived and for little Bathurst, population thirteen thousand, in what became of little Swift Current, population sixteen thousand. "Both small towns," says Sakic. "Both involved their teams. You never do forget. They say time heals, and it does, but you remember everything. You never forget."

Sakic can even recall the weather conditions that December 30, 1986: temperature dropping to around freezing, the radio talking about high winds, storm concerns for the game that night in Regina, a 2½-hour ride away on the team's old Western Flyer. Four of the guys had even arrived early—Scott Kruger and Trent Kresse, the scorers, Brent Ruff, the promising rookie, Chris Mantyka, the enforcer—and had claimed the prized card-playing seats at the very back of the bus.

Sakic, a rookie at seventeen and already the team's leading scorer, sat near the front with Sheldon Kennedy, his best friend and fellow billet at the busy McBean house in Swift Current. The third McBean billet, team captain Daniel Lambert, was off playing for the national junior team, the "C" taken over by popular Kurt Lackten, who was going with the McBeans' daughter, Karen.

The old bus pulled out of town and onto the Trans-Canada, rising quickly to pass over the railway tracks in a wide loop to the southeast. Sakic felt the bus begin to slide as it went into the long turn, then he felt the wind punch it sideways. He heard volunteer driver Dave Archibald yell "Hold on" just as the bus flew off the rise into the bank of an access road, crumbled over onto its right side and slid through the snow. The driver was thrown out the windshield and, miraculously, pushed to safety by the sliding bus. Sakic and Kennedy were shaken up but that was all. "Neither of us was hurt," Sakic remembers. "We were both fine. We just walked out where the windshield had been."

As Sakic made it back up the embankment, cars and trucks were already stopping. He was placed in one of the first vehicles— he doesn't remember if it was a truck or a car—and hurried off to the little hospital in town. He didn't even know if anyone had been hurt. Kennedy, who had walked around to the back of the bus, knew otherwise.

The four card players had taken the brunt of the blow. Kruger and Kresse had been thrown out the windows and killed instantly. Ruff, the sixteen-year-old rookie and younger brother of Lindy Ruff, then captain and now coach of the Buffalo Sabres, was crushed under the bus. Mantyka, the tough guy, was frantically trying to push clear of the weight of the bus that had trapped him. He called out for help, but help was impossible. His teammates had to stand there helplessly, watching their most popular player die.

Sakic was checked at the hospital and declared fine. It was only then that the others came streaming in and he heard what had happened. "I couldn't believe it," he says. "I was in absolute shock."

How, Sakic wondered, could he simply walk out without a scratch and be oblivious to the carnage behind him? He hadn't heard Mantyka's screams. He hadn't seen the trainer and a travelling reporter trying to resuscitate the players. He hadn't noticed the blood on so many of his other teammates. "It was all sort of dreamlike," he remembers. And then, nightmare-like.

Colleen McBean was the guidance counsellor at Swift Current Composite High School, but also surrogate mother to most of the team who came from other communities. Sakic, Kennedy and Lambert were all billeted at the McBean house. Her lawyer husband, Frank, was on the community-owned team's board of directors.

Frank McBean had been part of the group that had spearheaded a movement to get a team in town. Swift Current would be the smallest centre in all of major junior hockey and the doubters thought it too small to support such an enterprise, but McBean and others managed to land a franchise that would be moving from Lethbridge, Alberta. They had the beginnings of a team; they hired a popular young coach, Graham James, who believed in fast, skilled hockey; and they had young budding stars like Sakic, Kennedy and the kid, sixteen-year-old Ruff.

To no one's surprise, the first-year team was struggling: by Christmas break an unlikely bet to make the post-season play-offs. December 30, 1986, had already been circled on Colleen McBean's calendar. She had a dental appointment in Regina. And since she was going there anyway, daughter Karen asked if she might come along and stay for the game. And if she was going to be allowed to watch her boyfriend Kurt play, then would it be all right if the girlfriends of Joe—Debbie, whom he would later marry—and Sheldon also came along?

McBean agreed and headed out with a full carload—a visiting nephew included—and they all met later at Regina's Cornwall Centre shopping mall for coffee. One of the girls came along looking ghostly: She had just heard a radio report in one of the stores that tonight's game between the Pats and the Broncos had been cancelled due to an accident. The girlfriends were frantic with worry. "This was pre-cellphones," the now-retired teacher remembers, "so I had to go to a payphone. I reached Frank just as he was heading out for the hospital. 'It's bad,' he said, 'some of the boys have been killed.'"

Her first instinct, of course, was that it might be her boys—the billets. But then she realized it didn't matter who it was that had been killed, it was a horrible thing. They were all so young. So seemingly indestructible.

Just before Christmas she had had a long talk with the youngest, Brent Ruff, and heard how excited he was about going home to Warburg, Alberta, for the holidays. He had beaten his early homesickness. "I love it here," he told her. "I'm so lucky. I'm playing more than I thought I would. Life is good."

"I never forgot that," McBean says twenty-one years later. "'Life is good.' When he first came here and I saw he was so young I told his parents, 'Don't worry: We'll take good care of him.' No one knew what to do. Should they head for home? Should they go to the Regina hospital where the more seriously hurt might be sent? In the end we all just sat under the bank of payphones and cried."

They eventually made their way to the Regina home of a McBean relative and waited for the call and the list. Kresse . . . Kruger . . . Mantyka . . . Ruff . . . "The next few days are kind of a blur," McBean remembers.

She immediately put to use her grief training and her own personal experience. Only two summers earlier, Frank and Colleen McBean had lost their two young adolescent sons in a car accident near their country retreat. The boys weren't old enough to drive, and the lake friend at the wheel hadn't been responsible enough to take care. The car crashed, killing the two McBean boys and injuring others.

McBean kept her own emotions to herself and threw herself into working with students at the high school and with players who started hanging out at the McBean residence around the clock, endlessly talking about what had happened and why. "Colleen helped," Sakic says. "She was definitely a big help to everyone."

However, the team coach, James, elected not to have psychological counselling for the players as a group, the feeling being that they could deal with this as all teams are supposed to deal with adversity: quietly, and by themselves. No one thought for a moment that he might have his own motives for keeping professional help at bay.

"The bus accident sent a great wave of emotion through the school," McBean says. "The shock waves felt in this little community were immense."

Three weeks ago, when she heard the news coming out of New Brunswick, she felt it all over again. "You just knew instantly," she says, "what they are going through."

Ryan Switzer's world fell apart that December day in 1986. He was nine years old when word came that disaster had struck the team he worshipped. The Broncos meant everything to the hockey-mad youngster. He idolized Ruff—"He was like a rock star to me"— partly because of the nifty way Ruff played but also because he was youngest and therefore closest in age.

But the connection ran deeper still. The man Switzer considered his "adopted father" ran the public relations for the junior hockey club. His mother sang the anthem before the Broncos' home games. Switzer's own dream was to grow up and go to work for the team.

It was vacation time and the Switzers had gone, as so many Prairie families do, to the West Edmonton Mall, the poor man's Disney World. He was staring into the dolphin tank when another family from Swift Current came along and passed on the news. "That," says Switzer, now thirty, "was my first experience with death. I just went silent. I didn't know at all how I should react. All the adults were breaking down and so I started to cry, too."

Switzer, who has lived all his life in town and did indeed grow up to work for the Broncos—he does colour analysis during the broadcasts—says that crash changed his town forever. "Strange as this may sound," he says, "it was our 9/11. It became our city's identity. It changed people. Suddenly all the usual animosities in a town didn't seem so important. People seemed friendlier. It was like what you heard happened in New York City. The tragedy had the effect of bringing everyone together. New York changed forever after that. So did Swift Current."

The town staged a packed memorial at the hockey rink: mourners included jersey-clad players from the other teams in the league. They held Scott Kruger's funeral in town and sent off representatives to show a Swift Current presence at the other funerals.

And then they had to decide what to do. Carry on? Cancel the season? Fold the team? "There was no talk of not going on," Sakic says. "You keep going. We talked, but it was about when do we want to start again? How long do we wait?"

Colleen McBean was anxious, for professional reasons, for them to get back to playing again as soon as possible. The fragile youngsters needed it. "Difficult as it was for them," she says, "all of those kids kept getting up each morning and getting through the day. I think in hindsight that the fact that they made such an effort to get back on track was good for them. Their days were structured. They were busy. I know from our own experience that is what gets you through the day."

"The best thing for us was to get back on the ice," Sakic says. "Once you start playing again, for those few hours you can take your mind off it. You just focus on playing hockey."

They started talking about an appropriate memorial, and today the refurbished rink still features a special window in the lobby dedicated to the four players. "Unchanged forever," the window says. "What we keep in memory is ours."

First game back was an away game, against the archrival Moose Jaw Warriors, and the Broncos had something new on their jersey arms: a crest with the four lost numbers — 8, 9, 11, 22 — in a four-leaf clover that trainer Gord Hahn had stitched on. "It was nice to put the uniform back on and just go out and play," Sakic says.

At Moose Jaw, the visiting Broncos were given a louder cheer than the home side. At every rink throughout the league it was the same: a long, emotional standing ovation to start each match, cheers of salute to end the games. When they played at home, nearly three thousand fans would pack into the tiny rink that is supposed to hold only twenty-two hundred. "The rink was where we went for our healing," says Ben Wiebe, the current governor of the Broncos.

"It was pretty amazing," Sakic remembers.

Whatever it was that took hold of the budding seventeen-year-old rookie at this moment — the luck of the clover, a fierce determination to honour his teammates — Joe Sakic became a far more commanding player and, undeniably, the team's leader. "He was seventeen," Colleen McBean recalls. "We had lost our two older star players. It just seemed like all the pressure shifted to him. Everyone knew he had the makings of a great player, but he stepped up in a way that no one could have imagined."

At the time of the accident, the Broncos were out of a playoff berth. There had been no high expectations for that first season in town. Yet Sakic, playing as if possessed, racked up 133 points as a rookie and carried the team into the post-season. He was named the Western League's most valuable player and presented with a new trophy named in honour of the four downed Broncos.

The Little Team That Could had made the playoffs. They would go out in the first round, but they had still made the playoffs. With ten minutes to go in the final game they would play that spring, not a fan in the stands was still sitting, the ovation continuing long after the buzzer had sounded.

"That was their goal," says Trent McCleary, who at the time was a budding fourteen-year-old allowed to practise with the team and who would ultimately serve as Broncos captain. "That was their Stanley Cup."

"I will never be more proud of a group of kids anywhere," McBean says. "After what they had been through, it was such an amazing accomplishment."

Two years later, with Sakic now starring as a nineteen-year-old rookie with the Nordiques but with six of those original Broncos still in the lineup, they went all the way, winning the Memorial Cup in Saskatoon against the local hope, the Blades. Appropriately, it was the goaltending of Trevor Kruger, Scott's brother, that got them to overtime. And it was a shot from the point by Darren Kruger, another brother, that was tipped in for the victory by Tim Tisdale, who had been on the bus when it crashed.

When the winning goal went in at SaskPlace, Colleen McBean and her daughter Karen didn't even cheer. They threw their arms around each other, hugged and wept.

They were hardly alone. Ryan Switzer was now twelve and even more of a committed fan than he had been at nine. "The crash was the first time I ever cried over grief," he says. "And then, when they won the Memorial Cup, it was the first time I ever cried out of happiness. Bronco hockey taught me emotion."

There has, in the past, been talk of a movie on the Broncos' remarkable journey from tragedy to triumph and, certainly, all the ingredients are there: the raw emotion, the determination to carry on, the amazing victory in the Memorial Cup, the admirable humility of Joe Sakic, the local boy, Tisdale, scoring the winning goal by tipping in a shot from the brother of one of the players who had died . . .

But the whole storyline is hardly so simple. While no one blamed Archibald for the accident, there were some feelings that they shouldn't even have set out in such conditions, though such risky travel is common experience in the Prairie winter. The Kresse and Mantyka families eventually tried to pursue a civil suit over the accident, but it turned out they were too late for any such claim and the idea was quietly dropped.

As for the coach who wanted nothing to do with psychological counselling for his team, Graham James was, in fact, hiding
something. In 1996, a decade after the accident, James—by now
part-owner, general manager and coach of the Calgary Hitmen—
was charged with sexual assault against minors. Two players who
would eventually testify against him had been Broncos, Sheldon
Kennedy and another, unnamed player. James would plead guilty
and be given a forty-two-month jail sentence.

An *ESPN Magazine* story last year by Canadian writer Gare
Joyce opened some old wounds in Swift Current when some of
the people Joyce interviewed wondered how those close to the
team could not have known what was happening. There had,
after all, long been suspicion and innuendo concerning James and
his manipulative hold on certain players. Kennedy, who has gone
through a very public and brave catharsis concerning the damage
inflicted on him by his old coach—and who now runs a foundation dedicated to assisting abused children—thought he had been
let down by certain people who may have felt winning hockey
games was more important than losing innocence.

Trent McCleary, the former NHLer who served two years as
team captain of the Broncos while James was still coaching, has
often asked himself, "What would I have done?" if he had only
known. But he did not know. "I didn't see it," says McCleary,
now a Swift Current investment dealer. "I just did not see it."

McCleary is hardly alone. Almost everyone else close to the
team says they missed it, too. Some are haunted by their failure—
perhaps not realizing that deception is the predator's greatest
tool. "Was there stuff going on?" McCleary says. "Yeah, plain
and simple. Everyone has had to make their peace with that."
Some have; some have not.

When the twentieth anniversary of the Swift Current tragedy
was approaching a year ago, the board that controls the team held
several discussions on what might be done to mark the occasion.
Joe Arling, who served as chair, thought it should be humble, as

befits the Canadian Prairie personality. They elected to go with a moment's silence before the home game against Medicine Hat that fell on the precise date, December 30, 2006. Nothing else. Some thought there might have been more but others, including Joe Sakic, thought simplicity the correct route. He could not have come anyway, being involved in NHL play—and, besides, he didn't need to be there. "You never forget," he says. "So it's not just that one day you want to remember. You remember it every day."

McCleary thinks it should be remembered, and by more than the people of Swift Current. "It's one of the most amazing hockey stories ever," he says. "A brand-new team, a small town, in the very first year four players are killed in a bus accident and the team continues on to win the Memorial Cup two years later. You look at the last fifty years in hockey—what's a better story than that?"

At the moment, little Bathurst, New Brunswick, is one story: a highway crash that killed the coach's wife, fifty-one-year-old Beth Lord, five seventeen-year-olds—Javier Acevedo, Codey Branch, Nathan Cleland, Justin Cormier, Daniel Hains—a sixteen-year-old, Nickolas Quinn, and fifteen-year-old Nicholas Kelly. The rest of the story remains to be written.

Saskatchewan premier Brad Wall, who grew up playing street hockey in Swift Current with Scott Kruger, believes Bathurst can take comfort from the Swift Current story. Life has to go on. There is no other option. "It's what happens in small communities from time to time," Wall says. "These two towns have a lot in common. We're places where everyone knows everyone else. And communities rally. They never forget, but they rally. They have to."

"It's tough," says Joe Sakic from his home in Colorado. "You can't believe what happened. You just don't believe it. It's tough to think about it and it's something you never forget. You want to overcome it all, but these are your friends. You can't forget. You don't want to forget.

"All you know for sure is that, in time, things will get better."

Joe Sakic retired in 2009 as one of the greatest players in National Hockey League history. He stayed away from the game for two years, but has since rejoined the Avalanche as a special adviser and alternate governor. The Swift Current Broncos failed to make the playoffs in 2010–11 and are in a rebuilding mode. An RCMP investigation into the Bathurst tragedy concluded that the van would never have passed a safety test and that six of the seven who died did not have seatbelts properly fastened. A public inquiry produced a number of safety recommendations, several of which have now been put in place. One year later, remarkably, the Bathurst High School basketball team, the Phantoms, won the provincial AA championship.

GUY LAFLEUR'S NIGHTMARE

(*The Globe and Mail*, June 18, 2008)

POINTE-CLAIRE, QUEBEC

"**N**ice gift." The smile was subtle—the sarcasm, not at all.

Guy Lafleur was thinking about his and Lise's thirty-fifth wedding anniversary, which fell on Monday. Next month, their new restaurant, Bleu Blanc Rouge, is scheduled to open in nearby Rosemère. Their first child, Martin, a full partner in the business, is currently building a house, which has his father looking tanned and fit from his new life as contractor, landscaper and manual labourer.

Life, you would think, couldn't be better for the fifty-six-year-old hockey legend known in Quebec as the "Flower." But his wife has not been well. Twice, recently, Lise's voice mysteriously vanished. Neither of them sleeps well. Guy Lafleur—winner of five Stanley Cups with the Canadiens, one of the province's greatest heroes since that February day in 1962 when the eleven-year-old sensation from Thurso scored seven goals in a single game in the Quebec International Pee-Wee Hockey Tournament—still in shock from having a warrant issued for his arrest in January. And their other son, Mark, appeared in Montreal court yesterday to plead guilty to fourteen charges, including uttering threats to his now nineteen-year-old former girlfriend who was a minor, forcible confinement and assault.

"I look back on all this," says the elder Lafleur, "and say it's a nightmare."

And it is far from over. There will be more court days, as Mark Lafleur also pleaded not guilty to two charges of sexual assault. And Guy Lafleur will have his own day in court this fall. The police records and newspaper clippings will say the nightmare began a year and a half ago with that long list of charges being laid against the younger son, who has been in custody for the past nine months since he broke the strict conditions of his bail—police say with his father's assistance.

More accurately, it is a shared nightmare, and it goes back twenty-three years, virtually to the moment of Mark Lafleur's birth and a nurse's comment to Lise that her squirming, squealing second child had a "big personality." Perhaps too big. The records and the clippings—and now the courts—speak to the demon side, but the family and friends will tell you of a young man who has remarkable people skills, who can be charming and funny when he is not lashing out irrationally.

Guy Lafleur is not here to argue his son's innocence in all that he has been accused of, and now in part admitted to. "I have nothing against my son paying for what he did wrong," he says. But he has agreed to talk so that people know what it is like to have been a child such as Mark Lafleur. And, by extension, what it is like to be a parent of such a child.

Guy Lafleur tells his friends, *"Ton enfant reste ton enfant"*— once your child, always your child.

Three weeks after that squirming, crying baby was born, Mark

Lafleur had surgery for a digestive problem. He was not much more than a child when he was diagnosed with Tourette's syndrome, a neurological disorder that is more often associated with curious tics—sometimes in action, sometimes in voice—and less often with sudden outbursts of obscenities and cruel insults. Mark Lafleur is one who has no tics to signal this disorder to others, but has had the outbursts in quantity.

The outbursts worsened as he hit puberty, the boy screaming terrible threats—including "I'm going to kill you!"—at father, mother, older brother and others from the time he was about twelve right up to his arrest. The strange thing, the father says, is that the son would carry no memory of such moments, claiming "I can't remember," and then falling into often-tearful spasms of remorse.

Compounding all this was the discovery, early on, that Mark suffered from attention deficit hyperactivity disorder. By the time he began elementary school, he was on four different medications, chief among them Ritalin. Before he even made it to kindergarten, he had been kicked out of two daycares that could not handle the whirling dervish and the angry outbursts.

The Lafleurs took their younger child—Martin, now thirty-one, had no such difficulties—to a long series of doctors, psychologists and psychiatrists, each seemingly with a new idea of what to do. When the ADHD medication kept him awake at night, one added on sleeping pills. At one point, when Mark was fourteen, he spent two months in hospital while doctors tried to find a proper chemical mix for him. By the time he left school, he had attended thirteen different institutions, including two private schools in Ontario especially designed to accommodate children with learning disabilities and behavioural problems.

"All that medication made him look like a zombie," Guy Lafleur says. "When you give that to your kid at five, six, seven years old, you're giving him drugs. I know it's supposed to be that you're helping him out, but you're still giving him drugs.

"I'm not saying everyone is affected this way. We know people who take Ritalin and are okay with it. But then, if you don't give them that, what are you going to give them to help out?" The problems with this severe disorder prevented the youngster from finding a place for himself in the same sports world that had been such a sanctuary to the father: hockey. Martin, who had been only mildly interested in his father's game, had played briefly but preferred skiing. Mark, on the other hand, showed early talent, but his temper was soon the ruin of him.

"Maybe this is a result of all the rejection he has had in his life," the father wonders. "I don't know if he understood from the first moment when we tried to find help. It's tough. You don't have the answers of what to do to get them out of trouble. You try to make him understand what's wrong and what's right . . . They are a type of kid who are very—miserable—inside. They're unhappy. They're trying to find a way out and they cannot. People who don't have kids like that, they can't understand."

Guy Lafleur thinks he understands, to an extent. "I truly believe I was ADHD," he says of his youth in a small mill town along the Quebec side of the Ottawa River. "But I trained a lot. I worked on the farm. I wasn't on Valium or Ritalin. Nothing." He threw himself into hockey as there was little else for an active child to do. He worries that today's privileged youngsters have too much opportunity granted by parents with too much themselves.

"It's tougher for them to hear a 'no' than it was in our day," he says. "Because our parents had so little." Guy Lafleur was never fabulously wealthy by today's hockey superstar standards—the most he made in a single season was $400,000, and about $5 million for the seventeen seasons he played in the National Hockey League—but he made superb money and was always generous to his boys. As with most parents, perhaps generous to a fault.

Guy Lafleur believes people can change. He did himself, several times. The hockey star who was once known for his between-period smokes and post-game beers hasn't had a real beer in more than fifteen years. He sees himself today not as a hockey god, but as a simple restaurateur trying to get a family business off the ground—hopefully, at some point, with all the family involved. He says his son never got in much more trouble than the odd traffic ticket prior to his January 2007 arrest. But that is only officially, as trouble was long brewing. The young girlfriend was one thing, drugs another.

As yesterday's plea was tabled, the court was told this had been a highly abusive relationship, and given that it also involved a girl who was a minor at the time, one that most assuredly would have been torturous to the young unnamed girl's family as well as difficult for the Lafleurs. And the hurt, on all sides, is not over yet.

Lafleur, rightly or wrongly, believes young people with severe ADHD are more "immature" than their peer group, and he and Lise had always hoped maturity would come for their son before serious trouble. They tried to talk their son and his young girlfriend into going back to school. They tried to give them jobs. But nothing seemed to work.

When Mark's bail hearing came up after his arrest, Guy Lafleur agreed to watch over his son and ensure that the court-imposed curfew was kept. He made a serious error, however, when he drove Mark to a hotel rendezvous with the girl last August and allowed the court to believe that Mark had, in fact, been at the family's home in Île-Bizard. The older Lafleur said the 12:30 a.m. curfew was still being met but, of course, it was the wrong thing to do.

Since that time, Mark Lafleur has remained in jail—his parents' best hope now being that, whatever his sentencing and whatever the outcome of the other charges, his incarceration will eventually come to an end. "It's been hell for her," Lafleur says of his wife. "She's been sick ever since Mark got arrested."

But then, almost exactly one year later, there was a warrant issued for the arrest of Guy himself. "How do you think she felt?" Lafleur asks. "'My son is criminally charged—now my husband is, too.'"

The warrant for the arrest of one of the province's most beloved sports icons caused outrage in Quebec. Lafleur's closest friends— former players Jean Béliveau, Gaston Gingras, Yvan Cournoyer, Stephane Richer, Réjean Houle and powerful sportswriters such as Red Fisher and Bertrand Raymond—were furious.

Why a warrant? people wanted to know. Why would the police officer involved not simply ask Lafleur to come down to the station? "She phoned me on my cell," Lafleur says. "So, if I'm tough to reach? . . . I just don't know why she would do that." Lafleur is now suing Montreal police and the Crown for $3.5 million, claiming that the warrant was unnecessary and that it, along with his subsequent arrest, severely damaged his reputation and potential earnings from that reputation.

That, however, is less important to the father than his son having a chance to one day build a new reputation and a new life. "There's time for him to go back and think about what he did," Lafleur says.

If there is any silver lining to this very dark cloud, it may lie in the fact that Mark Lafleur has had time for some, hopefully, clearheaded reflection. After his arrest, he underwent a month of psychiatric assessment. The family then got him into a detox centre, where he spent four months. Then came the nine months in jail. With luck, the father says, that could soon add up to two years of being away from drugs.

"I tell him, 'When you get out, we'll help you out. But go slow. Be patient. Try to understand what happened and why.' I will tell him, 'If you want to do that type of life, it's your call. If you want to change, fine. We'll help. But if you choose that life, that's it. You're going to have to forget us as a family. There's not going to be a second time.'

"We have a life, too. It's something that if you let it happen, he will ruin his mother's life, my life, too. So I say, 'If you want to ruin your life, ruin it on your own.'"

The tension of such talk plays on the familiar face, but Guy

Lafleur is determined. "Mark is capable of doing well and changing his life," he says. "I'm not going to change his life. But he's twenty-three years old and he's going to have to do it himself." It takes a fourth fill of coffee for the smile to return, and even when it does it is small and uncertain.

"I always say, 'There's only one past—but there's a lot of futures.' It's going to be up to Mark to make the best of it. The most important thing is to get him out of there and on the right track. There's no other choice."

Guy Lafleur was convicted in June 2009 and given a one-year suspended sentence. He appealed and, on August 17, 2010, was unanimously acquitted of all charges by the provincial Court of Appeal.

THE CLOUD OVER VIKING
(*The Globe and Mail*, February 16, 2005)

VIKING, ALBERTA

They came to say farewell to a man who loved black cows, sappy songs and "pull my finger" gags. They thought, for most of the day, that they would be burying the game he loved best as well—the National Hockey League, where six of Louis Sutter's seven sons went off to play a total of 4,994 games. They filled the community centre with as many mourners as the town has citizens, fourteen hundred, filled it on a cold clear day where the only lingering cloud was in the conversation before and after the service.

Is the NHL season over? Will it be, as everyone expected when they set out for Louis Sutter's funeral, officially cancelled this afternoon in a New York press conference? Or has it—through panic, through coming to senses, through the intervention of three key players—been salvaged just when fans were beginning to accept that the owners' lockout would mean no season at all this year?

No one at the funeral knew what was going on in the surprise last-minute meetings between the league and the players, not even Harley Hotchkiss, chairman of the board of governors. "I didn't even know the man," said Mr. Hotchkiss, one of the owners of the Calgary Flames. "But I came because, right now, I feel there's more of the Sutters in all of us than there is in what's been going on elsewhere."

Whatever was going on elsewhere was far, far away from little Viking. Here, they started arriving before noon for a 2 p.m. funeral service. Some came by chartered bus, some wheeled their own chairs down the snow-covered streets. Some wore Hugo Boss suits—the true official uniform of NHL players—and some came in jeans and cowboy boots. Some men tossed cigarettes away at the door and inserted toothpicks; some men gave up their seats to women and went and leaned against the walls.

They were here to honour Louis Sutter, seventy-three, the seventh of thirteen children and, surely forever, to stand as the Secretariat of hockey breeding. Sons Brian, Darryl, Duane, Brent and the twins, Ron and Rich, all learned the game on the farm slough and went off to play in the NHL where, as a family, they scored a total of 1,320 goals and 2,935 points. They won Stanley Cups and played on so many teams that it is easier to remember the one none ever did play for—the Oilers straight up Highway 14. All six are still involved in hockey. Darryl coached the Flames to the Stanley Cup final last June, and Brent coached Team Canada to the world junior championship last month.

But the gathering also paid tribute to Grace, the widow who celebrated her fiftieth anniversary with Louis last summer, the mother who sorted out the tube socks and washed the long underwear. By wide admission, Grace was the central force behind a family so smitten with hockey that it was said that, on weekends, you had to go out into the barn if you wanted a breath of fresh air.

What Louis Sutter handed down to his boys was stubbornness, a willingness to work hard and a strong sense that you are never better than anyone else. The Sutter boys—only Gary, who stayed behind to work the farm, did not pursue a professional hockey career—were consummate "soldiers" in a Canadian game that admires grinders and heart and determination above all else.

Sutters never complained, never whined, never believed in the self above the team. A stark contrast often noted by those who stayed around to chat while the direct family, with the boys all serving as pallbearers, went off to the cemetery for a private burial.

People spoke with great affection for Louis, who was obviously sometimes a handful. They told the story of him trying to sneak into town for a drink driving the combine. Even his grandchildren joked about his love for "happy hour," which sometimes went on "too long." His great-nephew, Perry Chernesky, talked about the great delight his uncle took in playing the old "pull my finger" gag on any kid silly enough to yank the older man's finger and suffer the consequences.

It is unlikely that Mr. Chernesky, a pastor, has ever told a similar story to his congregation in Edmonton. But Edmonton is not Viking. Only Viking has a sign by the elevators claiming to be "Home of the Sutters."

It was this recognition as a special hockey family that brought so many of the hockey world out to honour a man many of them had never even met. Kevin Lowe and Craig MacTavish were there from the Oilers. Bob Pulford was there from the Chicago Blackhawks. Former players Lanny McDonald, Jim Peplinski and Rich Preston were there. Hockey Canada president Bob Nicholson was among the mourners, as were numerous scouts and various present players.

They came to sit and listen while Louis Sutter's grandchildren took to the podium, their voices sometimes breaking, and told stories about their grandfather.

"He loved old cows, preferably blacks. He said black cows could calve up in a tree."

"Grandpa loved standing oat crops—every year they were going to run 110 bushels."

"He loved grabbing handfuls of wheat and chewing on it until he had gum."

"He loved country music, especially the old ones, and thought he could sing them all."

"Grandpa loved shooting gophers with his old twenty-two."

"He loved Grandma's desserts—especially rhubarb pie and pudding. And chocolate bars from town."

"He loved watching hockey and baseball on television."

"He loved the Toronto Maple Leafs"—and, apparently, cheered for them even when one of his own would be playing for the other side.

They played his old favourite songs, John Denver's "Back Home Again" and Hank Snow's "Old Shep," the story of having to put a sick dog down and not quite being able to do it—a slight stretch of a metaphor for whatever might be going on in New York that same afternoon between owners and players.

Colin Campbell, the NHL vice-president who has spent the past months looking at changes to the professional game and hearing, endlessly, that it is "broke" and just isn't like the old days, could only stand in the centre of the hall and shake his head. "You see something like this," he said. "It's not broke." But then he had to move.

They were putting up the tables and chairs for the community supper. And everyone was expected to pitch in.

Almost immediately after the funeral, NHL commissioner Gary Bettman officially cancelled the 2004–05 season. Hockey returned a year later with new rules against obstruction that heralded a new era of faster, more skilled hockey. Brent Sutter coached the New Jersey Devils but then returned to Alberta, where today he is coach of the Calgary Flames. Brother Darryl resigned as the Flames' general manager in late December 2010. His son, Brett, is an NHL prospect with the Carolina Hurricanes, where Brandon Sutter, Brent's son, is an assistant captain. Several other next-generation Sutters are also excelling in hockey.

★ ★ ★ ★ ★ ★ ★ ★ ★ ★

TEN

IT'S NOT JUST
"A MAN'S GAME"

A SCANDAL OF MINUSCULE PROPORTIONS

(The Globe and Mail, March 2, 2010)

VANCOUVER, BRITISH COLUMBIA

It was their Olympic moment—and, in an accidental way, mine. Never for a moment of any kind—Olympic or professional—did I think of it as a story other than a charming and endearing tale. Perhaps I should resign in disgrace from the profession of journalism. As it happened, I was one of the very few actual witnesses to the post-game, on-ice celebration by the Canadian women's hockey team last Thursday.

You will know it as the "booze and cigars" scandal that shook the Canadian Olympic moment to the very core.

The women had defended their gold medal wonderfully with a sparkling 2–0 victory over archrival United States. They had leapt upon their brilliant goaltender Shannon Szabados with a fervour that suggested, for a moment, that she would become the "Lucky Loonie" under the ice that the men would play last Sunday for their gold. They had screamed and screeched and hugged each other and burst into tears and, in a lovely gesture, had paraded about the ice with their Canadian flags and saluted a delirious crowd. Some actually shook and shivered as their medals were placed over their necks and the flag and anthem raised to the roof.

That, I thought, was the story, and had been happily reworking it with quotes later in the day, when the packed arena had long since emptied. The ice had just been resurfaced. It glistened invitingly. The ice-surfacing machine was still out when the first unmistakable scrape of a skate blade on ice floated up into the press area where a few of us were still working.

I looked down and smiled to see that the gold medal winners had still not taken off their uniforms or skates, still had not had enough of their special moment. Several came skating out, the ice resurfacer cheering them as he saw what they were doing, even though it meant he would have to do his work all over again.

Two of the women—Meaghan Mikkelson and Rebecca Johnston—moved to the far end and began making circles in the ice like figure skaters, unaware that from where those of watching stood, their freshly cut circles were very close to forming the Olympic symbol. How serendipitous. Several more players came out. They had cameras. One was carrying a bottle of champagne. Others had beer. One had an unlighted cigar. Another cigar appeared and a lighter. Soon, the almost-forgotten smell of cigar smoke floated into the press area.

The former captain of the Canadian women's team, Cassie Campbell Pascal (now married to Hockey Canada's Brad Pascal), was still there, packing up from her broadcasting job, and the players called her down. She congratulated them and, wisely, left them to their special moment. As everyone should have.

The resurfacer asked if he could have his photograph taken with them and they were delighted to accommodate, forming an impromptu team photo at centre ice with the ice machine as backdrop. He let them try the machine. All, presumably, had driver's licences.

Two of them skated to a quiet part of the rink, lay on their backs, lifted their legs high in the air and shook their skates like little children playing in the snow. I do not know if I have seen anything so sweet and so very, very, very Canadian.

It never occurred to me that I would write about this except, perhaps, to show that there is something special to being on an Olympic team that goes far beyond any games or medals. But someone must have thought it was scandalous. Women smoking cigars? Women drinking champagne and beer? Didn't they just win an Olympic gold medal—and aren't they a hockey team?

But then someone looking for a peg found a peg—the woman with the beer was not only the one who had scored both Canadian goals but was . . . wait . . . wait . . . *eighteen years old!* And what's the drinking age in British Columbia? Why it's . . . *nineteen!*

Stop the Games. Call out the police. Charges. Disgrace. Take away their medals.

To me, there is only one thing equal to the embarrassment of a wire service deciding this was a news story of issue rather than an anecdote of great charm. And that is that some people actually took it seriously.

Hockey Canada felt obliged to apologize for the women's behaviour. The International Olympic Committee even vowed to get to the bottom of this scandalous allegation of an eighteen-year-old Olympic gold medallist holding a beer—suggesting perhaps the beer in hand wasn't an official sponsor, who knows?

What Hockey Canada should have done, rather than apologize to women who had already been insulted that same day by the president of the IOC calling the future of their game into doubt, was offer a single response that might not exactly be in keeping with Canada's image of a people so polite they apologize as often as other people blink.

A raised middle finger.

This "scandal" reflected far more poorly on the journalist who wrote it and the newspapers that ran the story than it did on the women's team. Canadians embraced their women hockey heroes with all the admiration they showered on the men's team. Several members of the women's team said they appreciated someone taking a stand for them. One reader wrote to say that the true "scandal" belonged to me—referring to "a raised middle finger" at the end. Sorry, but I'd do it again.

WOMEN'S GOLD A RECORD

(*The Globe and Mail*, February 26, 2010)

VANCOUVER, BRITISH COLUMBIA

The Olympic gold medal game may not have been decided on an outdoor rink but this one, unfortunately, was played under a bit of a cloud.

While Canada claimed its third Olympic championship in women's hockey with a 2–0 victory over the United States, the sport itself was reeling from a headshot delivered earlier in the day by no less than the president of the International Olympic Committee. "We cannot continue without improvement," said Jacques Rogge. Either women's hockey improves, or it goes.

It would, however, be hard to improve upon this championship match played by the sport's two archrivals, Canada and the United States. With the medal, Canada has set a new high for most gold medals at an Olympic Winter Games: eight.

The game featured all of good hockey's essential features— speed, determination, strong goaltending, playmaking, shot-blocking and even a few hard bodychecks (which are illegal in women's hockey). After brilliantly surviving a U.S. five-on-three power play—Canada's Shannon Szabados sensational in net—

Marie-Philip Poulin one-timed a perfect Jennifer Botterill set-up to put Canada in front early in the opening period.

The Canadians survived yet another five-on-three American power play—no wonder Szabados was chosen top goaltender and named to the all-star team—and a second goal by Poulin gave Canada the win before a wildly cheering sellout crowd that included Prime Minister Stephen Harper, Wayne Gretzky and B.C. favourite son Michael J. Fox.

Botterill was ecstatic at the game's conclusion. "This is the moment. This is just amazing. I wanted to soak up every last second of it out there." Szabados was equally overwhelmed. "I looked up in the stands and saw a sign that said 'Proud to be Canadian,' and that's what I am today." Reflecting on the battles against the U.S. team over the years, she said, "This rivalry will never end, it will just keep going on and on."

Carla MacLeod heaped praise on her goaltending teammate. "After the third shot of the game, I thought, 'Oh boy, she is on.'" The United States' Monique Lamoureux was also effusive in praising Szabados. "She played awesome. I tip my hat to her."

After the Canadian team almost floated to the dressing room, they returned in full uniforms and skates to celebrate at centre ice, taking pictures, drinking beer and champagne and posing with the ice resurfacing driver. The team called former Canadian captain Cassie Campbell, who won gold medals in 2002 and 2006, down to the ice to join them. Campbell was working on the TV broadcast of the game. To watch this unabashed display of joy, to see the tears on both sides—unbridled joy with the Canadian women, shattered dreams for the Americans—and to watch the pride as the medals were handed out on the ice to the Canadian, American and Finnish players, it would seem impossible that a sport with such obvious fan support could be so under the gun.

No one argues that there is not a gap problem. The Canadians opened with an 18–0 defeat of Slovakia and the aggregate semi-final score for the two gold medal contenders over bronze medallist Finland and Sweden was a distant and disturbing 14–1. And yet, while it is obvious that the parity some predicted back in 1998, when women's hockey was introduced to the Nagano Games, has not come about, it is obvious that, at its highest levels, the game is worthy of the Olympics.

The problem lies in making it a true contest of country rather than a flipped puck every four years between the two North American powerhouses. To accomplish this, the two power-houses will need to reach back and pull along those who will one day challenge them. It is a matter of self-preservation. At its best, these are elite athletes every bit the equal of the downhill skiers and snowboarders and ice skaters that do not have the head of the IOC saying get better or get out.

Men talk endlessly about "team" and, while they do give more than token loyalty to the concept, their game is far more indi-vidual, even greedy, when compared to the far more socialistic game the women play. What women play is a game of sharing and support. It has its peculiarities—sometimes they pass too much, sometimes they need to be more greedy—but it also has a genu-ineness to it that can be extraordinarily emotional.

All you had to do was be in Canada Hockey Place yesterday afternoon to watch the Canadian women pile onto each other with screams of joy, while at the other end, the American women held on to each other with cries of anguish, to understand that.

Ask the crowd if it's an Olympic sport. For that matter, ask the Canadian men's hockey team—also on hand to cheer on the women, as the women will surely be on hand today to cheer them against Slovakia.

Improve it must. And improve it will. Until one day, that cloud is forever lifted.

THE TRIUMPH OF THE CLARKSON CUP
(*The Globe and Mail*, July 11, 2006)

All bow down to the hockey lockout.
It put skill and speed back into a game that had become Velcro and duct tape. It put confidence back in the Canadian small-market teams. And now it may have saved women's hockey.

Hayley Wickenheiser, who is rarely lost for words or, for that matter, goals, took a long breath yesterday before commenting on what the unveiling of the Clarkson Cup meant for the women's game. Finally, the Olympic gold medallist said it all as succinctly as she could, eyes closed, cheeks bursting: "Phhhewwww!"

"It's absolutely true," said former governor general Adrienne Clarkson, who made the first presentation of the trophy to the Olympic champions. "If there hadn't been an NHL lockout, this whole thing would never have occurred to me."

It was Clarkson who, in the late winter of the 2004–05 lockout season, insisted that "the Stanley Cup belongs to Canada" and should be played for annually, even in a year with no NHL hockey. The famous sports trophy, after all, had been given to Canada 113 years earlier by her predecessor, Governor General Lord Stanley of Preston, and was to be emblematic of hockey supremacy in the Dominion.

The NHL, she argued, did not own the Cup, as the league had long claimed. And after legal action by a group of Toronto recreational players, an out-of-court settlement backed her contention. Clarkson's initial idea was to have women play for the Stanley Cup, but when that proved impossible—and women players, in fact, insisted that the Stanley Cup was a men's trophy—she turned her attention to a new trophy suggested to her by people who wrote and e-mailed in support: the Clarkson Cup.

"This, to me," said Cassie Campbell, captain of the Olympic team, "completely legitimizes women's hockey. This is our Stanley Cup—there's no turning back now."

The obvious relief expressed by both Wickenheiser and Campbell, the two biggest stars of the women's game, had to do with a growing sense that women's hockey was beginning a downward turn. With elite competition boiling down to only two teams, Canada and the USA, the legitimacy of the sport had reached a point where, as Campbell said, "there was a real fear it might be dropped from the Olympic program." In fact, this was precisely the talk at the Turin Winter Games up until Sweden stunned the Americans, and all women's hockey, by reaching the finals against Canada. The emergence of a third force and the creation of a serious cup could not have come at a better time for the game.

"This is big," said Campbell. "It's not just about Canada, it's about the world."

"We needed something that the world of women's hockey can focus on," added Wickenheiser. "It's something people can relate to. That's going to be our Stanley Cup."

Initially, Clarkson's intention was to have the trophy played for by the best women's teams in the country, but negotiations between the east and west elite leagues faltered to a point where she decided, instead, to turn it over to Hockey Canada to administer. The first band will hold the names of the women who won Olympic gold, but future bands are expected to be for individual teams.

The new silver trophy was built by Inuit artists working under Beth Biggs, who teaches art at Nunavut Arctic College in Iqaluit. Pootoogook Qiatsuk, who did the engraving, says he was "speechless" when asked to work on it. Clarkson, known for her love of the North, never thought of having it built anywhere else. "It's out of the North that ice comes," she said. "Get it?"

Bob Nicholson thinks everyone will. "Young boys have their dreams of winning the Stanley Cup on the streets and ponds," said the head of Hockey Canada. "Now young girls have their own dream."

Clarkson is acutely aware that, for the general public, only two governors general in Canada's 139-year history have registered: Lord Stanley, who left his name on a hockey trophy, and Lord Grey, who attached his to the one for football. "You hope you do something that catches on," she said. "But you just can't know."

The Stanley Cup has been hoisted in American cities since 1994, and it's just possible that if the Clarkson Cup is still being awarded when it too is 114 years old, the Swedish or Chinese woman raising it will not have a clue where it came from or who Clarkson was.

If that happens, said Clarkson, the Cup will have accomplished her goal. In 1892, Lord Stanley spent ten guineas on the silver bowl that has been hoisted, dropped, kicked, bent and even lost for periods of time—only to survive as the most recognizable sports prize in North America. Yesterday afternoon during the photo shoot to honour the gold medal winners in junior hockey, sledge hockey and, of course, women's hockey, a cry suddenly went up from the front row.

"Where's the Cup?"

"Where did we put it?"

Hopefully, in the history books.

The Clarkson Cup did indeed become a major focus for women's hockey. Montreal defeated Toronto 5–0 at the Barrie Molson Centre after a four-day tournament that also featured teams from Brampton and Minnesota. Several Canadian and American Olympians were on the teams, as well as players from Europe.

IN PRAISE OF HOCKEY MOMS
(*The Globe and Mail*, March 3, 2005)

Not much is known about her . . . She always stayed in the background . . .

They were, understandably, at a loss for words when it came to describing Phyllis Gretzky, when her family announced this week that this special woman—mother of Wayne, Canada's greatest hockey hero, wife of Walter, Canada's national hockey dad—is undergoing treatment for lung cancer.

They don't even know her age. And that, of course, would be just fine with Phyllis Gretzky. She'd just as soon have it that no one even knows she is ill. But when your last name is synonymous with the national game . . .

"The funny thing is," her son said in his 1990 autobiography, *Gretzky*, "my mom isn't even that big a hockey fan. She only wanted the kids to be happy."

She raised four sons and a daughter, and insisted on equal treatment even if the media had eyes for only one. She drove the kids to their games, pinched budgets to pay for new equipment and stood up for her children as any other parent would. When the extraordinarily gifted Wayne shone so brightly that other jealous parents would boo him, she froze them out; there are still people in Brantford, Ontario, Walter once said with a chuckle, whom she refuses to speak to for things they yelled at her son thirty years ago. She once told hockey great Bobby Hull to mind his manners around her boy.

Hockey mothers are an understudied group when compared to hockey fathers, who are forever being analyzed as the guiding light, the inspiration, at times the overbearing, even destructive force in a hockey star's life. Even Wayne Gretzky is too often seen as the creation of the easygoing, decent Walter when common sense argues that Wayne Gretzky did not pop, fully dressed, from a hockey dressing room.

"A lot of people know about my dad," the younger Gretzky

wrote back in 1990, "but the sacrifices my mom made to put me into the NHL never get talked about."

True, and there are a great many other stories of hockey mothers who should be better known:

★ How Mike Modano, the captain of the Dallas Stars, developed one of the hardest shots in the game in the family basement back in Michigan, his mother, Karen, standing at the far end in goaltending equipment and holding up a battered garbage can lid for him to fire away at.

★ How Pierrette Lemieux would shovel snow into her Montreal home, spread it over the floor and pound it down hard so that young Mario and his brothers could continue their street hockey under indoor lights.

★ How Tatiana Yashin, who had once been a national volleyball player in Russia, would ask for a coach's tape after each NHL game her son Alexei played for the Ottawa Senators, the two of them staying up into the early hours of the morning going over his positioning and plays.

★ How Laurette Béliveau had industrial-strength linoleum installed in her Victoriaville, Quebec, kitchen so that her boys, Jean and Guy, could keep their skates on while eating and then head right back out to the backyard rink.

★ How Katherine Howe gave her cripplingly shy son, Gordie, all the support and encouragement that her brusque husband (who thought the gawky child "backward") could not.

"It was through the kindness of my mother," Gordie once told an interviewer, according to Roy MacSkimming's fine *Gordie: A Hockey Legend.*

She took a couple of hard-earned dollars, either one or two or whatever it was. There was a lady who was trying to feed her family during the Depression and she needed some milk money, so my mother gave it to her. She in return gave her a gunny sack, and when that was dropped out onto the linoleum, there was a pair of skates fell out. My sister grabbed one, I grabbed one, and we went outside. We skated around on the pond at the back of the house. She got cold and went in and took the skate off, and that was the last she ever saw of it. I fell in love with hockey that day.

There is, today, a new breed of hockey mothers who play the game themselves and who, like Olympic champion Hayley Wickenheiser, bring their little boys out onto the ice to share moments of triumph.

And yet there will always be something to celebrate in those parents who, like Phyllis Gretzky, merely offer unconditional support, usually quietly. She offered it to her five children; she gave it to Walter after he suffered an aneurysm in 1991. His remarkable recovery, he says, was only possible with the support and patience and, yes, prodding of Phyllis.

Calgary poet Richard Harrison has a poem he calls "Hockey Moms" in which he speaks of those mothers who sit in the stands "with nothing but your breath to hold."

That situation has now been reversed. It is the ones Phyllis Gretzky watched who now hold their breath. And trust that, as has so often happened in the past, the game turns in their favour.

Phyllis Gretzky died in December 2005.

AMERICAN DEFENDER: ANGELA RUGGIERO

(*Ottawa Citizen*, February 6, 1998)

NAGANO, JAPAN

They will still point to the $25 million that Canadian centre Joe Sakic will be paid this season alone by the Colorado Avalanche, and they can, if they have the adding machines capable of doing so, total the annual payroll of the Canadian men's team until it reaches approximately $125.7 million.

But the most important dollar of all at these, the twenty-eighth Winter Games, may turn out to be a soggy, sweat-stained bill that is taped to the inside of Angela Ruggiero's helmet. It has been there for more than three years; it will stay there until the United States of America, not Canada, wins the Olympic gold medal in women's hockey.

There are two players instantly noticed on the ice any time the Americans and Canadians play—and they are expected to meet again here in Nagano for the all-important championship game in the first-ever women's hockey final. Both players are remarkable for their youth, their size, their hard shots and their passion for extremely physical, passionate play.

The Canadian, of course, is Hayley Wickenheiser, the big, nineteen-year-old forward from Calgary upon whose shoulders so much of the rising pressure to win is starting to fall. The American is Angela Ruggiero. Slightly larger and slightly younger, having just turned eighteen, the big American defender is the one player who most rattles the Canadians, the one the Americans look to to change the flow, to block momentum, to make the statement that this is not just another hockey game, it will be a battle for Olympic supremacy.

Both young women know they are endlessly compared. Wickenheiser was asked this week which of the two is "tougher," and she diplomatically sidestepped the issue. People debate their shots—both slapshots wildly beyond the weak flips of most of the other players—and referees pay particular attention to both for very good reason.

In a game that is, so far, supposed to be non-contact, the two strongest teenage players in the world have spoken out this week in favour of playing full body contact, just like the men. "I wouldn't mind seeing it," says Ruggiero. "I have a size advantage—why not use it?"

She already does, says Wickenheiser. "She's physical," the Canadian star says of her American alter ego, "and she definitely takes the body."

Ruggiero grew up in California, where her first hockey role model was, of all people, then Los Angeles Kings enforcer Marty McSorley. Unusually for women's hockey, she calls herself a "role player." She gives better than she gets, and if someone dares try and get her, she smiles and says, "I'll get a number."

The smile is enchanting, slightly mischievous, and says nothing about Ruggiero being perhaps the only woman hockey player who has lost a tooth to the game—mind you, she did it running into a door last summer while filming a Visa commercial on the U.S. women's team at Lake Placid. There is also a scar on her chin where she took three stitches after colliding full force with another player when she was the only girl playing in Conejo Valley, California.

She began playing the game almost by accident. Her father, Bill, then a glass worker, had grown up in Connecticut and wanted his boy, Billy, to play the game, and when he took six-year-old Billy down to the local rink to sign him up, the organizer complained that there might not be enough kids interested to make a team.

To help out, Bill Ruggiero also signed up Billy's sisters, Angela, then seven, and Pamela, then eight. Pamela soon quit, but Angela liked the game and stayed with it. She was bigger than any of the boys. She eventually became the protector for the entire team.

This is a truly remarkable athlete. She has starred in soccer, lacrosse and basketball, as well. She holds junior state records in javelin, discus and shot put. And she has her choice of Ivy League colleges offering her any number of athletic scholarships. "Lucky for us," says U.S. coach Ben Smith, "somebody gave her a pair of skates."

She hated it when they made her switch over to play with women. "The first women's game I ever saw," she says, "I played in." But gradually her size and skills began to pay off. At fifteen she received an invitation to try out for the women's national junior team.

Her father took a dollar bill out of his wallet—"a lucky dollar"—and taped it to the inside of her helmet. It will help you win, he told her. It is still there, she hopes still working.

Only just turned eighteen, she feels a pioneer in something very, very special. "In Canada," she says, "hockey already is their national sport. But if we could walk away with the gold here, the game would explode in the States." Besides, she adds, "We're the only team sport in these Olympics that America can really grab onto."

Her father now runs a small rink in Grosse Point, Michigan, just outside Detroit, and last June she went home for the first time, pulling into downtown Detroit on a train just as the parade was getting under way for the Stanley Cup champion Red Wings. She got a sense there of what winning can mean, and what it will feel like if the Americans can triumph over the powerful, and favourite, Canadians.

But she also knows that such sweet victories are meant to be shared, and that her father cannot be here for the simple reason that he cannot afford to come. Unlike their NHL counterparts, the women players have no league, or players' association, or personal wealth to take care of such matters. Which only makes Bill Ruggiero's lucky dollar bill all the more valuable—and, perhaps, all the more powerful.

Angela Ruggiero was only eighteen when she led her Team USA to an upset victory in the 1998 Winter Games. She is now thirty-one and still a fixture on the American defence as well as a member of the Boston Blades of the Canadian Women's Hockey League. In 2003, the Hockey News *named her the best women's hockey player in the world. She graduated cum laude from Harvard University and has written a memoir of her incredible athletic career.*

THE WAYNE GRETZKY OF WOMEN'S HOCKEY:
HAYLEY WICKENHEISER
(*Ottawa Citizen*, April 7, 1997)

I t is a story that, in time, may enter the sacred mythology of the game. They will tell of Hayley Wickenheiser's midnight skate as they tell the story of the neighbour dropping off a pair of old skates in the poor Floral, Saskatchewan, home where Gordie Howe was growing up.

It will become women's hockey equivalent of Pierrette Lemieux packing snow onto her living room carpet in Montreal so her child, Mario, could play indoors, of Walter Gretzky taking his son, Wayne, out onto the backyard rink in Brantford, Ontario, and teaching him to carry a puck around Javex bottles, of Réjean Lafleur going into his son's bedroom in Thurso, Quebec, and finding ten-year-old Guy sleeping is his hockey gear, fully dressed for the weekend.

Hayley Wickenheiser's story takes place in Shaunavon, Saskatchewan, on a clear, cold December night in 1985. Tom and Marilyn Wickenheiser are lying in bed when they hear a mysterious noise. It is not the baby, Jane. They know it cannot be the four-year-old, Ross, nor seven-year-old Hayley, both of whom went to bed earlier, exhausted, from a long day of playing on the neighbour's rink.

Tom Wickenheiser hears the noise again. They have just had

the kitchen redone, so perhaps it is just new wood settling. He gets up and goes downstairs: nothing. He goes to the sink for a drink and stands there, staring out at the night. A clear sky, probably twenty below and still only a little past midnight. The sound again. He leans into the window, staring, and across the yard and across the alley, he sees something moving. A small shadow moving up and down the rink in the dark. And the sound again, of course: the sound of a puck on a stick.

"I knew there would only be one person who'd be out there," he laughs.

His seven-year-old daughter had been out for more than an hour. She had slept, awakened and slipped out with her equipment after she knew her parents were asleep. "It didn't matter about the light," Hayley Wickenheiser remembers, "I could feel the puck."

Perhaps no one in women's hockey feels it better these days. Only eighteen years old, Hayley Wickenheiser is referred to as "the franchise" by officials in Canadian hockey. She is the inspiration for tomorrow's players; she is the hope for today.

When this country emerged triumphant in the Women's Hockey World Championship in Kitchener, Ontario, on Sunday much of it depended on the way the puck felt on the stick of Hayley Wickenheiser. "I'm very excited," she says.

And with good reason, for consider for a moment how Hayley's comet has shone: most valuable player in the gold medal game, 1991 Canada Winter Games, named to the national team while still a fifteen-year-old bantam, gold medal winner in the 1994 world championships in Lake Placid, New York, and earlier this month chosen player of the game as she led the Edmonton Chimos to the national championship.

In theory, she could be nineteen years old next year with two world championships and an Olympic gold medal to her credit and still with her best playing days ahead of her. The first-year general sciences student at the University of Alberta is one of the larger players (five foot eight, 163 pounds) in the game, but also one of the most skilled. A fine puck carrier with an excellent shot and extraordinary strength, she models herself on her childhood hero, NHL star Mark Messier, though she has often been referred to as "the Wayne Gretzky of women's hockey."

Messier, and to a lesser extent, Gretzky became her role models when she was that seven-year-old in Shaunavon, and it never occurred to her there was anything to prevent her from one day joining their team, the Edmonton Oilers, and playing alongside her male hockey heroes.

"I hadn't even heard of women's hockey until I was about thirteen," she says. "My aspirations were to make the NHL, just like any other kid. I was given that freedom to dream."

Since she was barely able to walk, she had pestered her father, a science teacher, to let her play the game he played for fun and the neighbourhood kids seemed to play obsessively. She was only four years old when, at the end of one of his recreational games, Tom Wickenheiser brought her out onto the ice and, for the first time, let her try skating with a stick and a puck. "I was pretty bad," she says. But she also knew that she had found her calling.

Shaunavon may have been a small town, but it was enlightened. Ken Billington and Jerry Mitchell were minor hockey coaches more than willing to welcome and encourage the youngster. Tom Wickenheiser also coached her, and her mother, Marilyn, became the team's chief fundraiser. The other kids on the team, all boys, were glad to have her. "I don't think they treated me any different," she says. But, in fact, they did. She was, after all, the best player, the leader. "Really," she says. "I had to be, being a girl. It was easier that way."

"They were very good about her being a girl," says Tom Wickenheiser. "Actually, the parents gave us a harder time than the kids did." The Wickenheisers are uncomfortable talking about it, but there were often scenes when the Shaunavon team travelled to other small towns. Parents would scream and swear from the stands; once three boys on an opposing team chased a frightened Hayley through the rink lobby. "Sometimes parents have a difficult time if a girl scores four or five goals and beats their team," says Tom Wickenheiser.

It is a parent's tale Walter Gretzky would identify with. His own superstar child, Wayne, used to have to switch jackets with teammates before making the run from the visitors' dressing room to the parking lot. "No one writes about how bitter parents are," Walter Gretzky once said. "I have been on both sides of the fence and the saddest part is they don't realize they have the best gift of all, a normal healthy boy. They are so busy resenting others who they think are better. They cannot accept that some boys are twice, three or four times as good as their son."

Or worse, that a girl could be twice, three or four times as good. "She's very quick," says Marilyn Wickenheiser of her daughter. "Her strong ability is to read the play so well, that's helped her avoid any bad hits."

A few years ago the family moved to Calgary so Marilyn could return to teaching and Hayley could find more competitive teams. She has played both women's and young men's hockey, though the games are dramatically different. Women's hockey, she believes, is far more "European" in its approach, with much more passing and far more emphasis on team play. Men's hockey, with its hitting, is far more physical, far more concerned with scoring goals. Two years ago she was a late cut from a superior midget male AAA team, but she still likes to play the male game because of its high competitiveness.

"It's a different game," she says of women's hockey. "People are surprised at how fast it is. They can't believe how much passing we do. There's more to women's hockey than scoring.

"There's respect out there."

Hayley Wickenheiser is now thirty-two. She is captain of the Canadian women's team that won the Olympic gold in Salt

Lake City (2002), Turin (2006) and Vancouver (2010). Twice she was named the tournament MVP. An accomplished softball player, she represented Canada in the 2000 Summer Olympics. She has played professional hockey against men in both Finland and Sweden. In search of competitive hockey, she returned to university in 2010 and played the 2010–11 season with the University of Calgary Dinos and was named Canada West Player of the Year.

★ ★ ★ ★ ★ ★ ★ ★ ★ ★ ★

ELEVEN

THE WORLD'S GAME

O COME, ALL YE FAITHFUL

(*The Globe and Mail*, December 31, 2009)

Let the others put "In God We Trust" on their money—
Canada puts its faith in different gods, with numbers on
their backs.

Abraham Lincoln is on the American five-dollar bill, pond
hockey on the Canadian. The U.S. dollar coin depicts an eagle,
symbol of liberty; the Canadian a loon, symbol of Olympic gold
since it was secretly buried at centre ice at Salt Lake City to bring
the men's and women's hockey teams luck—which the "Lucky
Loonie" did.

It is impossible to know this country without deep consideration of its national game and what that game will mean—for
players and fans of both sexes—once the 2010 Winter Games get
under way in Vancouver.

This, after all, is a country where more people sing Stompin'
Tom Connors's "Hockey Song" than the national anthem, a
country where the "second national anthem" is a television theme
song for the game, a place where the nightly news must wait each

spring until the final scores are in, a culture where the most significant national event for Canadians of a certain age is not the end of war or the first step on the moon, but a puck going into a net on the other side of the world at 19:26 of the third period on September 28, 1972.

It seems only right that Christmas is followed immediately by Boxing Day, when the country begins what has become an annual two-week celebration of a tournament played by teenage hockey players from around the world—whereas the rest of the world barely even notices. The World Juniors, however, pale considerably when compared with the Winter Games, which come along only every four years and have featured the best National Hockey League players only since Nagano in 1998—when Canada suffered collective heart failure during a lost shootout against the Czech Republic.

Four years later, in Salt Lake City, six million Canadians tuned in to watch a great Canadian women's team defeat their American archrivals for the gold medal. Three days later, a record 10.6 million Canadians—the northern equivalent of the American audience for Neil Armstrong's 1969 moon walk—watched the Canadian men defeat the American men's team for a second gold in the national game.

This year, with the Paralympics immediately following the Vancouver Games, the goal is three golds in the national game— those gold medals unfairly, but accurately, mattering in a way that no other victory in any other sport can match. It is not just the national game, but the national sense of self. If Canada truly owns the game it invented, gold is a required confirmation. As the late poet and avid fan of the game, Al Purdy, once put it, hockey is "a Canadian specific to salve the anguish of inferiority by being good at something the Americans aren't."

The Olympics, in fact, have arguably come to matter more than the Stanley Cup. No Canadian team has won the Cup since 1993 and the likelihood of this year producing both Olympic gold and a Canadian city staging a Stanley Cup parade is unlikely indeed. The Olympic gold—let slip away in 1998, won in 2002, blown in 2006—is within reach, while the Stanley Cup is increasingly out of reach.

Little wonder, then, that such obsessive attention was paid over the preceding months on the naming of the final men's roster, which took place yesterday. So breathless had the country become about this otherwise rather routine moment that one national media organization actually broke news that it had learned, from sources, when the team would be named. Such over-the-top attention puts enormous pressure on the players. But then, Canada is surely the only hockey nation to call a press conference, broadcast live across the country, to announce that no decision had yet been made on who would be the third goaltender on the team—a player who would not even be dressing for the actual games.

At times, the pressure is so intense it explodes even off the ice. No one watching Canada's 5–3 loss to the Soviet Union in Vancouver back in 1972 will ever forget Phil Esposito's impassioned plea: "To the people across Canada—we gave it our best. To the people that booed us, geez, all of us guys are really disheartened. We're disillusioned and disappointed. We cannot believe the bad press we've got, the booing we've got in our own building. I'm completely disappointed. I cannot believe it. Every one of us guys—thirty-five guys—we came out because we love our country. Not for any other reason. We came because we love Canada."

Thirty years later, in Salt Lake City, the outburst came from Team Canada executive director Wayne Gretzky. "Nobody understands the pressure these guys are under," a livid Gretzky told a post-game press conference after a lacklustre start by the Canadians. "The whole world wants us to lose!" Not quite. A more accurate claim would be "The whole country demands that we win."

Such expectations are hardly new. When the very first Winter Games were held in Chamonix, France, in 1924, Harry (Moose) Watson of the Toronto Granites sent a telegram from London to a Toronto newspaper, saying it had been a fine sail across the ocean but "our only hope now is that we can get to Chamonix at the earliest opportunity, so that we may start heavy training again and justify the confidence that has been placed in us and retain for Canada supremacy in the hockey world."

There was nothing to worry about. Canada won gold and big Moose set an Olympic scoring record—36 goals, including 13 in a 33–0 drubbing of the Swiss—that neither Alexander Ovechkin nor Sidney Crosby is likely to challenge.

Sixty-two years later, however, little Switzerland shut out Canada 2–0 in Turin, Italy, sending Canada to its worst showing ever in Olympic hockey, a seventh-place finish that stunned, embarrassed and angered both players and fans. It has only served to ramp up the pressure heading into Vancouver, home ice advantage, home pressure disadvantage.

The expectations, despite the disaster of Turin, will be nothing less than gold. Gold for men, gold for women, gold for sledge hockey. The one medal Canadian fans insist on.

"That's what you expect," Cassie Campbell said in Salt Lake City when she captained the women's team to victory. "And that's what you want."

The Canadian men and women both won Olympic gold in Vancouver. Peak television ratings had more than 80 percent of Canadians tuning in.

THE DOMINATOR: HASEK AT NAGANO

(*Ottawa Citizen*, February 23, 1998)

NAGANO, JAPAN

"I think I hurt one of my teammates," he said after. "I was so happy."

A half-hour later, the man Wayne Gretzky calls "the greatest player in the game today" sat at a press table and talked about what it meant to beat the Russians in the final of the first Olympic Games to feature the very best players of the National Hockey League. He didn't know if there was any money involved. "There might be a bowl," he said. "I don't even care."

Sitting beside him, Robert Reichel picked up the glittering gold medal that hung from his neck and held it out to remind Hasek of what his country had just accomplished. "We care about *this!*" Reichel said.

So too did anyone who had seen how the Olympic gold medal for hockey came to be placed around the necks of a team with the ugliest jerseys in the competition, a team where half the players aren't even in the National Hockey League, a team where the greatest hero, Hasek, hides his face behind a wire cage.

"A strange tournament," Czech defenceman Jiri Slegr had called it. Strange indeed—and riveting, emotional and wonderful, as well. The Czechs had beaten a team, a fine team, of Russian superstars. Using a defensive system that had proved impenetrable to, in order, the best NHLers the USA could ice, the best NHLers Canada could dress and, finally, the best NHLers from Russia, the Czechs had taken their first Olympic gold medal in hockey.

Russian head coach Vladimir Yurzinov had called it "a brilliant victory," and it was. Russia's Pavel Bure, the Olympics' most exciting player, had staged rush after rush, but never once was he able to get in on Hasek. Hasek had, in fact, been required to make only two good stops in the game, one off Valeri Kamensky early on, and one off Andrei Kovalenko, who was left alone with the puck in front of the Czech netminder.

"My job is to stop the puck," Hasek said. As usual, he did his job to perfection.

The moment of victory had come on a third-period point shot from Petr Svoboda that went in past the glove of Russian goaltender Mikhail Shtalenkov—giving Shtalenkov his first Olympic loss in thirteen matches—but the hero of the victory was Hasek. Perhaps he wasn't much needed this final day, but without him, they never would have been in the final.

Czech co-coach Slava Lener tried to downplay the significance of Hasek, but to little avail. "Maybe for the media and spectators," he said, "they were stars like Dominik Hasek and Jaromir Jagr and Robert Reichel . . . but seeing them as coaches in the dressing rooms, there were no stars on this team." It was, for the starless Czech players, a magnificent moment. They tossed their bouquets of flowers into the crowd and blew kisses at the singing, ecstatic Czech fans. Immediately after they left for Prague, where the party was already under way.

Those who were left behind were left with two weeks of hockey from which many of them might never recover. The most significant point being made this final day of play was that the three medals had gone to three European teams, the Czechs, the Russians and the Finns, and that both the Czech team and Finn team were laden with unfamiliar names playing in leagues that have nothing to do with North America. "I am very happy," said Yurzinov, "with the way European hockey was played at these Games."

Yurzinov, who did a masterful job of turning such Russian superstars as Bure and Kamensky and Sergei Fedorov into a surprisingly disciplined, effective team, took the opportunity to slap the NHL for treating European hockey as if it were nothing more than "a fun club"—not to be taken seriously. The time has come, he suggested, for a little "mutual respect."

"We're not all supposed to pray to just one god," he said.

Whatever the various hockey gods were up to, in Nagano they produced what many are calling the greatest hockey tournament ever played. There was not a bad game played. There was not a bad team in the tournament. The Canadian team may have missed out on the medals, but nothing has been said here about shame or mistakes or bad luck.

The Canadian team—well constructed, well behaved and well coached—missed going into the gold medal game by a single shoot-out goal that ticked in off both posts before it beat Patrick Roy. They missed a bronze medal by another goal, in a game against the feisty Finns where it cannot, and must not, be said that the Canadians did not try. They lost, fair and square—this time—to better players and better teams. There will be other chances, for it is also certain that the Olympic tournament, with NHLers, is here to stay.

To those who might criticize Eric Lindros for failing to come through, let them know that he threw so much of himself into the game against Sweden—on one unforgettable shift taking three tough Swedes out before heading back to the bench—that he threw up before reaching the dressing room at the end of the game.

Many Canadians had fine tournaments, particularly Rob Blake, who was named top defenceman in the tournament, even if popular opinion had Slegr tagged for that spot. Hasek, of course, was named top goaltender, but Roy was a close second. Bure, to no surprise, was the choice for top forward. Wayne Gretzky, at thirty-seven, might not have been a candidate for that honour, but it was an honour to watch him put everything he had into the Canadian effort.

There is much to reflect on what was on display here in Japan. The hockey was fabulous—as Canadian head coach Marc Crawford put it, "remarkably entertaining." Puck movement was the story— and, it must be said, where Canada came up short—and speed and skill were allowed to show themselves. There was plenty of hitting, often the equal of Stanley Cup playoffs, and the officiating— predominantly NHL—was awful.

Players were ecstatic about the pace of the games. How quickly they were played and, with no time outs for commercials, how much momentum can count for, whether a team be in full assault or full panic. It should give the NHL pause to rethink its packaging of games.

The key factor turned out to be, as expected, the size of the ice surface. That extra fifteen feet of width, the deeper corners and the extra space behind the net creates an invigorating added dimension to the game, opening up matters just enough to remind fans how creative, how quick, and how thrilling this game can be. Sadly, the National Hockey League, while either building or renovating virtually every rink in its twenty-six-city loop this decade, failed to take the hint when it was suggested that they shift to the larger ice surface.

"It becomes a different game," Sweden's Mats Sundin said after he had led his country to victory over the USA. "I didn't think it was going to become a big issue, but I guess it is."

"Big ice is a big advantage, for sure," said Slegr. "It's the ice we grew up on."

"Definitely the bigger ice surface was an advantage to the Europeans," said Czech co-coach Lener. The Americans and Canadians tried to adjust, but "they kind of get lost too often."

Some openly admitted they were lost, and most of them were the pure NHL snipers: Brett Hull of the United States, Brendan Shanahan of Canada. The Americans, however, fared far worse than the Canadians when it came to adapting. "That ice is so big you can get lost out there," said Mike Modano of Team USA. "We're a little bit out of our element," admitted United States head coach Ron Wilson.

By tournament's end, there had been a profound shift in thinking about European hockey, and mostly due to what the ice surface had done. With no more "excuses" to fall back on, as had always been the case before, the North Americans could only accept, finally, that the European players are every bit as good—and in this case, better.

"European hockey has to be given a lot of respect now," said

Canada's Steve Yzerman, who probably adapted better than any other North American to the ice surface. It's too simplistic to keep saying that a lot of Europeans come over to the NHL and fail, Yzerman said. It now goes both ways. "I don't think a lot of NHL guys would have success over here."

It certainly did not work out as the NHL had hoped, though the NHL still says it is delighted with much of what transpired. The idea, however, was to "showcase" the game in markets not yet familiar with the game, including those U.S. markets the league and the Fox Network still wish to penetrate. The ideal situation, obviously, would have been to reach a gold medal game between the United States and Canada. It was not to be so. Russia, with different stars, and the Czech Republic, a non-starter with American hockey fans, played the key game. Wilson stated the obvious: "They didn't rig this tournament."

But some of what took place could not be pre-arranged. How sweet, for example, that Finland's greatest player, Jari Kurri, should score against Canada in the bronze medal game. It would be his final game for his country. "I'm happy for Jari," said Gretzky, who had set up so very many of Kurri's NHL goals, "but disappointed for us."

And Gretzky himself, causing a national sensation when he arrived at the Nagano train station. Always saying the right thing, always conducting himself as Canadians like to think of them-selves being represented abroad. Gretzky was "devastated" by the loss, and said that he too had probably played his last game for his country. But first, he made sure to pass on, to the next generation of Canadian players, what it means to have the chance. "I love to represent Canada. Every time I've put that sweater on, it's been something special for me."

And for us. Win, or lose.

Dominik Hasek played sixteen seasons in the NHL. He won back-to-back Hart trophies as league MVP in 1997 and 1998, while playing for the Buffalo Sabres. In 2002, with the Detroit Red Wings, he became the first European starting goaltender to win the Stanley Cup. He retired in 2008 but soon returned to play again, first in the Czech league, then for HC Spartak Moscow in the Kontinental Hockey League.

RYAN SMYTH: CAPTAIN CANADA

(*National Post*, September 8, 2001)

CALGARY, ALBERTA

Once a rink rat, always a rink rat.

The final practice of Team Canada's Olympic orientation week was over, the Zamboni was out of the chute, and still Ryan Smyth was on the ice—more accurately, on his knees, his stick tossed to the side as he quickly shovelled dozens of pucks into a large pail while the regular arena attendant looked on in stunned silence.

Millionaire hockey players are not supposed to behave this way. The other thirty-three members of this four-day orientation camp were already in their dressing rooms, relaxing between the last practice and a short final-day scrimmage before heading off to their respective homes and teams. Yet Smyth was out there pitching in, still the small-town rink rat from Banff willing to do whatever it takes for an extra few minutes of ice time.

"I just wish this week would never end," he said when, finally, it did.

For Smyth, however, the week was also closing on a good note. For while there remains a profound difference between meaningless shinny and the pressure of a full-contact Olympic medal game, he had shown he had the speed and the skills necessary to be a factor. At twenty-five and one of the younger players in camp, with Nagano missing from his resumé, he was nonetheless being counted among those almost certainly headed for Salt Lake City come next February. "My parents taught me that the first impression is important," he said.

This, however, is hardly the first. He is now entering his seventh season of impressing the Edmonton Oilers with his gritty, drive-to-the-net, never-say-die, kamikaze style of play. And this spring, as the stubborn Oilers fell so valiantly to the richer and more experienced Dallas Stars, the high-scoring forward made a profound national impression on television viewers that is today paying dividends as the country looks to players who can accomplish in Salt Lake City what others failed to do in Nagano.

"I like to get my nose dirty out there," he says. And, some would add, bloody as well. In Game 4 against Dallas, he took eleven stitches over his left eye. In Game 6, nine more stitches over his left ear. He missed only two shifts, racing back out onto the ice with the stitches barely tied to try to accomplish what would eventually prove impossible.

"It hurts," he admitted at the end of Dallas's deciding victory in Game 6. "It will hurt for quite some time. It may hurt till we play them next year."

He is what is known in hockey circles as a throwback. While most of today's pampered and rich players form close friendships off the ice with players from other teams, the quiet, self-effacing Smyth came to Calgary and said he had no interest in getting to know goaltenders like Dallas's Eddie Belfour and Colorado's Patrick Roy. In a few weeks he would have to be playing against them, and he had no interest in seeing possible friendship come between him and literally driving an opposing goaltender through his own net.

Canadians have always played the composite hockey player game, imagining a mythical perfect Canadian player who might bear, say, the shot of a Bobby Hull, the stickhandling of a Jean Béliveau, the hands of a Mike Bossy, the legs (but not knees) of a

Bobby Orr and the eyes of a Wayne Gretzky. If such a player had been built here this week, Mario Lemieux would supply the hands, Eric Lindros the muscle, Paul Kariya the head—but the heart, that most sacred of all Canadian hockey qualities, would more likely come from Ryan Smyth, among the least known of the stars gathered here at Father David Bauer Arena.

What he found hardest this week was simply overcoming the "awe" he felt by being in the presence of so many of hockey's household names, particularly that of his lifelong idol, Wayne Gretzky, who will have the task of deciding whether Smyth is part of the final Team Canada or not. It is a worship that goes back to 1987, when a former edition of Team Canada was preparing for the upcoming Canada Cup by spending a few days practising in Banff. An eleven-year-old rink rat named Ryan Smyth was asked if he'd like to run water and handle the sticks for the Canadian squad and, from that moment on, his dream has been to follow the likes of Gretzky and Lemieux and play for his country.

Even as a youngster, he did everything he could to help. When the 1987 team held a golf tournament, he loaded and unloaded their clubs, only to have former Oiler Glenn Anderson accidentally back a golf cart over Smyth and badly twist his ankle. No problem, he told the players, just drop me off at the hospital and get back to your golf games.

He is, in the age of whiners, one who never complains about anything. They can cut him, they can try and break his knees—as happened a few years ago in a game against the Phoenix Coyotes—and he might go down, and he might need medical attention, but he never says a word and he comes right back with the best answer his skates and stick are capable of delivering.

"I'm just a guy," he says, "who likes to stay on the ice."

Ryan Smyth did make the team and won a gold medal for Canada at Salt Lake City. The fan favourite left the Edmonton Oilers in 2007 and currently, at age thirty-five, plays for the Los

Angeles Kings. He holds the record for the number of games played, 78, in a Team Canada uniform.

"THE WHOLE WORLD WANTS US TO LOSE"
(*National Post*, February 19, 2002)

SALT LAKE CITY, UTAH

In three stunning hours last night, two of Canadian hockey's greatest icons—The Magnificent One and The Great One—served notice that Team Canada is for real, and ready to take on all comers. Including international public opinion.

Mario Lemieux, The Magnificent One, scored the key goals in Canada's feisty 3–3 tie with the defending Olympic champion Czech Republic. And Wayne Gretzky, The Great One, went one-on-one with the rest of the hockey world later in an emotional press conference in which the executive director of Team Canada claimed, "The whole world wants us to lose."

Both Gretzky and Team Canada coach Pat Quinn accused the Czechs of dirty hockey—in particular a Roman Hamrlik cross-check on Canada's Theoren Fleury late in the third period—and promised there will be "payback" later in the National Hockey League season that resumes once the Olympics are over. Gretzky further blamed the U.S. media for spreading rumours about disenchantment on the team over Quinn's coaching during a humiliating 5–2 loss to Sweden and an equally embarrassing 3–2 win over lowly Germany. Having taken on American hockey, Gretzky then moved on to the rest of world hockey, claiming that European players do not return the same respect afforded them by Canadian players.

"I'll tell you what it is," the former NHL superstar said. "They don't like us. They love beating us."

Gretzky's outburst was similar to one by former player Phil Esposito halfway through the 1972 Summit Series. Esposito's Vancouver plea was widely embraced by Canadian hockey fans at the time; how Gretzky's will be taken is yet to be seen. Certainly many Canadian fans will love it, while many fans outside Canada will see his outburst as Canadian whining.

"It sickens my stomach to turn the TV on," Gretzky said. "It makes me ill to hear what's being said about Canadian hockey. If a Canadian player had done what [happened to Fleury], he would have been suspended. We have to eliminate this from the game. He was speared and cross-checked on the same play."

"Am I hot?" Gretzky said. "Yeah—I'm tired of people taking shots at Canadian hockey. If we do something like that, we're hooligans. Americans love our poor start. Nobody wants us to win but our players and our loyal fans. We're very proud—I guarantee you we'll be standing at the end. They should remember that there's payback in this game, and it won't be pretty." The heated outburst threatened to distract from what should have been a welcome result in what had, so far, been a rocky start for the team that has repeatedly said it wants only the gold medal out of these Games.

"We were a better team tonight," Quinn admitted after he had let off considerable steam concerning the rough play of the Czechs. It was Lemieux, the team captain, who led the Canadian effort with two goals, despite still being bothered by a bad hip—or, more likely, back—that had kept him out of Sunday's game against Germany. There will be no more sitting out, Lemieux vowed at game's end. "I'm ready to go," he said. The win, added Lemieux, "means a lot to everybody who is here trying to win the gold medal. There is certainly a lot of pressure out there. It means a lot just to play well."

The Canadians now head into the playoff round, which begins Wednesday against Finland. Any single loss from now on would exclude Canada from the gold medal round they have said they must reach this year. "It's going to get tough from here on in," said Joe Nieuwendyk, who batted a Fleury pass out of the air late in the third period to give Canada the tie. "But we feel good heading into the next round."

The game marked the first meeting since the famous Olympic shootout four years ago in Nagano, Japan, a Czech victory that dashed the dreams of the first Canadian gold medal in Olympic hockey since 1952.

This time, however, there was no shootout for Canadian fans to wring their hands over, as overtime and shootouts will only decide games from here on out. Martin Brodeur, who had played the German game, was back in goal, only this time backed by No. 3 Canadian goaltender, Ed Belfour. Curtis Joseph, the Toronto Maple Leafs goaltender who had been expected to carry the net-minding load in Salt Lake City, was scratched and sat in the stands looking on. Brodeur played well, highlighted by a spectacular third-period glove save off Czech forward Jan Hrdina. His play virtually guarantees him the start in the playoff round, though Quinn was adamant that all three goalies remain in the mix.

Lemieux, who had played terribly Friday and not at all Sunday, answered his doubters by scoring twice on his first three shots, the second goal somewhat dubious as it seemed inconclusive from replays as to whether it had gone in—which in NHL games results in no goal, but was deemed a goal by Olympic standards. The puck was smothered by Czech netminder Dominik Hasek, but his body appeared to cross the line and, after considerable review, a goal was counted. "The only thing that I was afraid of was that they could not see the puck from above," said Lemieux. "But it was clearly over the line."

Martin Havlat, the twenty-year-old sophomore with the Ottawa Senators, scored twice for the powerful Czech team, Jiri Dopita scored the other Czech goal on a rebound in the third period, briefly giving the Czech Republic a lead which the unexpected Nieuwendyk goal soon negated. "We made a mistake in our end," said Czech defenceman Richard Smehlik, "and it ended up in our net."

Quinn and his coaching staff had clearly made adjustments for this third game. No more "pretending" there was a red line. No more endless dump and chase. No more acting like the stultifying NHL game was by some mysterious cant transferrable to the vastly superior international game. The inspired play soon paid off, with first Kariya hitting Lemieux for an excellent chance that Hasek, the Human Gumby, managed to get a pad on, then Lemieux again coming in on the off wing and slipping a soft shot between Hasek's pads for a 1–0 Canada lead. With less than two minutes to go in the opening period, the slight Havlat physically knocked big Eric Lindros off the puck, scooped it up, danced in and ripped a shot past the glove of Brodeur to tie the game.

Havlat then put the Czech Republic ahead 2–1 early in the second, when he was set up all alone in the slot and slipped the puck under a diving Brodeur. Lemieux's controversial second goal—the puck was deemed to cross the goal line when Hasek went down to smother it—tied the match and gave the Canadians renewed confidence for the third period.

Hasek was, as always, brilliant, preventing several excellent Canadian scoring chances. "When you play against Dominik Hasek," said Canadian forward Owen Nolan, "you have to put everything aside because he doesn't give up on a single play."

A loss or tie by the Canadians would ensure that they would be playing the Finns, who earlier had surprised the Olympic tournament with a 3–1 victory over the powerful Russians. The Czechs now go on to meet the Russians in the next round, while the Swedes, winners of the group Canada found itself in, will meet Belarus and the surprising USA squad, winners of the other grouping, will meet Germany.

"This was an important game for us," said Brodeur. "We played hard and we have a big rivalry with the Czechs. We didn't win—but in our hearts, the way we played we felt like we won."

SALT LAKE CITY GOLD

(*National Post*, February 25, 2002)

SALT LAKE CITY, UTAH

Fifty years ago today. Maybe some things are meant to be.
—Canadian defenceman Al MacInnis

Four minutes left in the biggest hockey game in the thirty
years of his life—biggest in the last fifty years of Canada's—
and Owen Nolan suddenly bolted from the bench to the dressing room.

Nothing to do with injury, but an equipment problem. He
wanted his camera. Sixty seconds to go in the final match at the
2002 Winter Games and Nolan, like his teammates, was on his
feet at the Team Canada bench. The big Canadian forward,
however, was the only one not holding his stick. Gloves off and
stick down, he was recording the final seconds so he would never
forget. As if he will ever be allowed.

All around him, the crowd was singing "O Canada"; behind
him, coach Pat Quinn was dealing with the first of many tears,
so perhaps he didn't notice. Nor would it have mattered if
Quinn had and tapped the player to take the next shift. "I wasn't
going on!" a smiling Nolan said when it was all over. "I was
too busy."

His camera lens had captured what all Canada had been dreaming about for four long, torturous, soul-searching and at times
panic-inducing years: the first Olympic gold medal in hockey in
fifty years, to the very day. Canada's perfect golden anniversary.
"Words can't describe what was going on," said Nolan.

They can try: The horn went and the scoreboard said Canada
5, USA 2. Sticks and gloves and helmets were in the air. Goaltender
Martin Brodeur—he of the endless doubts—was being mobbed
by those who now believed they had believed in him forever.

Quinn used the back of his sleeve to wipe away a tear. They rushed Brodeur and someone tossed a Canadian flag to Team Canada captain Mario Lemieux and he thought about wearing it and then thought it would be too much and carried it to the bench. Paul Kariya blew kisses up to his mother and girlfriend in the stands. Lemieux then led his team in a handshake with the Americans that ended, charmingly, with Brodeur hugging American goaltender Mike Richter.

Such a modest, gracious, classy celebration—the moment the horn blew the Canadians ceased to be fierce, driven hockey players and suddenly turned back into the shy and humble men who have taken their lead from the likes of Gordie Howe and Bobby Orr and, yes, the one who put this team together: Wayne Gretzky.

They shook hands and the American team saluted the crowd that cheered for them all over again, and they gave out the medals—the classless Russians not even bothering to show up for their bronze—and the Canadian flag rose highest in the E Center for the second time this week. And Quinn wiped away a tear, just as he had when the Canadian women took the gold medal Thursday night.

"A big monkey is lifted off Canada's back," said U.S. forward Jeremy Roenick, who played his junior hockey in Hull, Quebec, and knows what this day meant to Canada. "Today was their day."

"This," said Quinn, "is a legacy for Canadian hockey we want to pass on."

"Fifty years ago today," mused Canadian defenceman Al MacInnis. "Maybe some things are meant to be."

Asked what he thought the reaction might be back home, MacInnis smiled and suggested, "They're having a cold one on us—and well deserved."

The Canadian team, assembled over this past year by Gretzky and his Team Canada brain trust, was widely held to be the greatest hockey team ever iced by the country that invented the sport—and yet it had been plagued by questions. Patrick Roy, the best goaltender, had elected not to play. Other key players—Lemieux, Nolan, Steve Yzerman—were injured coming in. The team collapsed against Sweden, struggled against Germany, but seemed to find itself against the Czech Republic. They then beat Finland and Belarus to reach the final, which they won in convincing fashion.

"There's no question there was a great deal of pressure on us," said a relieved Gretzky. "There was pressure on all the teams, but ours seemed to be a little bit greater, maybe because we hadn't won in fifty years."

Gretzky himself conceded he "probably" handled the pressure better as a player, and claimed his emotional outburst last week had been deliberate, in order to "get all the focus off those guys and turn the focus in a different direction." Whatever—the players still felt the pressure intensely. Paul Kariya said he was so "numb" he found it difficult to play the third period. "It was like I got shot by a shotgun," defenceman Adam Foote said when it was over, "and all the air was seeping out, all the pressure."

The pressure going into this match was extraordinary. No Canadian team had won since the Edmonton Mercurys in the 1952 Oslo Games. Canada had twice reached silver in the 1990s and fallen in a shootout four years ago in Nagano. The Americans were enjoying their best Winter Games ever, and were talking up their own anniversary: twenty-two years since the "Miracle on Ice" at Lake Placid that had given the USA its last gold medal in hockey. The Americans had not lost an Olympic hockey game on home ice since 1932—a seventy-year anniversary to lord over Canada's fifty-year benchmark.

It was not quite the game expected. The Americans had dominated throughout the tournament but could not use their speed against the pounding Canadian defence. Nor could the Americans get the Canadians to play their European hybrid puck-control game. The Canadians simply played NHL hockey on a big ice surface, up and down, dump and chase, pound and jam—and it worked wonderfully.

Herb Brooks, the American coach in both 1980 and today, sounded the only sour note, claiming that the Canadians had been given an easier route to the final and Team USA's tougher matches had meant the Canadians had "better legs" when it counted. It had been anticipated that Canadian nerves and American patriotism would fire up Team USA right off the mark, and the USA did score first when Tony Amonte came in on a two-on-one and fired a hard, low shot through Brodeur's pads. It was Brodeur's only bad moment of the day.

Canada tied the game on a gorgeous cross-ice pass from Chris Pronger to Kariya, moving fast up the left side, and Kariya had the open side to put the puck in behind Richter. The Canadians went ahead on a second lovely pass, this time from Sakic to Jarome Iginla, the NHL scoring leader, and Iginla jammed the puck in along the post.

Canada should have run away with the match in the second but for an extraordinary number of missed opportunities. Theoren Fleury flubbed a chance, Scott Niedermayer failed to slip a puck into the open set and—in the shocker of the day—Lemieux missed a wide-open net, hitting the goalpost as Canada enjoyed a two-man advantage and Richter was so far out of the play that Lemieux could have shoved it in with his nose had he so chosen.

In a brief but ominous turn, the Americans then immediately tied the game 2–2 when a power-play pass from defenceman Brian Rafalski was tipped by Pronger into his own net. Canada took the lead again, however, when Sakic fired a floater from the top of the left circle that seemed to deflect off American defence-man Brian Leetch, for there seemed no other explanation for Richter missing so easy a shot.

Richter, incidentally, was named all-star goaltender for the tournament, in a media vote that must have been counted in Florida. He was joined by American defencemen Chris Chelios and Leetch, U.S. forward John LeClair, Swedish forward Mats Sundin and, mercifully, Canada's Sakic. The best forward in the tournament, however, may well have been Canada's Steve Yzerman. The Canadians put it away in the third period when Iginla one-timed a nice pass from Yzerman and the puck simply trickled on in after an initial stop by Richter.

It was 16:01, and Nolan was already hurrying down the hallway in his skates, racing for his video camera. Gretzky, high in the stands, was also on his feet, pumping his fist in the air and shouting something we will presume was "Hip, Hip, Hurrah."

Then, with only 1:20 left in the game, Sakic broke up the right side, drove to the net and slipped a quick low shot into the far side.

The crowd was already singing "O Canada." Nolan had it on film, just in case anyone ever doubted that Canada won the gold medal at the 2002 Winter Games.

And Pat Quinn was wondering if anyone was noticing that he was crying.

DEBACLE IN TURIN
(*The Globe and Mail*, February 24, 2006)

TURIN, ITALY

It's hard to look ahead when everyone else insists on looking back.

But that was the situation yesterday at the Palasport Olympico, where the rest of the hockey world was gearing up for today's semifinal matches—Russia against Finland and Sweden against the Czech Republic—while the Canadian hockey world was still trying to figure out what went wrong a day earlier.

"It's like being dead without being buried," long-time minor-league coach Gene Ubriaco once said of an unacceptable string of losses. Team Canada head coach Pat Quinn would surely agree.

The list of reasons Canada fell flat on its face in its attempt to defend the Olympic gold continues to grow by the hour:

★ No Scott Niedermayer to carry the puck up ice and run the power play;

★ No Sidney Crosby, no Eric Staal, no Dan Boyle, no Ed Jovanovski and no (fill in the blank) to do what all the others failed to do;

★ Not enough speed;

★ Not enough shooters;

★ No chemistry;

★ Not enough mobility in defence;

★ Not enough creativity on offence;

★ Not enough adjustment by the coaching staff;

★ Not enough time;

★ No luck.

Such a waste of time and energy. They lost because, as they openly admitted, they weren't good enough. Unlike Nagano in 1998, when a loss to the Czech Republic in a shootout sent Canadian hockey into a spin with demands for a complete make-over of Canadian hockey, it's pretty hard to get worked up when Canada hasn't lost so much as a game in the world junior championship in two years.

Hockey Canada president Bob Nicholson also met with the

media to assure Canadians there is no need for a royal commission on hockey. "We don't have to tear our game apart," he said. "We have to continue to work hard."

Nor, he suggested, is there need of another snap election to decide the next leader of the country—when it comes to something that matters far more than politics. Executive director Wayne Gretzky, the architect of the team that failed, is welcome to stay for as long as he wishes. "Hockey Canada needs Wayne Gretzky," Nicholson said.

At the same time, Nicholson conceded that the results in Turin had been disastrous for the Canadians. Shut out in three games. Seventeen power plays without a goal. A team that never came together in any sense. "It just wasn't their tournament," he said.

And yet, even with Canada out of it, it was still in some ways Canada's tournament—simply because of losing. As the Finns and Swedes and Czechs and Russians came to practise for their semifinal matches, the players were besieged with questions that often had far more to do with what went wrong for Canada than what must go right tonight to put them into Sunday's gold medal game.

Sometimes the players even volunteered to look back rather than look ahead. Tournament sensation Alexander Ovechkin, the twenty-year-old Russian who scored the goal that put Canada out, joked that his agent, Don Meehan, wouldn't be coming to watch the final games because "he's at home, probably wondering what happened to his Canada."

When that caught the media's attention and the Canada questions began, Ovechkin tried to move on. "Right now" he said, "we have to forget about this game with Canada."

It would not, however, be that simple. Was the problem the big ice, players were asked, Europeans having grown up on it and North Americans having to adapt to it? "I don't see it as an advantage," Swedish forward Daniel Alfredsson answered. He prefers the smaller North American ice. Maybe, suggested Czech star Jaromir Jagr. "It's a different game. You skate more on the big ice and you have to be smart. If you have a chance, you go for it. If not, sit back and preserve energy."

Canadian coaches Quinn and Ken Hitchcock both repeatedly said their team had to forget they were on the big ice and play "the Canadian game." It didn't work. When Nicholson and his staff get together to "reassess," as promised, one question they will have to ask is whether this is intelligent strategy. The Canadian game, it seems, simply does not translate to the larger ice surface.

Is it, then, that the Europeans care so much more about the Olympics than they do about the Stanley Cup? Again, Alfredsson, the captain of the Ottawa Senators, shook his head. "The No. 1 trophy for me to win would be the Stanley Cup. No question. It's so much harder to win."

Eventually the questions and answers were forced to the real story at hand: the four remaining teams and their chances of winning the gold medal. "I think the Russians have the best team," Jagr said.

So too does everyone else. And yet, as the Canadians found—apologies for returning to the past—hockey is also a game of lucky bounces, bad bounces and unexpected whistles. The phrase "anything can happen" was used so many times in the mixed zone it hardly requires attribution. "You've got to have some luck and some great goaltending," said Swedish coach Bengt-Ake Gustafsson, "especially at the right time."

While goaltending is always pivotal, it's intriguing that goaltending has been a question for all four of the remaining teams—whereas goaltending was the only non-issue for Canada. The Finns did not have Mikka Kiprusoff, but Antero Niittymaki has been sensational. The Czechs were counting on Dominik Hasek, but injury has put third goalie Milan Hnilicka in the spotlight. Russia's top goaltender is supposed to be Nikolai Khabibulin, but he didn't come and Evgeni Nabokov has been superb. The Swedes traditionally lack good goaltending, but Henrik Lundqvist has been fine.

Sweden will play the Czech Republic in today's first game, and the Czechs are slight favourites. Though they lost 3–2 to Canada in a meaningless earlier game, the Czechs completely dominated play when it struck their fancy. The Swedish players, several of whom play in Ottawa, Toronto and Vancouver, are hoping that Canadian fans will now switch loyalties.

"I hope they're cheering for us," said Mats Sundin, who is also captain of the Toronto Maple Leafs. "We'll take any support we can—we're going to need it."

In the later game, Finland against Russia, the Russians have to be the heavy favourites, given the way such youngsters as Ovechkin, Ilya Kovalchuk and Evgeni Malkin are playing. "That team is scary one-on-one," said Finnish forward Ville Nieminen. "We must take away their time and space—and excitement."

"Obviously, they have more talent and more skills than we do," Finnish star Teemu Selanne said, "but there is only one puck."

One puck and one game.

And the secret to winning that one game is so simple, young Ovechkin said, that it says as much about the Canadian disaster as anything: "Score more goals."

In a surprise outcome, Sweden and Finland met in the final, with Sweden claiming the gold medal. The great Russian team also sputtered when it mattered. Wayne Gretzky declined to be involved with the selection of the 2010 Canadian team, handing over the job to his friend Steve Yzerman.

THE GOLDEN GOAL

(*The Globe and Mail*, March 1, 2010)

VANCOUVER, BRITISH COLUMBIA

He says he did not even see it, though he had dreamed of that exact moment "a thousand times growing up." The over-time winner in the most important hockey game of a lifetime—in this case, the gold medal game in Olympic men's hockey that gave Team Canada a 3–2 victory over a stubborn Team USA.

Sidney Crosby took the shot—the scoresheet will say the country's heart both stopped and started up again at the 7:40 mark of overtime—and suddenly Canada had gold. "I didn't see it go in the net," said Crosby. "I just heard everyone screaming. Every kid dreams of that opportunity—it could have been anyone else."

Not likely. Though Crosby had been effectively checked in games against Russia and Slovakia, as well as for most of this game, there was always a sense that he would be most likely to rise to the occasion if occasion presented itself.

This winning goal will now stand with the ones scored by Paul Henderson, hero of the 1972 Summit Series, and Mario Lemieux, hero of the 1987 Canada Cup and, coincidentally, Crosby's land-lord in Pittsburgh. He will be forever known by it, the ultimate highlight—though he is still only twenty-two—of what has already become a fairy tale on ice for the shy, soft-spoken young-ster from Cole Harbour, Nova Scotia.

His linemate, Jarome Iginla, says Crosby was screaming himself just before the goal. "*Iggy! Iggy!*" Iginla said he heard from the corner, where he was attempting to protect the puck against the boards. "There are different pitches to a yell," said Iginla. "Sounded pretty urgent so I figured he was open—I was just hoping I wasn't too late."

He was not too late. The pass came to Crosby and the shot he never saw squeaked through the pads of Team USA goaltender Ryan Miller to cap a remarkable week that saw Canadian doubts turned to Canadian delirium—no moment cheered so wildly as Crosby's fairy-tale goal.

One week earlier, the Canadians had lost 5–3 to the United States in the preliminary round, and it had seemed this game that fate might be working against the Canadians, as they hit posts twice in the third period and Crosby, on a clear breakaway, was caught by the USA's tiny Patrick Kane, who had outshone Crosby in the tournament and set up both American goals.

Kane, the twenty-one-year-old Buffalo native who plays for the Chicago Blackhawks, was left in tears when it was over and Crosby's earlier struggles in the game were instantly forgotten. For Miller, who was named the tournament's most valuable player, it was a crushing moment of defeat. Asked how he felt, he responded only "I feel like shit" and walked away.

Crosby, on the other hand, was jubilant, piled on by his teammates and glassy-eyed as the gold medals were awarded and the Team Canada players locked arms for the singing of the national anthem and the raising of the Canadian flag.

The cheers for Crosby were so loud that International Olympic Committee president Jacques Rogge had to pause for several seconds before placing the gold medal around the Canadian hero's neck. "There's nothing that kid can't do—or hasn't done," said twenty-one-year-old Jonathan Toews, Canada's top forward, of Crosby. Toews and Corey Perry also scored for Canada.

Crosby refused to be drawn into a choice between the Stanley Cup, which he led his Pittsburgh Penguins to last spring, and the Olympic gold. "I wouldn't put one ahead of the other," he said. But he added that, for his teammates and himself, there was "a ton of pride" in being able to bring home Canada's fourteenth gold medal at these Games, which the players knew would mark a new Olympic record.

Canadian defenceman Chris Pronger, who also won gold in men's hockey at Salt Lake City in 2002, said this one was far more special—"because it's on home soil."

The American team had forced overtime after pulling Miller for an extra attacker and scoring with only twenty-five seconds left in regulation play. After Crosby's goal, the American players stood around in shock and wept while the Canadians littered the ice with their gloves and sticks and helmets and jumped into each other's arms.

"It stings," said Zach Parise, who scored the final-minute tying goal and is the son of J.P. Parise, who played in the '72 Series. "It's a fitting finish for Canadian fans."

Nervous Canadians were relieved by the victory, but so too was Canadian goaltender Roberto Luongo, playing doubly at home in that he is the goaltender for the Vancouver Canucks of the National Hockey League. Luongo, long held to be Canada's top netminder, has also long had a reputation of coming up short in important games. When the Americans scored in the dying seconds, it seemed possible that reputation might be cemented here this day. But it was not to be, thanks to the heroics of Iginla and Crosby.

"I've got a gold medal around my neck," said a smiling Luongo. "Nobody can take it away from me."

As for Crosby, even after the medals and the anthem and several interviews, he was still stunned by what had happened out there on the ice. "It doesn't even feel real," he said. "It feels like a dream."

But it is real. And it was also a dream.

INTERNATIONAL TOURNAMENTS
VS. THE STANLEY CUP

(*The Globe and Mail*, January 7, 2003)

HALIFAX, NOVA SCOTIA

Two o'clock in the morning, Duke Street in downtown Halifax, and nothing but the flicker of a cigarette lighter to show off a gold medal. It may never have shone brighter.

The Russian teenagers walked the snow-choked streets below the Citadel until the early hours of Monday morning following their world junior hockey championship victory over Canada. They smoked cigarettes, some of them walked a bit unsteadily, and they periodically yelled out in English—"Gold! Gold! Gold!"—while lifting their medals from their chests to show all who happened to drive or stumble by.

There were no hard feelings. There was, instead, a congratulatory air about the streets, as if the kids and the city and the game itself had won—and no one at all had lost.

What a difference a year makes. Eleven months ago in Salt Lake City, the Canadian men's and women's hockey teams won Olympic gold. Had they not, and had the Canadian juniors come here and failed to win, not having won this tournament since 1997, there would likely be a few wringing hands today over the state of Canadian hockey. But not this time.

Out of the Olympics came a refreshing confidence in Canadian hockey and a new, and deep, appreciation for the way other countries have taken to the national sport. "Canada gave the world this wonderful game," says Art Berglund, Team USA's director of player personnel, "but the rest of the world now plays it, too."

They do indeed. The Russians won because they had the necessary skill and size, but they did not win by much. The Canadian juniors, also highly skilled and swift, put up a wonderful battle. The Canadians, like the Russians, went five games straight without a loss in this extraordinary tournament, and they went into the third period of the gold medal final with a 2–1 lead, only to lose 3–2 in a game that could easily have gone either way but for a goalpost, a missed check, a lost opportunity. The two teams that fought for the bronze medal—Finland winning by the same tight 3–2 score over the United States—might have reached the final as well but for some other momentary tick of a puck. The six other teams in the tournament all showed, at times, remarkable skill.

The fans obviously adored it. The combined attendance totals for Halifax and Sydney set a new world junior championship record of 242,173—breaking previous records that had also been set here in Canada (173,453 in Winnipeg in 1999 and 148,632 in Hamilton back in 1986). Obviously, Canadian fans like their junior hockey. Such an undeniable national embrace of the junior international game cannot help, at this particular time, to contrast with what is obviously less enthusiasm shown for the overpriced professional product.

"It's the purity of the game," says former Canadian Hockey Association president Murray Costello. "These kids aren't yet spoiled."

International Ice Hockey Federation president René Fasel thinks the fan interest has risen as the junior competition changed over the years and, increasingly, became impossible to predict. This 2003 version stressed skill above all else. Skill and speed, and aggressive but clean play. "In the end," said Fasel, "sportsmanship is so much more important than bad feelings. It wasn't always this way in the past."

Such positive feelings may also have something to do with the possibility that, ever so slowly, Canadians have been shifting their allegiances away from the Stanley Cup toward the international game. There has been a grudging acceptance that not only are the small-market Canadian teams increasingly on fragile footing, but the Stanley Cup—last seen in Canada a decade ago when the

Montreal Canadiens defeated Wayne Gretzky's Los Angeles Kings—now only returns to go on exhibition at the Hockey Hall of Fame.

There has not been a Canadian team in the finals since 1994, when the Vancouver Canucks lost to the New York Rangers, but it does not follow that this marks any concern for Canadian hockey talent. It simply means that the Colorado Avalanche can afford Joe Sakic, the Detroit Red Wings Steve Yzerman. Canadian teams continue, it seems, to excel during the regular NHL season, but once the tougher, differently officiated playoffs begin, the expensive free agent—the tough old guy on the third line making a few million a year—rises out of the tangle and the younger, inexperienced Canadian teams are soon gone.

Canadians, however, have discovered that there is both national and personal joy in the international game. The Canadian men are the best in the world, as are the Canadian women, and Canadians anxiously look forward to the 2006 Winter Games to see the men and women defend their titles.

Just as Canadian hockey fans are already looking forward to next year's world junior championships in Finland, where a Russia–Canada final, for the third year in a row, would be perfect.

And, just maybe, third-time lucky.

CANADA'S LITTLE BIG MAN: RYAN ELLIS

(The Globe and Mail, January 2, 2009)

OTTAWA, ONTARIO

The most feared power play at the 2009 world junior hockey championship is in hands that look more like they should be carrying one of the flags the house-league players ripple around the ice at the start of each match. Jersey a size too large, body several sizes too slight, face hidden by the full mask seventeen-year-olds must wear in this tournament for eighteen- and nineteen-year-olds, Canada's Ryan Ellis has become a crowd favourite since his first shift.

The Team Canada power play has come out of the preliminary round running at a stunning 60 percent efficiency (18 goals in 30 chances). While much of this has been the John Tavares story—five of his eight goals coming on the power play—the sideshow has been the little guy on the blueline.

It is not so much his scoring—though Ellis's six points in four games have him in the tournament's top twenty—but rather his uncanny ability to keep pucks inside the opposition's blueline and set up teammates for clear shots. Against Germany, Canada's little big man—generously listed at five foot nine, 180 pounds—knocked one clearing shot down with a back kick that would have had soccer legend Maradona doing a double take.

Ellis protects the blueline and sees the ice so well that when the final roster was named in December, he was the surprise "extra" defenceman added when the usual choice is to carry another forward. Head coach Pat Quinn figured Team Canada would have him solely to quarterback the power play—only to use the quick little defender increasingly in even-strength situations, as well.

He is an accidental defenceman, going back from forward in atom hockey when flu and injury struck his little team. "I was captain," Ellis remembers, "and the coach says, 'You want to fill in for a few games until they get better?' I said sure—and never looked back."

Tomorrow, Ellis will turn eighteen on the day the tournament truly begins—with every game a must-win situation if Canada hopes to win a fifth successive gold medal in this tournament. Canada and Sweden, the first-place finishers in the two pools of the preliminary round, have byes into the semifinals. Tomorrow afternoon, Sweden will meet the winner of today's match between the United States and Slovakia; Canada will play tomorrow night against the winner of today's game between Russia and the Czech Republic. If Canada wins, it will play Monday for the gold medal.

If Freelton, Ontario's Ellis is standing on the ice Monday while "O Canada" is played, it will mark his fourth gold medal in a year. He's already captured the top prize at the summer under-eighteen tournament, world under-eighteen and the world under-seventeen championships. The Windsor Spitfires defenceman is also the OHL's scholar of the year—an honour he says is the delight of his parents and the subject of a great deal of ribbing by his teammates.

A decade or less ago, such a slight young man would not likely be playing defence and, if he played junior hockey at all, he would be looking toward a hockey scholarship. But not this seventeen-year-old. Ellis has his sights set on being picked high in the NHL entry draft in June and then moving on to an NHL career that in previous years would have often been denied the small of stature.

One spectacular exception was on hand New Year's Eve to watch Ellis's team defeat the United States 7–4, with Ellis setting up the winning power-play goal by Cody Hodgson. "It's about time," Theo Fleury says about hockey's recent embrace of smaller players such as the Chicago Blackhawks' brilliant Patrick Kane and Daniel Brière of the Philadelphia Flyers.

Fleury, at five foot six, 180 pounds, played 1,084 NHL games, mostly with the Calgary Flames, and represented Canada nine times in international play, picking up an Olympic gold medal in 2002 to go with his Stanley Cup ring from Calgary in 1989. "The game has definitely changed where smaller guys can excel at the NHL level," Fleury says. "I don't know if the game's necessarily better or not. I loved my era."

Fleury, now living in Calgary, was captain of the 1988 Canadian junior team that won gold in Moscow, a team that featured fast, fluid and small defenceman Greg Hawgood, who scored nine points that tournament—a Canadian world junior record that Ellis may surpass.

Hawgood went on to play 474 NHL games for eight teams in the era of clutch-and-grab and teams seeking ever-larger players. "I tell my parents I wish they would have waited a little bit longer," laughs Hawgood, who coached the WHL's Kamloops Blazers for a partial season last year. "It's good to see that there's a place in hockey for this kind of player," he says of Ellis.

There once was, of course. Roy (Shrimp) Worters stood five foot three and played goalie for New York, Pittsburgh and Montreal in the 1920s and '30s. King Clancy was tiny in the same era. Camille (the Eel) Henry weighed 152 pounds and starred for the New York Rangers in the Original Six years. But hockey players kept getting bigger. Frank (The Big M) Mahovlich came into the league in 1957 at six feet, 205 pounds, a tally that, in recent years, would make him below average in NHL size and necessitate a nickname change to "The Medium M."

Following the 2004–05 lockout and lost season, the league cracked down on obstruction, freeing up the swift and skilled and sometimes small. Kane—even more generously listed than Ellis at five foot ten, 176 pounds—was the 2008 NHL rookie of the year.

"I had a great career," Hawgood says with a sigh. "I wouldn't change anything. But when I see how the game is today without all the clutching and grabbing that we had to fight through . . . It would be a different way of playing, for sure."

Ellis can only hope the style holds. If, say, Toronto Maple Leafs general manager Brian Burke succeeds with his plan to build a bigger team with what he terms "proper levels of pugnacity, testosterone tenacity, truculence and belligerence," then copycat hockey will follow suit and, just possibly, smaller players will once again be suspect.

Ellis doesn't think so, though. "I think it's not a factor anymore," he says. "So long as you're hockey smart and you can battle, I think you're set. Once I get a chance, I try to prove myself night in and night out. Obviously, some people are going to think 'he's too small' and things like that, but I think for the most part I let it just kind of light my fire."

Seeing Fleury and watching a video presentation of Fleury's passionate role in that 1988 junior team win is just one more inspiration for the little defenceman. "He took it the right way and used it for motivation when people said bad things about him," Ellis says. "I want to do that."

There is also the chance, however slim, that Ellis will not always be first noticed for his size. "My mom's still taller than me," he says, "so I think I got a chance to grow a couple of inches. And if I do, it won't hurt me.

"But if I don't, I'll still be happy. I'll just play my game and not worry about height or anything like that."

Ryan Ellis was named captain of the 2011 Team Canada junior team. It marked his third year in the tournament. The Windsor Spitfire star was drafted eleventh overall in the 2009 entry draft by the Nashville Predators. In May 2011, he was named Canadian Hockey League Player of the Year.

DÉJÀ VU, 1972?

(*The Globe and Mail*, January 5, 2011)

BUFFALO, NEW YORK

Happy New Year—and welcome, again, to 1972. Or so it feels these past few days, as Canada seems pitted against Russia each time the puck drops in this rather unexpected *Back to the Future* twist to the national game.

First it was the Winter Classic in Pittsburgh on New Year's Day, with HBO, NBC and the hockey media world fixating on a wildly overhyped outdoor clash between Sidney Crosby of Cole

Harbour, Nova Scotia, and Alexander Ovechkin of Moscow. Crosby, captain of the Pittsburgh Penguins, and Ovechkin, captain of the Washington Capitals, are today the two prime faces of professional hockey: Crosby, the polite, studious, respectful Canadian; Ovechkin the brash, fun-loving Russian who cockily raised his stick in victory as the final seconds ticked down in his team's 3–1 victory at Pittsburgh's Heinz Field.

And this Wednesday in Buffalo, it will be Team Canada against Team Russia to decide world supremacy in junior hockey—a gold medal match that no one saw coming until Monday's semifinal rounds, when the Russians stormed back to defeat the highly touted Swedes 4–3 in a shootout and the Canadians rode roughshod over tournament-favourite USA, winning 4–1 to reach the final.

While it may feel a bit like 1972 at times, it most assuredly is not. That Summit Series—renowned in Canada for the Paul Henderson goal that won it with only 34 seconds left in the final game—was seen as a match between the flamboyant superstars of Canadian hockey and the faceless, emotionless Soviets. All passion—from Phil Esposito's tearful Vancouver speech ("We came because we love Canada!") to Henderson's leaping victory dance—seemed clothed in the red maple leaf.

Monday night in Buffalo, however, it was virtually impossible to pick a Canadian star, so surgical was the Canadian team effort in dissecting the much-vaunted American speed and skill. Canada's head coach Dave Cameron said that as long ago as last summer his staff had been working with these young men "to convince the players to give their skills to the team." They did so, and no matter what the final score turns out to be Wednesday, the strategy has been a remarkable success.

While Canadian hockey has evolved increasingly into team play and stringent coaching systems—three coaches back of the bench, one sending messages down from above, some even using iPads between shifts to point out errors—Russian hockey has gone in the opposite direction. Gone are the days when a tyrannical coach could treat his players as if they were soldiers, which they usually were. Today's Russian coaches bemoan their lack of influence in what happens on the ice. In the years following Mikhail Gorbachev's perestroika and glasnost, individualism and self-determination became part of the Russian character, in hockey as well.

Renowned Soviet defenceman Slava Fetisov—who referred to his former teammates as "ice robots"—was one of the first to leave the crumbling totalitarian system for the NHL. Already an older veteran, he eventually came to the Detroit Red Wings where he and old Russian teammates like Igor Larionov were able to practise the "creative hockey" they had always dreamed of playing.

Fetisov and Larionov set in motion a Russian revolution in professional hockey that is still sorting itself out. Brilliant youngsters like Alexander Mogilny and Pavel Bure followed. While the traditional Canadian hockey hero is cast in a humble style set by Jean Béliveau and Gordie Howe and carried on by Bobby Orr, Wayne Gretzky and others, Russian hockey heroes have been more like movie stars, with all the glamour and problems that can entail.

Modern Russian hockey players seemed, at times, so determined to show that they were different from their old image that when young Darius Kasparaitis dropped the gloves with respected NHL fighter Rick Tocchet, Kasparaitis later explained to the press that Tocchet had "called me a 'commie'—I didn't like that."

Russian players have certainly entertained, but they have also disappointed and frustrated fans who, early on, embraced them. Alexei Yashin may have been brilliant at times as an Ottawa Senator, but the lingering memory is of contract headaches and disappointment. Two of today's most gifted NHLers—Alexei Kovalev of the Ottawa Senators and Ilya Kovalchuk of the New Jersey Devils—are having years in which their lack of interest and lack of production have outraged fans, Kovalchuk all the more so in that only last summer, the Devils signed him to a fifteen-year, $100-million contract.

NHL teams have grown increasingly wary of Russian talent in recent years, the number of drafted eighteen-year-old Russians dropping to a half-dozen in 2009 and only eight in 2010, despite the proof that this junior team in Buffalo holds that Russian teenagers obviously still excel at the game.

There is a long string of stereotypes that the hockey world applies to Russian players. They are called "enigmatic"—sometimes referred to as "the Russian factor"—and often dismissed as greedy players interested only in themselves, not their teams.

While that may hold up in some instances, it does not in others. Washington's Ovechkin is not leading the individual goal-scoring race as he usually does, but he has led his Capitals into an ongoing battle for the very top of the NHL's Eastern Conference. The Washington captain is praised as much these days for his team leadership as for his wrist shot.

His example seems to be filtering down, as well. "It doesn't matter who scores the goals," said Denis Golubev, who scored the key shootout winner against Sweden. "It's not about me—it's about the team."

Golubev also, it might be pointed out, crossed himself just prior to taking that shot—something more in keeping with, say, Claude Provost jumping on the ice for the old Montreal Canadiens than with any heritage from the old Soviet Union. "God was with us," added Russian captain Vladimir Taresenko.

Another intriguing change in the stereotype of the Russian game is that what was once considered the Achilles heel of Russian hockey—an inability to fight back late in a game if they are behind—has been put to rest in Buffalo. These Russian teenagers staged a stunning comeback Sunday against the Finns after being down 3–1 to win 4–3 in overtime, then tied the Swedes in the dying seconds of Sunday's semifinal game to force overtime and get to the shootout, which they won.

Wednesday's game will be played in an atmosphere rather reminiscent of the great Canada–Russia clashes of the past, including the 1972 Summit Series and the 1987 Canada Cup. Buffalo may be in northwestern New York State, but it has blushed red throughout this long tournament as fanatical Canadian fans have driven from as far away as Alberta and Nova Scotia to attend and raise signs calling the HSBC Arena "Canada's house."

So dominant has the Canadian presence in Buffalo been that before Monday's match against the Americans, the arena mascot, Sabretooth, tweeted that "Tonight will be strange. I will be hated by about 18,000 people in my own arena."

No such message need be sent to either team scheduled for Wednesday's final, however. Canada knows from experience to beware the Russian bear. And Russia has to be wary of the power of the Canadian Maple Leaf.

Just as matters turned out, much to Canadians' surprise, in 1972. Just as it should, to no one's surprise, in 2011.

This column would prove surprisingly prescient in the final period of the final game of the 2011 world junior hockey championship.

MARK VISENTIN AND THE THIRD PERIOD FROM HELL

(*The Globe and Mail*, January 8, 2011)

Let us begin around midnight on Wednesday on the Peace Bridge leading from Buffalo, New York, to Fort Erie, Ontario. Dan Visentin, a high-school math teacher, is driving. His wife, Liz, also a teacher, is in the car, as are his parents, Italo and Rita Visentin.

Italo Visentin knows something about dreams. More than a half century ago, he and Rita came from Italy to nearby Niagara Falls with no idea what would happen to them in this strange new country where they didn't even speak the language. Yet it all worked out wonderfully. He became a crane operator, their children excelled in school and life, retirement gave them time to spend with grandchildren. They had just witnessed one of them have a dream shattered.

Mark Visentin, who turned eighteen only last August, was in goal for Team Canada at the world junior championship when the unimaginable happened. Canada was ahead 3–0 going into the third period of the gold medal game and seemed on a cruise to avenge the championship lost to the Americans last year in Saskatoon. But then, in what felt like the snap of a finger, the Russians scored twice, then tied the game and stormed on to a stunning 5–3 victory.

Even without the radio on, everyone in the car knew what was being said: the greatest collapse ever . . . the team had choked . . . the goalie was the goat. They hoped that Mark, travelling behind in another car with his girlfriend, Harmony, didn't have his radio on. He didn't.

"How ya doin' tonight?" the border guard asked as Dan Visentin handed over the four passports.

"Depressed," Visentin answered.

The guard, flicking through the passports, paused and looked up, surprised. "Oh, shit," he said, "you're a Visentin."

"I'm the father."

The guard handed back the passports. "Don't worry," he said. "You have a great kid there—you got to be proud of him."

"We are."

"He's going to be a great goalie one day."

"We know."

Mark Visentin made it through at another border booth and drove slowly to his parents' home in little Waterdown. No radio. Hardly any words. What was there to say? He had already said what he thought he had to say. He had sobbed on the ice and was still weeping in the dressing room when Hockey Canada's André Brin asked if anyone was ready to speak to the media.

"I'll come out," he volunteered. Many goaltenders would have refused. Some members of the media reacted with surprise when the black curtain split open and out stepped the Canadian goaltender of record, eyes clear, head held high, and prepared to talk as long as there were questions. "I like to get stuff done and not leave it," he said Friday in an interview.

He put no blame on the defence that, at times, let him down, no blame on the forwards who had their own breakdowns. He took full responsibility. "I'm not the guy who blames his team," he said. "You really wish you could have provided a couple of saves when they were needed."

He had felt the tide turning, as coach Dave Cameron later put it. He watched the "spark" go into the Russians and knew that it had gone out of his own team. "We pushed the panic button a bit," he said. "We tried to get back, but . . ."

He knew he could talk forever and the score would never change. "No one to blame but me," he said. "I try to make myself accountable for what happens."

It is, in fact, the accountability and responsibility of that crucial position in hockey that first appealed to him. The first time he tried playing goal he "fell in love with it. The goaltender can be a game-changer," he said, "and that is a great feeling. But if you're going to do that, you have to accept the ups and downs."

Growing up, his great hero was Curtis Joseph, then the goaltender for the nearby Toronto Maple Leafs. He and his friends would play on the backyard rink and he would imagine he was "CuJo" kicking out the pucks — at least when Sheeba, the family's golden retriever puppy, wasn't running off with them.

At sixteen, he made the leap to Major Junior, drafted by the Niagara IceDogs, a team that plays out of St. Catharines, Ontario. At seventeen, six weeks short of his eighteenth birthday, and much to his own surprise, he became a first-round draft pick (chosen twenty-seventh overall) of the Phoenix Coyotes.

He hopes to have a professional career, but he is also an excellent student and calls his decision to take courses at Brock University his "backup plan." He was one of nine goaltenders invited to the summer junior camp, one of four at the December camp. His roommate was Olivier Roy, who got an early-morning call that he'd made it, convincing Visentin he had not.

"Who's your partner going to be?" the disappointed youngster asked.

"You!"

It seemed that partnership would be in the backup role, with the year-older Roy pegged to get the most work, but after Canada lost 6–5 in a shootout to Sweden, the switch was made to Mark Visentin, and Cameron stuck with him right to the final, going with an eighteen-year-old in a tournament meant for nineteen-year-olds.

The young goaltender prepared as usual—have a meal of chicken parmesan, listen to some music (everything from rap to country), get to the rink, work on his sticks—but no one, not the coaches, not the country, was prepared for that third period.

It has been described as the greatest collapse ever in Canada's time in international hockey, but there are comparables. Alan Eagleson says what happened in Buffalo reminded him of Game 5 in the 1972 Summit Series. Team Canada was up 4–1 into the third period in Moscow, only to have the Soviets score two very quick goals on Tony Esposito and then two more before the period was out to win 5–4. Tony Esposito, it might be worth pointing out, went on to a Hall of Fame career.

"People lose perspective," said Dan Visentin. "Mark will be fine. He's got his whole future in front of him."

Mark Visentin had that future to consider that night as he drove home to Canada. "It was weird," he said. "There was just so much to take in." He was grateful for Ben Vanderklok, a coach with the IceDogs, for working so hard on his personal mental toughness.

"It was a tough pill to swallow," he said. "But I think I'm a better person for it." He knew now he could handle the worst imaginable adversity. He knew he was strong enough to leave it behind him.

No one was up when he came through the front door, but then came the sound of an old dog's nails moving along the floor. Sheeba, the old puppy still going at fourteen, came hurrying toward him, wiggling and tail wagging.

"She was just happy to see me," he said.

Mark Visentin inspired an entire hockey nation when he spoke so openly about his own feelings in the days immediately following that astonishing loss to Russia. He returned to form quickly on return to the Niagara IceDogs and led them into the 2011 Ontario Hockey League playoffs by posting a stunning .977 save percentage and allowing a mere three goals as his team swept the Brampton Battalion in the opening round. He was indeed "a better person" and, still, a first-rate goaltender. At season's end, he was named the Ontario Hockey League's Goaltender of the Year.

ACKNOWLEDGMENTS

The author is forever indebted to those many editors and sports editors who either assigned me these stories, agreed with me that these were stories or, in a few instances, forced me to do stories they thought needed doing and I could not see why until I was well into it: Peter C. Newman, Don Obe, Mel Morris, John Aitken, John Gault, Hal Quinn, Walter Stewart, Lou Clancy, Keith Spicer, Nelson Skuce, Scott Honeyman, Jim Travers, Lynn McAuley, Graham Parley, Tom Casey, Ken Whyte, Jim Bray, Ed Greenspon, Steve McAllister, David Walmsley, John Stackhouse, Tom Maloney.

Thanks, as well, to *Maclean's*, *The Canadian*, *Today*, *Toronto Star*, *Ottawa Citizen*, *National Post* and *The Globe and Mail* for a lifetime of opportunity.

A huge note of appreciation to Natasha Haines and Bruce Westwood of Westwood Creative Artists for their continued support. And gratitude, as well, to Craig Pyette of Random House Canada, who pushed and prodded and polished and knows enough about hockey to write his own book.

Roy MacGregor is the acclaimed and bestselling author of *Home Team: Fathers, Sons and Hockey* (shortlisted for the Governor General's Literary Award), *A Life in the Bush* (winner of the Author's Rutstrum Award for Best Wilderness Book and the CAA Award for Biography) and *Canadians: A Portrait of a Country and Its People*, as well as two novels, *Canoe Lake* and *The Last Season*, and the popular Screech Owls mystery series for young readers. A regular columnist at *The Globe and Mail* since 2002, MacGregor has received four National Magazine Awards and eight National Newspaper Award nominations for his journalism. He is an Officer of the Order of Canada, and was described in the citation as one of Canada's "most gifted storytellers." He grew up in Huntsville, Ontario, and now lives in Kanata, Ontario.